Facilitating the Future?

Facilitating the Future?

US Aid, European Integration and Irish Industrial Viability, 1948–73

PETER MURRAY

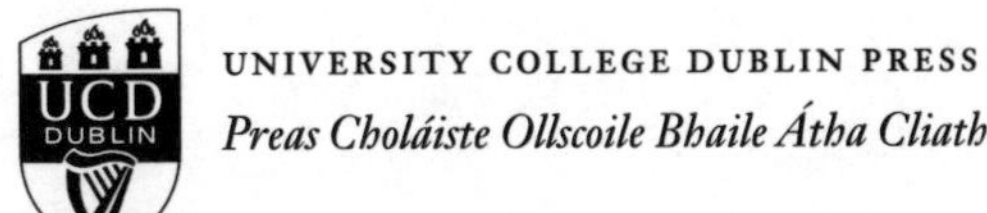

First published 2009
by University College Dublin Press
Newman House
86 St Stephen's Green
Dublin 2
Ireland
www.ucdpress.ie

ISBN 978-1-906359-38-6

Cataloguing in Publication data available from the British Library

The right of Peter Murray to be identified as the author of this work has been asserted by him

Typeset in Ireland in Adobe Garamond, Janson and Trade Gothic by Elaine Burberry and Ryan Shiels
Text design by Lyn Davies
Index by Jane Rogers
Printed in England on acid-free paper by Athenaeum Press, Gateshead

In memory of my parents
Eileen and Harry Murray

Contents

Acknowledgements

A number of scholars have given me invaluable assistance and encouragement without which this book could not have been written. Here I would like to thank Bent Boel, Francis Devine, Brian Girvin, Gary Murphy, Peter Rigney and Bill Roche. Less directly connected with this project, but greatly influential along the road that has led me towards it, have been Eamonn Slater, Chris Whelan and James Wickham. I owe a debt to the Sociological Association of Ireland (SAI) and to the National Institute of Regional and Spatial Analysis (NIRSA) in NUI Maynooth for the opportunities to present my research work in progress with which the annual conference of the former and the Working Papers series of the latter provided me.

The Irish Research Council for the Humanities and Social Sciences (IRCHSS) awarded me a project grant that enabled me to take a year's sabbatical devoted to researching this book. For part of that sabbatical year Maria Feeney worked with me as Research Assistant. Maria made a hugely significant contribution to the work of the project. I would like to thank her for this and to wish her every success with the PhD in Sociology she has since gone on to undertake.

I would also like to thank the staff of the archives and libraries in Ireland and the USA in which the research for this book was carried out – the National Archives of Ireland, the National Library of Ireland, the Dublin Diocesan Archives, the Irish Jesuit Archives, Trinity College Dublin Library, John Paul II Library in Maynooth, the National Archives and Research Administration in College Park, Maryland and the Ford Foundation Archives in New York. Within these institutions I am particularly indebted to Brian Donnelly, Noeleen Dowling and Jim Moske. I also thank the National University of Ireland for a generous grant under the NUI Publications Scheme.

Barbara Mennell at UCD Press has been enormously helpful at every stage of the book's development and production. I am deeply grateful to her for this.

A long-suffering family is an essential requirement for any author. Mary, Francisco and Marta make up mine. I thank them warmly for their support and encouragement.

PETER MURRAY
Maynooth, May 2009

Acknowledgements

Abbreviations

AACP	Anglo-American Council on Productivity
ATGWU	Amalgamated Transport and General Workers Union
BIM	British Institute of Management
CIÉ	Córas Iompair Éireann
CII	Confederation of Irish Industry
CIO	Committee on Industrial Organisation
CIR	College of Industrial Relations
CIU	Congress of Irish Unions
CSO	Central Statistics Office
CTT	Córas Tráchtála
CWC	Catholic Workers' College
DDA	Dublin Diocesan Archives
DEAC	Dollar Exports Advisory Committee
DETE	Department of Enterprise, Trade and Employment
DF	Department of Finance
DFA	Department of Foreign Affairs
DIC	Department of Industry and Commerce
DL	Department of Labour
DT	Department of the Taoiseach
ECA	(Dublin) Economic Co-operation Administration
ECA	Economic Co-operation Administration (USA)
EDB	Economic Development Branch (Department of Finance)
EEC	European Economic Community
EFTA	European Free Trade Association
EPA	European Productivity Agency
ERI	Economic Research Institute
ERP	European Recovery Programme
ESB	Electricity Supply Board
ESRI	Economic and Social Research Institute
FFA	Ford Foundation Archives
FII	Federation of Irish Industries

FIM	Federation of Irish Manufacturers
FUE	Federated Union of Employers
GATT	General Agreement on Tariffs and Trade
HSC	Joint Committee on the Human Sciences and their Application to Industry (Human Sciences Committee)
IAC	Industrial Advisory Council
ICA	International Co-operation Administration
ICC	Industrial Credit Company
ICFC	Industrial and Commercial Finance Corporation
ICTU	Irish Congress of Trade Unions
IDA	Industrial Development Authority
IIRS	Institute for Industrial Research and Standards
IJA	Irish Jesuit Archive
IMI	Irish Management Institute
INPC	Irish National Productivity Committee
IPA	Institute of Public Administration
IPC	Irish Productivity Centre
IRB	Industrial Reorganisation Branch
IRC	Industrial Reorganisation Corporation
ISI	Irish Supervisors Institute
ITGWU	Irish Transport and General Workers Union
MBA	Master of Business Administration
MDU	Management Development Unit
MSA	Mutual Security Agency
NAI	National Archives of Ireland
NARA	National Archives and Research Administration (USA)
NATO	North Atlantic Treaty Organisation
NCIR	National College of Industrial Relations
NCLC	National Council of Labour Colleges
NIEC	National Industrial Economic Council
NLI	National Library of Ireland
OECD	Organisation for Economic Co-operation and Development
OEEC	Organisation for European Economic Co-operation
OSTP	Office of Scientific and Technical Personnel
PUTUO	Provisional United Trade Union Organisation
RG	Record Group
RGDATA	Retail, Grocery, Dairy and Allied Trades Association
S&T	Scientific and Technical

SFADCO	Shannon Free Airport Development Company
SRC	Social Research Committee
SSISI	Statistical and Social Inquiry Society of Ireland
TA	Technical Assistance
TUAB	Trade Union Advisory Body
TUC	Trades Union Congress (UK)
TWI	Training with Industry
UCC	University College Cork
UCD	University College Dublin
UCG	University College Galway
USTAP	United States Technical Assistance and Productivity Program
VEC	Vocational Education Committee
WEA	Workers Education Association
WUI	Workers Union of Ireland

CHAPTER ONE

Protected Irish Industry and Post-war European Free Trade

Introduction

As the second half of the twentieth century began, the Department of Industry and Commerce in Dublin received the following enquiry from Cork, the county from which Henry Ford's grandfather had emigrated to the United States one hundred years earlier:

> Are there any facilities for the study of Mass Production, Industrial Management, Time and Motion and Trade Unionism in Ireland[?] If not in Ireland does your Department know of any College where these subjects are taught, or would it be possible to receive instruction in America under the ECA scheme, if possible what conditions are necessary[?] I am a production engineer, and have studied and worked on the Continent but I still feel that more 'know how' is needed to cope with our problems in industry in Ireland.

The reply stated that 'so far as this Department is aware there are no such facilities available in this country'. It went on to suggest that 'you might communicate in the matter with the British Institute of Management at 17, Hill Street, London W.1'.[1]

These two letters offer confirmation of southern Ireland's position as a poor, peripheral agrarian region of an industrialised British Isles economy – a position not fundamentally altered by or since its achievement of political independence three decades earlier. But through the specific institutions the letters refer to – the ECA and the British Institute of Management – our attention is drawn to a significant change process just getting under way.

The Economic Co-operation Administration (ECA) was the US government agency set up in 1948 to implement the Marshall Plan and a key actor in the post-war 'americanisation' of Western Europe (Bjarner and Kipping 1998;

Zeitlin and Herrigel 2000). The British Institute of Management was a body shaped within this 'americanisation' context, as the Attlee government embraced a programme of industrial modernisation that sought to close the productivity gap between British industry and its US counterpart (Engwall and Zamagni 1998; Gourvish and Tiratsoo 1998). Becoming a Marshall Aid recipient drew Ireland into wider European economic co-operation that would eventually deepen into the integration of the European Economic Community (EEC). This integration would create an environment within which Ireland would very significantly reduce its dependence on the United Kingdom and acquire – to a degree that continues to be debated – the kind of sophisticated industrial capacity so patently absent in 1950. Between Ireland's receipt of US aid (1948–51) and its entry into the EEC in 1973, technical assistance and productivity programmes sought to promote the upgrading of Irish industry. Their effects rippled out into the field of education. They also fed into a remoulding of Irish public opinion on the desirability and inevitability of becoming outward-looking and embracing economic and social change. These US, European and Irish domestic programmes are the subject of this book.

The Sinn Féin road to industrialisation

The partition of Ireland in the early 1920s separated an industrialised north-east that remained within the United Kingdom from an agricultural, self-governing south and west. Carried out in 1926, the first Census of Industrial of Production in the Irish Free State found 60,000 people, or just over four per cent of the labour force, employed in manufacturing industry. Under the Anglo-Irish Treaty the Free State had acquired the right to determine its own tariff regime. It could therefore break with the free trade *status quo* and pursue an active industrial development policy if it wished to do so. As the movement seeking separation from Britain was spearheaded by Sinn Féin, a party which had since its foundation advocated protection 'to give Ireland back her manufacturing arm', this was a policy initiative that might have been expected to follow self-government quickly. But at first it did so only in the most cautious fashion.

The Free State's agricultural economy was highly export-orientated towards the British market. Most trade with Britain was conducted free of tariffs, and the party in government, Cumann na Gaedheal, formed by the faction favouring acceptance of the Anglo-Irish Treaty when Sinn Féin split in 1922, maintained this arrangement. Its industrial development strategy in these circumstances amounted to concentrating on the expansion of food exports to increase spending power in Ireland and thereby stimulate the creation of new Irish industries to meet higher consumer demand. In this 'wager on the strong' farmers, policy aimed at holding down taxes which would help to keep production costs low and make Irish food competitive on the British market. Some new tariffs were introduced but only after applications were exhaustively investigated with consumers or importers being given the chance to present a case against their imposition. The returns from this strategy in terms of employment creation were modest. By the end of the 1920s, with most of the opponents of the 1921 Treaty now in Fianna Fáil, a party whose leaders had ended parliamentary abstentionism and entered the Dáil, the protectionist alternative began to be advocated with renewed vigour.

By the time Fianna Fáil came to power in the general election of 1932, debates about free trade versus protectionist industrial policies had become largely academic. Britain had joined in the general movement towards throwing up tariff walls in response to the Great Depression ushered in by the Wall Street Crash of 1929:

> For a few months at the turn of 1931 into 1932, between the introduction of the British tariff and the change of government in Dublin, [the Free State] was the last surviving example of a predominantly free-trading state left in the world. Within another few months it had passed to being one of the most heavily tariffed countries that could be found (Meenan 1970: 141–2)

The Fianna Fáil election victory 'marked the transition from the free-trading beer, biscuits, cars and cattle lobby of the early Irish state towards an attempted realignment based on smaller protected industries in alliance with protected, more tillage-oriented agriculture' (Daly 1992: 56). High tariffs, quotas and licences became the order of the day in relation to manufactured goods as the old cautious case-by-case approach was swept away. Tit-for-tat measures instituted in the course of the 'Economic War' with Britain helped roll this movement forward. Anglo-Irish economic peace was restored, and a durable cross-party Irish consensus on economic strategy established, by a 1938 Trade Agreement that accommodated both export-oriented cattle farmers and protected industrialists – 'the former recovered their traditional access to the British market on the best terms available given Britain's policy of promoting domestic agriculture, while the latter were not forced to cede industrial protection' (Daly 1992: 170).

With the depression drastically restricting emigration outlets, protection delivered impressive Irish industrial employment gains – an estimated 25 per cent increase between 1932 and 1936 – but 'industrial policy in the 1930s was better geared towards generating employment throughout the country in the short run than towards building up a self-supporting Irish industrial sector' (O'Gráda 1995: 398). There may be justification for a tariff designed to allow an industry time to grow so that it is able to reach an efficient scale and method of production. But a tariff which becomes a permanent fixture because its continuance is needed to save a local producer from going under in the face of outside competition is a welfare-diminishing subsidy local consumers are forced to pay to an inefficient producer. Crucial features of the industrial base established in Ireland during the 1930s militated against protected industrial infants ever growing into independent adult entities. Of particular significance was the large extent to which the new enterprises – legally required to be majority Irish owned and directed – were dependent on foreign expertise, finance and technology (Daly 1992: 172–3; Jacobson 1989: 176–7).

Increased fuel, raw material and semi-finished manufactured good imports were stimulated by the operation of new industries that were not generating any foreign exchange earnings with which to pay for these imports. Confined to a small home market, the surge in employment associated with the establishment of these industries was quite quickly exhausted. The massive dislocation experienced in the Second World War years, owing to shortages of raw materials, energy and spare parts, obscured the full scale of these problems for a time. But even before war broke out in 1939 there were industries such as footwear where short-time working and production cutbacks had been introduced to adjust output to the prevailing level of demand (Press 1989: 50–72)

Between 1945 and 1950 industrial output in southern Ireland almost doubled and employment grew by nearly half. But, as post-war recovery was proceeding, serious concern among policy makers about the efficiency of Irish industry was clearly evident. In February 1946 the Minister for Industry and Commerce Seán Lemass proposed a bill that would create an Industrial Efficiency Bureau:

> The bureau was to have unprecedented powers to ensure 'reasonable standards of efficiency' which, according to Industry and Commerce, were lacking in 'those industries which enjoy the benefit of tariff or quota instruments on imports'. At first the bureau was to be a 'friendly advisor' with some price control powers. For those businesses which didn't respond adequately, a court of inquiry would be set up with power to subpoena documents on quality,

> price, methods of management, labour recruitment and training, materials used, marketing, overhead charges, capital structure and other matters. If businesses did not then comply to the bureau's directives, the state would be empowered to stop the distribution of profits, fix prices, fix maximum profit limits, confiscate excess profits and remove protection. Under certain conditions, the Minister of Industry and Commerce would be empowered to seize a company's assets and run it as a state concern. (O'Hearn 1990: 14)

The bill approved by the cabinet opted to extend the functions of the Prices Commission rather than create a new investigative body. It was also shorn of its more severe sanctions and had added to it proposals for the creation of industry level development councils composed of management and labour representatives as well as independent ministerial nominees 'to promote efficiency in industry by voluntary efforts'.[2] This still controversial measure lapsed when the Dáil was dissolved for a general election in February 1948 and the first Inter-Party government thereafter succeeded Fianna Fáil in office. The new government adopted a different approach to the pursuit of industrial efficiency in deciding to set up an Industrial Development Authority (IDA). With four appointed members, this body was given less drastic powers and a wider-ranging brief 'to investigate the effect of protective measures', 'to initiate proposals and schemes for the development of Irish industry' and 'to advise on steps necessary for the expansion and modernisation of existing industries'.

In 1945 Irish political estrangement from Britain and the USA co-existed with ongoing relationships of economic dependence. While trade with Britain remained overwhelmingly predominant, the relationship with USA was much more important than it had been before the war. Of Irish imports, 25 per cent came from the USA in 1947 compared with 10 per cent in 1938, a growth that mirrored the general European pattern. From the establishment of the Free State, Irish governments had foregone the option of having an independent currency by maintaining the Irish pound's parity with sterling. Ireland thus formed part of the Sterling Area whose policy was controlled by Treasury officials in London. In 1947 the British government suspended the convertibility into dollars of sterling. For a time Ireland was still able to draw on the sterling area dollar pool – a fund centralising the British Empire's dollar earnings from products like Malayan rubber or West African cocoa under Treasury control – to acquire the wherewithal for its imports from the USA.

The economic and political dimensions of its relations with Ireland were brought together when the US government launched the Marshall Plan in

1947. Here, 'the US wish to isolate Ireland in retaliation for her wartime neutrality was counterbalanced by a perceived need, for security reasons, to incorporate Ireland into some American-sponsored organisation' (Whelan 1992: 51). Ireland was seen by US policy makers as being capable of aiding broader European recovery through increased food production. Its involvement in a US-orchestrated programme could ease British financial difficulties by lessening pressure on the sterling area dollar pool. Seen in Cold War terms, Irish hostility to communism was overwhelming but dangerous destabilisation might, it was feared, occur in the future as a result of deteriorating economic and social conditions. Finally, the exclusion of Ireland from a European programme might prompt a revival of agitation in the USA on the issue of partition. Irish acceptance of a US invitation to attend the inaugural Paris meeting followed exchanges in which Agriculture, External Affairs and Industry and Commerce favoured participation but Finance expressed strong reservations (Whelan 1992).

The first Inter-Party government had replaced Fianna Fáil by the time an offer of US aid within the framework of the European Recovery Programme (ERP) was made to Ireland in mid-1948. Non-repayable grant aid had been sought: only repayable loan aid was offered. The Irish government was initially inclined to turn this offer down, but accepted it when it was informed by Britain that Ireland's already restricted access to the sterling area dollar pool was to be entirely cut off with almost immediate effect. Although some grant aid was later forthcoming, close to 90 per cent of the ERP dollar allocations to Ireland between 1948 and 1951 were made in loan form. During the lifetime of the ERP dollar aid for technical assistance projects was added to dollar allocations for commodity purchases. Yet when security strings were attached to US aid from the start of 1952, the Irish state – which had reaffirmed its neutral stance by refusing to join the North Atlantic Treaty Organisation (NATO) in 1949 – was cut off from a flow of US technical assistance funding that continued in the case of most other Western European states through the 1950s.

With the dollar flow ending, Ireland became firmly locked during the 1950s into a cycle of low economic growth and high emigration by a combination of structural weakness across several sectors of its economy and government austerity policies. These policies were prompted by recurrent balance of payments crises. As well as choking off the demand for imports, state policies also began to focus on promoting export growth. While ERP activity was heavily focused on agriculture, the US ECA pressed Irish policy makers to tackle the 'dollar gap'. This was the large difference between the quantity of dollars Ireland needed to acquire the US goods it was importing and the quantity it was earning from its exports. This pressure resulted in the establishment in 1950 of a Dollar Exports Advisory Committee (DEAC) whose examination of possibilities ranged across all sectors of the economy. Subsequently the IDA (with its remit greatly narrowed after Fianna Fáil returned to office in 1951) and Córas Tráchtála (a purely dollar export agency until its remit was widened in 1954) led the push to increase exports. By the mid-1950s, grant aid to new export-oriented industrial projects, tax relief on profits earned from exports and the relaxation of restrictions on foreign ownership of Irish industry were being introduced. By the end of the decade, with the publication of *Economic Development* (Department of Finance 1958), and subsequently the First Programme for Economic Expansion, key elements of a strategic move away from import substitution industrialisation were in place.

OEEC, EEC and EFTA

The international environment within which export growth could be pursued was also changing. Participation in the ERP began the process of reducing Ireland's international isolation when, as a condition of ERP participation, the state became in 1948 a member of the Organisation for European Economic Co-operation (OEEC), a membership that continued after the cessation of Ireland's US aid. Among the specific forms of co-operation on which OEEC focused was the promotion of trade by establishing the European Payments Union system which operated until currency convertibility was generally prevalent towards the end of the 1950s. Early OEEC measures aimed at the freeing of trade targeted quantitative restriction, a device of relatively slight importance to the Irish system of protection:

> Over the years it may be said, Ireland discharged its obligations in relation to trade liberalisation in an exemplary fashion. At the same time it must be acknowledged that the suppression of quantitative import restrictions is much easier for a high tariff country than for a low tariff country . . . the virtual elimination of quantitative import restriction was seen by the low tariff countries – Sweden, Denmark, Switzerland and the Benelux countries – as having put them at a disadvantage *vis-à-vis* high-tariff partners which continued to enjoy a significantly greater measure of protection. The high tariff countries were reluctant to face the increased competition which tariff reductions would entail and, in any event, argued that the GATT [General

> Agreement on Tariffs and Trade] was the appropriate body within which to negotiate such reductions. (Maher 1986: 27 and 52)

Division between high and low tariff countries was cross-cut by a divergence between those who wished to construct an integrated area presenting a common tariff to the rest of the world and those who favoured a free trade area that left its members free to choose the rate of tariff imposed on imports from non-member states. By 1956:

> On the one side were the six [European Economic] community countries with their plan to found a customs union and common market with strong central institutions: on the other side was an assortment of mainly Scandinavians and neutrals led by the United Kingdom, all of which preferred a free trade area within the OEEC context . . . Furthermore. . .Britain wanted only industrial free trade with agricultural products excluded and also wanted arrangements for her own Commonwealth preferential trade (Archer 1990: 68)

Outside both of these groupings were the OEEC's peripheral members – Greece, Iceland, Ireland, Turkey and (from 1959) Spain – Archer's 'forgotten five' in a Europe 'at sixs and sevens'. Exploration of the possibility of setting up a free trade area that would encompass both the customs union of the EEC and the organisation's other member states had spawned three OEEC working parties by the time the Treaty of Rome was signed in the spring of 1957. One of these – Working Party 23 – dealt with countries in the process of economic development. Irish efforts during 1957–8 focused on establishing a claim to come within this category and on formulating a common position with Greece and Turkey. Working Party 23 was chaired by the Irish Ambassador in Paris, W. P. Fay, who observed in his summing-up at the end of its first meeting:

> That the introduction of Free Trade in the 19th century had had catastrophic effects for some regions and countries (including Ireland); that it was false to assume that the unrestricted application of the so-called economic laws (without any regard to human factors) was going to solve economic problems. He added that members of the working party should realise that there was no need to apologise for the existence of this special committee, that no country was excluded from the circle of European friendship, that it was not so long since all the countries of Western Europe had come together in OEEC and declared themselves to be in need of special outside assistance, and that they should not emulate the unjust steward in the Gospel.[3]

Experts attached to Working Party 23 visited Dublin for discussions in May 1958 where they were told by Finance Secretary T. K. Whitaker that 'we were now in the position . . . that taxation was high, productivity was low, we had insufficient training in management and supervision, inadequate technical education and more restrictive practices than were good for economic progress'.[4] What struck the experts most forcibly was the 'absence of an overall plan to co-ordinate individual projects into one general policy objective':

> The experts were somewhat hampered in their examination by the absence of production targets, investment objectives etc. They would like to know, for example, how much investment the Government expected would take place over the next, say, five to ten years. Even the Greek attempt at the formulation of a development plan, with all its deficiencies, was preferable to the complete absence of any plan. While the Greek programme was not altogether realistic, it, at least, provided some indication of the thinking of the authorities regarding the pattern of future development.[5]

'Some indication of the thinking of the Irish authorities' was in place by the autumn of 1958 with the publication of *Economic Development* (Department of Finance 1958), as was a common formula with Greece and Turkey for special treatment within the Free Trade Area. This would provide the countries in the process of development with a transition period for dismantling protection with a minimum length of 30 years and also – influenced by the Treaty of Rome's provision for the European Social Fund – with grants to develop or adapt their infrastructure from the resources of the more advanced OEEC members (Maher 1986: 82–4).[6] However, the OEEC free trade area negotiations broke down at the end of 1958 owing to the divisions between these more advanced members, united though they were in their disinclination to provide the funding envisaged by the proposals being put forward in Working Party 23.

During 1959 Greece and Turkey applied for association with the EEC while Britain and six other OEEC member states moved towards the formation of an industrial free trade area. This, it was envisaged, would as a bloc negotiate a wider free trade arrangement with EEC whose terms would be better than those available through individual bilateral deals. Since, from a British viewpoint 'the OEEC-sponsored [free trade area] negotiations had placed the peripherals in a powerful position to block or veto progress if their individual demands were not met' (Fitzgerald 2000: 75), this approach sought to sideline claimants for special treatment such as Ireland. It did so by the simple expedient of not allowing them to take part in negotiations – at least not until they would be faced on a take-it-or-leave-it basis with the *fait accompli* of whatever accommodation the EEC and the British-led group had arrived at.

The formation of the European Free Trade Area (EFTA) in January 1960 imperilled Irish interests because it threatened to seriously erode the actual and potential benefits Ireland derived from the 1938 and subsequent trade agreements with Britain. In relation to manufactured goods, these had given Irish goods duty free access to the British market. Few Irish manufacturers had had the competitive capacity to exploit this opportunity and, after an initial period focused on the 'dollar gap', attempts to foster industrial exports in the 1950s concentrated on Irish firms turning this provision from a potential into an actual benefit. For Ireland, formation of a free trade area meant 'we have the dilemma of (a) having to secure an extension of industrialisation and (b) of having to try to do that in circumstances in which not only the home market but such a large proportion of our export market would be put in jeopardy'[7]. At the end of the 1950s, over 70 per cent of Irish exports of industrial goods went to Britain and close to 80 per cent of these goods enjoyed a tariff or quota preference over competing European goods. Losses of £4m from a trade currently running at around £18m were projected, with half of the loss attributed to paper and board products.[8] Agricultural goods were, of course, still Ireland's principal exports to Britain. Under the 1938 settlement Irish farmers 'had recovered their traditional access to the British market on the best terms available given Britain's policy of promoting domestic agriculture' (Daly 1992: 170). By the later 1950s these terms had become increasingly less advantageous:

> The effect of the British system of deficiency payments was to insulate the domestic producer from world prices while continuing to give the consumer the benefit of low retail prices, the cost of deficiency payments being borne by the British Exchequer. Britain was virtually the only market which operated an open door policy for agricultural products. As world food production rose, surplus supplies of temperate zone products tended to flow to that market. Price competition was intensified with adverse effects on Irish export earnings (Maher 1986: 120)

The British door had not, however, been equally open to all comers, with Commonwealth producers enjoying more favoured access than non-Commonwealth ones like Argentina and Denmark, from whom concessions had also been extracted under pressure in relation to non-agricultural trade

(O'Rourke 1991: 360). By putting EFTA members like Denmark in a position to link better terms of agricultural trade with Britain with the movement to industrial free trade, the new grouping threatened to further worsen the Irish position. In the summer of 1959 Britain concluded a new bilateral agreement with Denmark that reduced duties on products such as bacon. Here the speedy conclusion of the agreement for EFTA was a principal British consideration (Archer 1990: 122–4; Fitzgerald 2000: 80–1; Maher 1986: 99).

It was to a bilateral agreement with Britain that Ireland also now turned, although Irish diplomats had just presented an *aide-mémoire* to the six EEC members and the seven states in the process of forming EFTA somewhat optimistically seeking that:

> As an interim measure and pending the negotiations of a multilateral association comprising all members countries of the OEEC, which would precisely define Ireland's obligations concerning the reduction and eventual elimination of trade barriers *vis-à-vis* other OEEC countries, the members of the European Economic Community and the members of any other grouping which may be formed by other OEEC countries should, without obligation of reciprocity, extend to Ireland the benefit of tariff reductions and quota enlargements made in favour of one another (quoted in Fitzgerald 2000: 85)

In a memorandum prepared under the supervision of the Committee of Secretaries and submitted by the Minister for Finance on 8 July 1959, consideration was given to offering to dismantle Irish tariffs over an extended transitional period in a manner that gave preference to British goods in return for a 'joint responsibility' for Irish development approach that would see the British government encourage British companies to invest in Ireland in the way its regional policy encouraged industrial investment in its own 'development areas'. An Irish memorandum presented to the British at the end of July drew attention to 'the advantages to be gained by British industry in locating factory extensions in Ireland, where various costs were lower and social problems arising from excessive urbanisation did not exist to the same degree as in the United Kingdom' (Maher 1986: 94–101) However, in the discussions that took place against the background of expected British participation in a seven-country free trade area, emphasis was placed on offering Britain better access to the Irish market for industrial goods in an attempt to secure benefits 'which amounted to a proposal for an Anglo-Irish agricultural common market' (Maher 1986: 101). These proposals held no attraction for the British:

> The Irish ministers talked in terms of economic integration with this country and were prepared to offer us substantial concession on industrial trade; but since we already gave the Republic of Ireland free entry both for agricultural and industrial products there was little we could offer them . . . it appeared that they wanted to receive the benefit of the agricultural prices given to our home producers and that in return they might suggest that they might give us preferences in their market and instruct their state undertakings to buy British products, but these suggestions would be embarrassing in view of our relations with other countries (quoted in Fitzgerald 2000: 89)

In February 1960 the President of the Board of Trade, Reginald Maudling, told the Taoiseach that 'he could not think of any price that Ireland could offer in matters of trade which would enable Britain to grant the concessions on agriculture which Ireland wanted' and that 'it would not be possible for the British Government to take any positive steps to steer investment into Irish industry' (Maher 1986: 104). The Anglo-Irish Trade Agreement signed in April made very limited adjustments to the *status quo*.

Ireland's becalmed and isolated position was not to last for long, however. Within a year Britain had shifted its strategy from leading a European industrial free trade area intent on negotiating as a bloc with the EEC to applying for EEC membership. Ireland followed suit, its farming lobby having already begun to advocate that Ireland should join the EEC even if Britain did not. In applying to the EEC Ireland sought full membership rather than the association that its erstwhile OEEC Working Party 23 allies, Greece and Turkey, had obtained. This necessitated foregoing extensive claims for an extended period of special treatment with regard to tariff retention. Moreover, the formation of EEC and EFTA had replaced the kind of lengthy transition which even the more advanced states had contemplated in the 1956–8 OEEC free trade area discussions with expectations of a much shorter period for adaptation (Whitaker 2006: 20). In May 1962, EEC enquiries elicited an Irish intention to complete tariff elimination by 1 January 1970. With the collapse of the British membership negotiations early in 1963, the prospect of early Irish accession to the EEC ended. But membership remained the central state policy objective and an agreement that phased in free trade with Britain over a ten-year period was negotiated in 1965 as a preparatory step since 'the long-term national economic interest requires that the transition from the era of high protection to conditions of free trade be commenced as early as possible' (quoted in Maher 1986: 184).

Against a background of flux and uncertainty in European economic and political alignments, the dominant perception of what strategy would best serve Ireland's national interests shifted significantly between the 1957–8 submission to OEEC Working Party 23 and the 1961–2 campaign to convince the six EEC members that Ireland had the capacity to take on full Community membership. Initially the Industry and Commerce view held sway. This was that existing protection must be preserved to the fullest extent possible for as long as possible if most of the progress made in industrial development since the attainment of self-government was not to be wiped out. But by 1959 the view that freeing of trade should be pro-actively embraced by Irish policy was being vigorously advanced by Finance in what Whitaker (2006: 14) has termed the final phase of the battle between the two perspectives. Central to the espousal of free trade was the belief in its efficacy as a discipline to enforce greater efficiency and higher productivity on Irish workers and industrialists. As a Finance memorandum of 14 December 1959 entitled 'Reasons for Reducing Protection' put it:

> A gradual but steady reduction in protection over a period of years would ensure more intense concentration by management and workers on the raising of efficiency and productivity and reinforce the fiscal and other incentives to increase production for export. The pace of technical development may be expected to quicken in the outside world. Some driving force is needed to bring our production and marketing methods up to competitive pitch and to keep them there . . . As far back as 1947 the Department of Industry and Commerce recognised the need for some discipline to increase industrial efficiency. In that year legislation was prepared and approved by the Government providing wide powers for continuous supervision of the efficiency of manufacturing businesses and, if necessary, for formal inquiries into the efficiency of such businesses. It was felt that there was a necessity to ensure reasonable standards of efficiency in industries which enjoyed the benefit of tariff or quota restrictions on imports. It would appear to be much preferable that the discipline necessary to secure a general increase in industrial efficiency should be applied by gradual exposure to external competition rather than by internal administrative measures (quoted in Whitaker 2006: 56–7)

Finance envisaged that application of the disciplinary free trade stick would be combined with an offering of carrot – 'state aid, in the form of loan capital on reasonable terms, technical assistance grants, etc., could be made available to assist in the process of adaptation and modernisation of industry'. The innovation of technical assistance (TA) had been introduced to Ireland by the ERP, but its transatlantic flow had been cut off in 1952 when Ireland would not adhere to the conditions attached to its provision by the US Mutual Security Act. The establishment of the European Productivity Agency (EPA) within OEEC created a new external TA source, which operated for almost a decade after 1953. As an OEEC member, Ireland joined the EPA, which worked in tandem with national productivity centres, when it was set up in 1953. Minimal Irish involvement during the EPA's early years was reflected in the ongoing failure to give effect to the government's approval in 1950 of the creation of an Irish national productivity centre. But by 1958 a coalition of state and civil society actors that saw the EPA as a source of vital resources for Ireland's development had formed and the Irish National Productivity Committee (INPC) was created.

Supported by EPA in its early years, and securing domestic state support after the EPA's disbandment, the productivity drive helped shape the new Ireland in significant ways. Its bringing together of government, business and unions made it a precursor of a sustained social partnership approach to issues of adaptation to ongoing change in the international economic environment. It provided a forum where emerging labour policy issues, such as workers' rights in a situation of redundancy, were initially raised. In addition to initiating support for social science research, its resources were crucial to establishing educational provision for managers and trade unionists. It also played a part in preparing the ground for the transformation of the mainstream of the Irish education system that occurred during the 1960s. By contrast with its trade liberalisation initiatives, the impact on Ireland of the technical assistance and productivity side of OEEC's activities has received little attention. One aim of this study is to remedy that situation.

Plan of this book

Chapter 2 looks at how the Marshall Plan provided Ireland with technical assistance as well as dollar loans and grants. As the Irish TA programme developed, the emphasis was drawn away from agriculture and towards the development of industry. An ambitious and innovative programme of technical assistance projects came to an abrupt halt in January 1952, however, when Irish standing apart from NATO collided with US Mutual Security legislation.

Ireland differed from most other OEEC states in the shortness of the period in which it received US TA and productivity aid. For other states this type of aid continued to flow until the end of the 1950s. In most other OEEC states there was extensive exposure of both management and labour to US influences in industrial TA and productivity programmes. In Ireland, however, there were few team visits to the USA and neither business nor union leaders had extensive contact with US aid providers.

Chapter 3 examines Irish productivity and TA provision after the Marshall Plan. TA was retained as a sub-head of some Irish government department Votes – the departmental expenditure estimates authorised by the Oireachtas – after US aid ended in 1951. Thus some planned projects proceeded using Irish rather than US funds. TA was conceived by Industry and Commerce as a tool for promoting greater efficiency and lessening the reliance of industry on very high levels of protection but great difficulty was encountered in attempting to implement a TA-driven upgrading policy on the ground. The eventual conclusion of agreements with the US government for the spending of the Grant Counterpart Fund and the Irish move to play an active role within EPA gave a major fillip to TA and productivity projects in the later 1950s. The 1961 disbandment of EPA coincided with the Irish government's decision to apply for membership of the EEC. For Ireland to continue to access external sources of TA would involve accepting the status of being 'in the process of development'. This might have undermined the state's claim to be able to fulfil the obligations of full – as opposed to associate – membership of the EEC. At the same time, the massive task of adapting protected Irish industries to give them a chance of surviving in free trade conditions was underlined by the Committee on Industrial Organisation's surveys. This set the stage for the simultaneous domestication and expansion of Irish industrial TA and the productivity promotion drive that would be pursued throughout the 1960s.

Chapter 4 notes how from its initiation in 1950 discussion of organisational arrangements to promote TA activity and preach the gospel of productivity in Ireland took it for granted that government, business and trade union support would be essential to achieve success. However, the circle of those actually involved in addressing the question of whether an Irish national productivity centre should be set up was for several years restricted to ministers and state officials. From the late 1950s, Irish non-government actors became engaged in bipartite and tripartite bodies promoting first a productivity drive and later a wider process of planning for economic expansion within a European free trade context. Industry-level joint action did not root itself successfully in Irish soil. By the late 1960s a series of industrial policy initiatives were filling the vacuum left by this failure – a reinvention of the IDA, an unsuccessful attempt to integrate the state 'field' services supporting adaptation and a governmental turn towards mergers as the most feasible means of rationalising Irish industry for free trade survival.

Chapter 5 is the first of three chapters dealing with the impact of TA and the productivity drive on Irish education. From the late 1940s through the 1950s, the education of Irish trade unionists was a bone of contention within a divided Labour movement with British-style secular provision struggling to survive in the face of initiatives that united espousal of the social teaching of the Catholic Church with anti-communist crusading. The Marshall Plan and the formation of EPA saw trade union leaders and their protégés exposed to new US and continental European influences. During the 1960s, first EPA, then OECD and finally INPC funding enabled a reunified Irish Congress of Trade Unions (ICTU) to run its own education programme. During the same decade the Catholic Workers' College (CWC) moved to change itself into a specialist industrial relations centre as its religious and social contexts were radically altered. Acquisition of resources from the state became a feature common to the two formerly opposed tendencies of trade union education.

Chapter 6 continues the education theme but changes the focus from workers to management. Although many European countries had long-established schools of commerce, European managers were widely viewed as backward by their US counterparts in the post-1945 period. Bridging the education gap between European and US management came to be considered to be one of the principal ways in which the transatlantic productivity gap could be closed. Working with the Irish Management Institute and other bodies, the EPA provided an important channel through which American managerial techniques were introduced to Irish business organisations. Recipients of EPA help subsequently benefited from the 1960s expansion of domestic TA to promote adaptation to free trade conditions. In common with communism, if to a very much lesser extent, US-style capitalism was initially an object of Irish Catholic cultural suspicion. A non-American variety of management education was offered by CWC although philosophical difference was displaced by functional specialisation as the college transformed itself into a College of Industrial Relations and sought entry into the circle of institutions supported by TA funding.

In chapter 7, the focus on educational change is broadened out from specialist provision for trade unionists and managers to take in the national education system as a whole and the interlinked area of national science policy. Gathering pace during the 1960s, the key aspects of the transformation of Ireland's mainstream system of mass education were, first, greatly expanded levels of participation in secondary and higher education and, second, the rising emphasis on science and technology that diminished the predominant importance the Irish system attached to issues of denominational religious formation and language revival. Debate about the need for and organisation of an Irish national science policy proceeded in tandem with these new educational departures.

Preceding this process was a period in which OEEC, through its Office of Scientific and Technical Personnel (OSTP), had urged Irish policy makers to integrate economic planning with education and science policy initiatives. Both in education and in science and technology the bridge between a general commitment to planning and a concrete programme of action was subsequently supplied by OECD-initiated pilot studies drawing upon Irish resources of expertise across a range of disciplines.

Chapter 8 examines how, in addition to its general promotion of science and technology, OEEC particularly influenced the institutional shape of Irish social science research. At the prompting of EPA, the National Joint Committee on the Human Sciences and Their Application to Industry (HSC) was set up in tandem with INPC in 1958. Through EPA it sponsored the training abroad of young research workers, promoted awareness of ergonomic issues and participated in the development of plans to construct a model industrial community at Shannon Free Airport. It also unsuccessfully sought funding for the setting up of an occupational psychology research institute. As EPA was disbanded, HSC began to sponsor substantive research studies like the Tavistock Institute's Morale of the Dublin Busmen and J. A. Jackson's Skibbereen Survey. In 1964, HSC was merged with INPC and began to provide project grants to research projects based in the Irish universities. Much of this research was published in the Human Sciences in Industry series of monographs.

OSTP's influence was a significant factor operating in favour of Ford Foundation grant aid for the establishment of the Economic Research Institute (ERI) in 1960. Two figures active in the international economics of education network, Patrick Lynch and Henning Friis, were centrally involved in the developments that widened the remit of ERI and transformed it into the Economic and Social Research Institute (ESRI). Civil service discussion of planning for social development that would complement ongoing economic expansion plans provided another context for this move.

Integration between the HSC and ESRI had been envisaged but the two remained separate and did not collaborate to any significant extent. The HSC declined after the chronically strife-prone INPC was reconstituted in the early 1970s as the Irish Productivity Centre (IPC) under the joint control of the Federated Union of Employers and the Irish Congress of Trade Unions. Starved of money by IPC, HSC's eventual death helped to establish the sharp division between the 'sociology of the research institutes' and the 'sociology of the universities' that has characterised Irish social science research.

Chapter 9 offers concluding reflections on the how TA and the productivity drive of the 1950s and 1960s have contributed to the making of modern Ireland. As regards education and science, a significant effect through the creation of new institutions and the remoulding of existing ones can be discerned. But success in bringing together government, unions and business to effectively adapt a largely inefficient Irish industrial base to coming conditions of free trade can hardly be claimed. Industry-level joint action simply did not get off the ground while education in the trade union movement, management development in the business world and planning in the civil service all remained minority enthusiasms. Here a number of long-term (and one short-term) factors that combined to limit the positive response to these innovations are identified.

CHAPTER TWO

Marshall Plan Innovations: Technical Assistance and the Productivity Drive

Introduction

Between 1948 and 1952 Marshall Aid provided Ireland with $128m in loans, $18m in grants and less than half a million dollars in technical assistance (TA). Accounting for a fraction of one per cent of the monetary value of the aid received, TA might appear insignificant and deserving of no more than brief discussion. Against this view, however, is the argument that 'with its delayed fuse, the United States Technical Assistance and Productivity Program, or USTAP, qualifies as the Marshall Plan innovation with the biggest bang for the buck' (Machado 2007: 46). Certainly more developmental benefit to Irish society might plausibly be attributed to the small TA expenditure than to the whole $34m or so of the aid spent on importing tobacco.

In addition, the coming on stream of Marshall Aid TA in Ireland's case coincided with a shift from providing solely loan aid to a mix of grant and loan aid. When a state received US dollar aid under the European Recovery Programme (ERP), it was obliged to deposit in a special account a local currency sum equivalent to the value of the dollars it had been given. These local currency funds were known as counterpart funds. The power to decide on their allocation to specific uses varied according to whether the dollars to which they formed the counterpart were loaned or granted. If loaned, then the recipient country's government determined how the counterpart funds should be spent. If granted, the expenditure of counterpart funds had to be agreed between the recipient government and the US authorities. The combined advent of grant aid and TA from the middle of 1949 significantly intensified the interaction between US and Irish government officials while simultaneously increasing the leverage the USA might deploy to influence Irish government policies.

Although in per capita terms Ireland was one of the European countries benefiting least from the overall Marshall Aid provision, by late 1951 its authorised TA programme had become 'proportionately much larger than that of any other country'.[1] Moreover, whereas agriculture and food production had been given priority by US planners as the area in which Ireland could contribute to overall European recovery, this authorised TA programme then consisted almost entirely of industrial projects. When US aid to Ireland was suspended in January 1952, the losses incurred took almost entirely the form of cancelled TA projects. The fact that the USTAP represented the only form of US non-military economic aid to continue (and dramatically expand) in Europe after 1951 also meant that the ongoing opportunity costs of what proved to be a permanent Irish aid suspension also took the form of TA foregone.

This chapter charts how, as the Irish TA programme developed, the emphasis was drawn away from agriculture and towards the development of industry. An ambitious and innovative programme of such TA projects came to an abrupt halt, however, when Irish foreign policy collided with US Mutual Security legislation. Ireland differed from most other OEEC states in the shortness of the period in which it received US technical assistance and productivity aid. For such other states this type of aid continued to flow until the end of the 1950s. In most other OEEC states there was extensive exposure of both management and labour to US influences in industrial technical assistance and productivity programmes. In Ireland, however, there were few team visits to the USA and neither business nor union leaders had extensive contact with US aid providers. The shorter duration of the TA programme was only partly responsible for this: the way in which it was shaped by US and Irish official actions also played a significant role.

The initiation of the TA programme and its turn towards industry

Although a formal approach from the Dublin Economic Co-operation Administration (ECA) Mission on participation in the TA programme was only made to the Irish government in March 1949, documentation about the availability of TA was circulating around government departments six months earlier and discussion about projects that might be put forward for funding was under way before the end of 1948. Agriculture initially accounted for the lion's share of TA projects but by the end of 1949 a number of factors combined to switch the programme's emphasis towards the involvement of industry.

In the last months of 1949 the Dublin ECA Mission found itself subjected for the first time to sustained public criticism from *Irish Industry*, a journal linked to the Federation of Irish Manufacturers. A statement by the Director of the Mission, Joseph Carrigan, that Ireland 'because it is mainly agricultural, should aim at becoming a very good agricultural country instead of trying to create an industrial life where there was no possibility of it succeeding' became the basis of an attack on foreign interference in the Irish economy that the monthly journal continued over successive issues. Such interference was depicted as promoting the same kind of narrow, stunted economic development that British conquest of Ireland had fostered, with Carrigan being compared to Thomas Wentworth, Earl of Strafford – 'England in 1635 and USA in 1949 selling us the same idea for similar reasons. Well! Well!' These attacks plainly affected the Mission's approach to the TA programme with Carrigan 'expressing a strong desire to have some industry projects going ahead while the agricultural projects were being proceeded with as he did not want it to appear to an uninformed outsider that the Mission was in any way antagonistic to industry'.[2]

Back in Washington, the *Irish Industry* criticism prompted a move to broaden the base of expertise ECA applied to the southern Irish economy with the assignment to Irish affairs of Harry Clement, 'previously a Consultant for the establishment of small industries' who 'operated in Central and South America and China as well as in the United States'. This assignment was intended to counterbalance any tendency to concentrate on agriculture to the exclusion of industry arising from the staffing of the Dublin Mission with agricultural specialists.[3] Clement's input shaped a policy letter dispatched from ECA Washington on 28 December. Here a role was identified for industrial TA in promoting movement away from a situation whereby the Irish desire for industrial development led to inefficient plants being created and towards 'intelligent plant development . . . based on processing Irish raw materials into products which Irish farmers want at a price equal to or less than the import price'. A number of categories of agricultural industries 'that seem to us to warrant further investigation' were then identified – fertilisers; 'by-products in connection with existing slaughter houses'; various types of livestock feed; 'cheap farm building and construction materials' as well as 'improvement in the efficiency and operation of such existing industries as slaughtering and the manufacture of dairy products'.

These, the letter stressed, were suggestions rather than recommendations – 'we recognise the difficulties involved in developing industries that could compete on a free trade basis, but significant steps might be taken during the ECA lifetime to help the Irish to determine what plant possibilities they should investigate'. Given the limited level of industrial development in southern

Ireland, a two-phase industrial TA programme was envisaged. In the first phase the focus would be broad. A small team would be assembled that combined varied forms of expertise and 'would have the experience and imagination to eliminate those possibilities which should not be further pursued, to suggest alternative possibilities which they will run across during their investigation and then specifically to be able to show what specific half dozen industrial plant possibilities remain'. In the second stage TA could be used to bring in specialists 'whose job it would be to pursue the line of attack suggested by the preceding team, to work up detailed cost and technical specifications, to aid in locating possible plant sites etc.'

The team of experts could, it was suggested, be assigned to the Industrial Development Authority (IDA) – which had been in existence for a little over six months and was awaiting a formal legislative framework – if the Mission rated this agency positively.[4] The Mission had already reported that the IDA 'are anxious to dispel, via our Department of Commerce or any other effective places, any notion that they would not welcome American industrial investment' to facilitate which 'the Control of Manufacturers Act can, and would, they say, be waived'. The IDA had requested and received the Mission's assistance to follow up a *Daily Telegraph* story of 9 November about 'thirty would-be American investors . . . refused permission to invest in the United Kingdom on the grounds that their production was not to be of a dollar earning type'.[5] However, ECA in Washington was unenthusiastic about the IDA pursuing US investment in this fashion. Referring to the *Daily Telegraph* article, the policy letter of 28 December commented that 'rather than run down these would-be investors, it might be more fruitful, in our opinion, for the Authority to exert its influence to obtain approval of the "Treaty of Friendship, Commerce and Navigation" now being negotiated between the US and Ireland', adding that 'this type of treaty does not assure any flow of private investment to a country, but it certainly is a necessary prerequisite to this flow'. The 'magnitude of the task of attracting capital' was then emphasised by spelling out in considerable detail the range of investment criteria upon which an investor would expect the IDA to be able to supply concrete information – 'resources, power, water supply, labour force, marketing conditions, availability of local capital (Irish pounds) for investment if foreign capital is brought in, and other key production factors'. This kind of information would only become available through the kinds of surveys of Ireland's industrial potential that ECA Washington was suggesting that the TA programme be used to carry out.[6]

On 27 February Carrigan, in reply to ECA Washington's request for the Mission's opinion of the IDA, wrote that 'we are not in a position to appraise the effectiveness of this agency':

> It is too new and is as yet feeling its way. The Chairman [J. P. Beddy] appears to be rather conservative and studious and has a good reputation here. I would expect that under his guidance and given a chance the Authority might prove effective in the long run; but it is not going to move very fast in comparison with the ECA tempo, which is, as you know, attempting to reorganise European economy in four years . . . Just how much support it will get from the Government it is hard to determine at this time.

In this letter Carrigan also reported on recent discussions with the IDA in which the ideas about TA utilisation contained in the policy letter had been raised. The response was not particularly enthusiastic:

> The members exhibited some interest but for the most part feel that such ['agricultural industries'] projects have already been given consideration; and thus they did not show promise of prompt action along these lines . . . This Authority feels that it is constituted to perform the industrial survey function and has such a survey in hand in preliminary form. At this stage the Authority does not appear to feel that it needs technical assistance for this over-all survey job. It seems more interested in specific fields as soon as these fields are determined.[7]

By contrast, the policy letter's proposals, as reported back to Dublin by the Washington legation, drew a much more positive reaction from the Secretaries of External Affairs (Frederick Boland) and Industry and Commerce (John Leydon) as well as from the Minister for Industry and Commerce, Daniel Morrissey, who was 'deeply interested in the proposal, and indeed classed it as the first sensible suggestion on the industrial side which had come from ECA'.[8]

Spending the allocated TA budget and widening participation in the programme

The likelihood that a large part of ECA's budget allocation for southern Irish TA in the US fiscal year July 1949–June 1950 would not be spent provided another source of pressure for greater industrial involvement during 1950. A letter from Carrigan to Seán MacBride on 5 January pointed out that to date only $25,000 had been committed out of the $100,000 allocated.[9] On 10 February MacBride circulated a memorandum to the government on the issue. TA projects could, he argued, help remedy Ireland's serious scientific and technical deficiencies while 'our failure to avail of the Technical Assistance offered to us by ECA is inevitably taken as a lack of interest and creates a most unfavourable impression'. Both Industry and Commerce and the IDA were identified as having been inactive to date and as having particular potential to generate projects. Here the memorandum did not confine itself to general exhortation to greater activity and named specific industrial sectors that would benefit from TA. The memorandum also called for 'visits to the USA of teams of Irish workers to study American labour production practices and methods'.[10] In response, the government agreed that the relevant ministers and agencies would send project proposals to External Affairs by 28 February.

In the first half of 1950 the Irish government, under pressure from ECA, also removed two interlinked obstructions to wider participation in the TA programme. One was the resistance on the Irish side to the involvement of those working in the private sector rather than the public service. The initial agricultural projects participants were scientists and educationalists rather than farmers, while the civil servant members of the Interdepartmental ERP Committee were initially dubious about ECA Mission arguments that businessmen should be encouraged to become involved. The second was the financing of TA on a grant with counterpart basis whereby ECA paid all the dollar costs (excluding travel) but the equivalent amount of local currency had to be deposited in the grant counterpart account. If a private individual or firm were required to make this counterpart deposit, 'the manufacturer financing the scheme would in effect be paying the whole cost of a training trip to the States or of a visiting advisor to Ireland, deriving only the advantage of the ECA's ability to arrange and select'.[11]

ECA had discretion to waive the deposit of counterpart subject to the limitation that no more than one third of projects could benefit from such waivers. The fact that Irish applications almost invariably sought to benefit from a waiver quickly brought matters to a head. Transmitting proposals drawn up by ECA, a memorandum to the government from External Affairs on 17 April proposed that the state would fulfil the obligation of TA project participants to make an Irish currency 'counterpart' payment whenever it arose, and would, as a general rule, relieve participants of 50 per cent of the travel and other non-dollar expenses for which they were liable.[12] A new Technical Assistance Vote was created for the purpose of providing the necessary funds. By late June, press advertisements were inviting applications for TA on the basis of these new financial arrangements and highlighting how they facilitated private sector participation in the scheme.

In the spring of 1950 Harry Clement spent several weeks in Ireland working to expand TA project activity. In the wake of his visit a rift became apparent between ECA and IDA views of how the TA programme should develop in relation to industry. ECA favoured US experts coming to Ireland (Type B TA) rather than Irish teams visiting the USA (Type A TA) as the appropriate programme emphasis with an 'over-all industrial investigation or survey' forming the programme's centrepiece. The IDA disparaged the importation of US consultants and canvassed Irish industrial groups for Type A proposals to send study teams to the USA.

When Clement returned to Dublin in August, the IDA was prevailed upon over a series of meetings to support the two-phase overall survey conception that had been at the centre of ECA's thinking on Irish industrial TA since the start of the year. In September ECA approval was forthcoming with counterpart waived for phase one and US consultants were invited to submit proposals.[13] Its acquiescence in this flagship Type B enterprise notwithstanding, IDA promotion of TA continued to focus on generating Type A projects. In late October it brought forward proposals for 'seventeen groups of industry to travel to the USA', the sending of a team of cost accountants, two firm-specific Type A visits and a lone firm-specific Type B project.[14] The tentative ECA Technical Assistance Budget for Ireland in the US fiscal years 1950–1 and 1951–2 into which these projects were incorporated had by now increased to half a million dollars and was about to take a quantum leap upwards.

The major 1951 expansion of an industry-skewed TA programme

As Clement moved to Dublin to become Deputy Director of the Mission in December, the Irish government was aware that ECA dollar allocations to Britain were about to stop and fearful that Ireland would be accorded similar treatment. Advised by Clement, the Minister for External Affairs, Seán MacBride, sought to stave off the ending of Ireland's dollar area commodity flow by massively expanding its take-up of ECA TA.[15] By the start of 1951, the heads of a $2.6m TA programme, giving primacy across all sectors to Type B projects, were in place, with some Type A missions coming on stream at a later date and only in contexts framed by the findings and recommendations of the visiting US experts. While this new programme was in its conception a comprehensive one within which agriculture remained the largest intended recipient of TA funding (see table 2.1), its movement towards implementation was to confirm the increasing concentration of TA activity in the industrial field which had begun a year earlier. Against a background of strained relations between the Mission and the Minister for Agriculture, James Dillon, no progress was made in developing the projects in the Agriculture category.[16] A similar, if less specifically personalised, standoff developed in the tourism field.[17] Only with Industry and Commerce – apart from its tourism section – and the IDA did Clement and his Mission colleagues forge the working relationships needed to bring forward fully developed project proposals.

Table 2.1 **Composition of TA programme circulated by Seán MacBride at the end of December 1950**

Field	*Cost* $
Agriculture	1,040,000
Industry	912,000
Dollar Exports	260,000
Tourism	290,000
Special Advisory Services[18]	90,000
TOTAL	2,592,000

The Industry element of the December 1950 programme had, as table 2.2 shows, ten sub-headings to which one of the five projects included in the Dollar Exports section could also be added since it was concerned with production efficiency.

Apart from the proposals relating to plant engineering – which logically followed the completion of the industrial survey's two phases – and merchant shipping, the other projects were all developed, sponsored and transmitted to Washington where they received approval by the end of the fiscal year on 30 June. At this stage they fell into two broad categories. One came under Industry and Commerce sponsorship and consisted of projects related to semi-state companies – Bord na Mona, Electricity Supply Board (ESB) and the Sugar Company. The other came under IDA sponsorship, was a mix of proposals that originally appeared under the Agriculture as well as the Industry heading, and was concerned in the main with either private sector manufacturing (projects 1, 2, 4 and 5 in table 2.3) or with exploring untapped industrial potential (projects 3 and 6 in table 2.3). Although IDA sponsorship of the production methods in potential dollar export industries project was mooted at one stage, it was handled by Industry and Commerce pending the coming into effective existence of the Irish dollar export corporation, Córas Tráchtála (CTT).

In relation to the existing as opposed to the potential Irish manufacturing base, the projects allocating US experts to the IDA (projects 4 and 5 in table 2.3: TA 44–76 and TA 44–77 in ECA-speak) were, as presented by the Mission to ECA Washington, wide-ranging and ambitious interventions. The proposals were 'designed by the Irish government to give direct practical assistance in the formation of an industrial productivity program' and 'between them hit a series of horizontal and vertical industrial problems'. Here horizontal problems were those affecting industry across the board, while vertical problems were specific to an individual industry. The five horizontal problems chosen for attention are summarised in table 2.4. Under the first two headings – management techniques and materials handling – what was envisaged was 'the introduction to Ireland of needed aspects of scientific management [which] could, if successful, be spread rapidly'. Standardisation and simplification had underpinned the historical development of scientific management in the USA and, even in the absence of the chaotic situation that was said to exist in Ireland, were logical accompaniments of any attempt to transplant US industrial management technique or technology. Institutional obstructions to private industrial investment in Ireland together with the fuel shortage problems, which had sent Irish industrial production plummeting during the Emergency and continued in the early 1950s to pose a serious problem for which there appeared to be no solution near to hand, made up the project's remaining horizontal issues.[19]

Table 2.2 **Industry projects of TA programme circulated by Seán MacBride at the end of December 1950**

	Cost $
American experts in this [Industry] field would work in conjunction with the Industrial Development Authority and the Department of Industry and Commerce in Ireland	**912,000**
1 General Industrial Survey (Phase 2)	*75,000*
2 Plant Specifications, Design and Engineering Under contract with specialists following Phase Two of the Industrial Survey, with estimated total construction cost of $400,000: 10% for engineering	*40,000*
3 Peat Gasification Contract with US chemical engineering firm, which would sub-contract with European peat gasification experts as needed . . .	*100,000*
4 Analysis of Sulphuric Acid Materials Services of two expert for evaluation of Avoca pyrites deposits versus the use of gypsum in terms of operations and costs: six months per expert	*30,000*
5 Rationalisation of Irish Power Potential Evaluation of present systems as well as potential in terms of efficiency and costs, recommendations etc. by two men for six months each	*30,000*
6 Specialists Assigned to IDA Six technicians to the Industrial Development Authority in special fields as requested to supplement IDA staff, and to undertake specialised industrial functions and servicing; at six months each	*45,000*
7 To assist IDA in servicing Existing Industries and Business Fifteen specialists to be made available to Irish industry for short periods each, on request, to advise re. production methods, costs etc. averaging $5,000 each (to be tied in with Productivity programme)	*75,000*
8 Merchant Shipping The services of two experts for six months each to examine the Irish mercantile marine question . . .	*17,000*
9 Sending of Irish Technicians to USA in connection with each of the schemes at (1) to (8) foregoing it may be desirable from time to time to send Irish technicians to the USA to study American practices (Type A projects)	*75,000*

	$
10 Mineral Exploration	*65,000*
in three areas recommended for evaluation by industrial survey	
DOLLAR EXPORTS	
4 Improvement of Production Methods etc.	*100,000*
Services of specialist to evaluate and make specific recommendations re. existing production methods, machinery and equipment, plant layout and processes employed in those Irish firms whose products are potential sellers in the US markets. Analysis should include evaluation of practices having a bearing on prices, quality and output in six such fields (e.g. speciality goods, stout etc.)	
TOTAL	1,012,000

Table 2.3 **IDA-submitted technical assistance projects, 9 June 1951**[20]

1 Survey of the animal protein-feeding-stuffs industry
2 Survey of the food processing and food storage industries
3 Allocation of an additional $75,000 for the Industrial Survey project
4 Allocation to the Industrial Development Authority of experts who would study specific industrial problems
5 Allocation to the Industrial Development Authority of specialists who would assist in servicing specified industries
6 Allocation to the Industrial Development Authority of experts who would assist in the evaluation of pyrites versus gypsum deposits in terms of mining and processing costs as raw materials for the production of sulphuric acid and/or sulphate of ammonia

When a vertical focus was adopted in TA 44–77, the aim was said by the Mission to be 'to provide through the Irish Government productivity centre (the IDA) practical technical help designed to show the Irish businessman how he might unravel specific production problems of his own and produce a better product (or more of it) from the materials, labour and machinery he now uses'. The 15 specialists envisaged in December 1950 had been reduced, initially at any rate, to six by the time of its transmission to Washington in the following June. The six industries chosen for initial study were leather and hides, low-cost furniture, industrial alcohol, files and hacksaws, cutlery and pharmaceutical products. Apart from industrial alcohol, which was produced by a state-sponsored company, all of these industries were composed of private enterprises. To win acceptance for funding TA in admittedly inefficient industries, mostly using imported raw materials and, in some cases, with a record of seeking to have high tariff protection raised even further, the Mission urged its Washington colleagues to take a longer, wider view of the issues at stake:

> The Industrial Development Authority. . . and the Department of Industry and Commerce are both aware of the desirability of concentrating upon those industries that have a firm base in agriculture, or that at least use local materials for the most part. Evidence of this exists in the Government's submission of a range of TA proposals that concentrate on this approach . . . However as the plants referred to in this proposal are here and in existence, and as they now operate, they are either causing problems or acting as a drain on the public as a whole, in seeking to solve these problems through TA, this proposal has the Mission's backing as a practical productivity measure . . . This proposal not only

involves strictly technical problems, but it also involves the government's position on many tariff items. During the 1930s the Irish Government adopted a policy of putting up tariffs not only to 'protect' existing industries, but to develop industries that might come into being if tariffs made it practically certain that they could succeed. When the IDA was established two years ago, it was given the responsibility not only of industrial development but also of tariff review and of tariff policy. It has stated now that it intends to go to work on the whole question of tariff review and it has adopted the line that certain industries are being given undue protection or are not in need of it at all. In other cases, the IDA has raised the question of whether from the national standpoint, it is desirable to continue protection for a given industry in instances where the industry will not or cannot operate effectively enough to permit serious tariff reduction or elimination. To put it another way, the IDA is seriously interested in seeing to it that the industries involved do everything possible to compete with similar plants outside Ireland and the IDA (by maintaining tariffs) is not maintaining an artificially low technical standard. More specifically the IDA wants to know the effect of lowering tariffs on a range of Irish industries, whether the industries really will be able to exist under those circumstances, what the industries themselves could do (with competent technical help) to reduce costs and improve production methods, and whether such improvements would then permit tariff reduction or elimination.[21]

Table 2.4 **Horizontal industrial problems to be tackled by IDA-attached experts**

Management techniques including cost and production control

'The Government feels that Irish business as a whole has lagged behind in adapting techniques of standardising, costs, quality control (processes) and systems of costings (including records, accounting etc.). Rather than attempt to get a foot in the door in all types of industry at once, the Industrial Development Authority feels that it would be preferable to confine this project to two fields of industry, get successful results and then spread out. The Industrial Development Authority, accordingly, has selected (a) the clothing industry and (b) the light engineering and foundry industry, and has stated that considerable cooperation could be obtained from the private firms involved . . . almost no work at all has been done on time and motion studies, on elimination of unnecessary handling and work etc. Generally antiquated production methods prevail, and there is a considerable lack of mechanisation.'

Materials handling

'The Irish are aware that a steady flow of materials will raise productivity by at least 15% using existing machinery, but this information is known only in a general way, and the techniques to be used are not widely known. The purpose of this project is to increase output, save costs and increase effectiveness in using labor. Therefore the specialist would work directly with business and labor groups; he would use his know-how and how-how wherever possible in a plant and he would encourage by such mean as he deems feasible the spread of a useful idea from one plant to another . . .'

Industrial fuel conservation

'Fuel conservation should help Ireland stretch its meagre fuel supplies and tend to stave off the collapse of many industries that are already feeling the pinch of fuel shortages . . . it is a heavy importer of soft coal from the United Kingdom which has been unable to deliver minimum requirements here. The outlook for the future is not very bright in this department. . . The increasing likelihood of difficulty in getting supplies of petroleum, oil and lubricants have forced the Irish to examine all possibilities of tightening their belts. . . . the Irish are aware that new techniques of fuel conservation not only make good sense from a national point of view, but provide good business operations as well. The Government is interested in launching a Save Fuel movement, and wants to start in industrial plants. . .'

Industrial finance and taxation

'The Mission has encountered repeatedly and often instances of the need for new industrial investment for the creation of new or expanded industries; all too often such investment has been stymied either by lack of real risk capital or by the Government's income tax code, particularly with regard to depreciation facilities . . . what is needed is an intensive analysis [by a "top-flight" specialist]'

Simplification and standardisation

'The rapid development of Irish industry during the past twenty years has resulted in a chaotic situation in the fields of standardisation and simplification. For example the range of variation in many products is much greater than actual need . . . As a result of lack of simplification, manufacturers need to make numerous short runs of many different varieties of the same product, resulting in materials wastage and in high costs. . . . [while] the Government has established the Institute of Industrial Research and Standards . . . the field is still wide open for assistance.'

The suspension of US aid

At the end of December 1951 ECA was replaced by the Mutual Security Agency (MSA). The legislation that created MSA changed the context of US aid provision from European economic recovery to strengthening 'the mutual security and individual and collective defences of the free world'. Crucially, its terms required the Irish government to explicitly adhere to the Economic Cooperation Act of 1948 – which provided the framework for its ongoing aid programme – 'as heretofore amended, including the statement of purpose contained in Section 2 of the Mutual Security Act of 1951'. This was deemed to be incompatible with Ireland's declared foreign policy,[22] and a memorandum to the government advised that should refusal to adhere 'entail the discontinuance of all further American aid to this country after the 31st December, 1951, the Minister for External Affairs considers there is no alternative but to accept the loss involved.'

The extent of the loss became clear in the middle of January 1952 with MSA deciding that 'the only rule that would fully meet their responsibilities under the legislation was that all assistance should be terminated as of midnight on the 8th January except to the extent necessary to relieve a government of a dollar commitment which they had entered into by firm contract and to which they were irrevocably committed'.[23] Just over six months after their authorisation almost all the Irish TA projects had, against the background of staff shortage bottlenecks in both the Dublin Mission and the Washington Embassy (Murray 2008: 30–1), yet to reach this stage of irrevocable commitment. As table 2.5 shows, of just under $900,000 authorised for Irish industrial TA projects, only a little over $20,000 was to be expended after the suspension. This sum was spread over five projects. Two were part of a set of projects for the semi-state sugar company. One – food preservation and canning – was sponsored by the Department of Education and related to domestic economy instruction rather than factory production. The remaining two (partially) funded projects surveyed private firms involved in one case in processing meat or meat by-products and in the other in processing fruit and/or vegetables. Together with the report of the first phase of the overall industrial survey, these fragments comprise the full extent of the Type B industrial TA received by Ireland under the Marshall Plan.

Table 2.5 **Actual provision of dollars for authorised technical assistance projects after aid suspension on 8 January 1952**

Project	*Submission Date*	*$*
Sugar Beet: maintenance engineering	4 June 1951	
Sugar Beet: factory design engineering	4 June 1951	
Sugar Beet: cost accounting study	4 June 1951	
Sugar Beet: mechanical engineering	4 June 1951	1,451.35
Sugar Beet: visit of pathologist	31 March 1951	1,860.00
Food preservation and canning	28 May 1951	1,635.76
Analysis of power potential	5 June 1951	
Peat gasification	26 June 1951	
Manufacture of Protein Feed etc.	26 June 1951	8,659.01
IDA: Special Industrial Problems	26 June 1951	
IDA: Direct Productivity Assistance	26 June 1951	
Food processing	5 June 1951	9,102.84
Sulphuric acid production	6 June 1951	
Phase Two of Industrial Survey	5 June1951	
Industrial minerals exploration	6 June1951	
Dollar export projects (Córas Tráchtála)	6 June1951	
CIE projects: maintenance, engineering and hotels	8 June 1951	
TOTAL		22, 753

The Ibec Technical Services Corporation's report, *Industrial Potentials of Ireland: An Appraisal* (often referred to as the Stacy May report), was researched during the summer of 1951 and – with its concluding references to a variety of disrupted TA projects – had been overtaken by the suspension of US aid to Ireland by the time it was published a year later. The report favourably contrasted Irish industry with Irish agriculture in productivity terms – 'all of the upward momentum in physical output terms has come from industry, since agricultural production has remained static . . . industry measured by output per worker has produced far more than has agriculture . . . the continuation of the employment shift that has been taking place should be further encouraged'. It then noted that 'there are, however, serious limitations on such shift imposed by shortages of domestically produced materials, a limited domestic market for manufactures, and competitive problems in producing for export manufactures based on imported materials'. It also attempted to estimate the dimensions of the 'productivity gap' between Irish and US industry (see table 2.6). The major limitations and competitive disadvantages of Irish manufacturing industry were identified as being unduly high materials costs, concentration on activities resulting in little added value as well as low productivity per person employed, 'in part, probably, because of inefficiencies in management and labor usages, but importantly because of low plant and equipment investment'.

Table 2.6 **Estimated operating ratios per person employed: US and Irish industry**

Category	*Ratio US to Ireland*
Gross output	2.1 to 1
Value added	3.0 to 1
Wage and salary payments	3.0 to 1
Materials costs	1.6 to 1
Profits before taxes	3.4 to 1
Investment in fixed assets	2.9 to 1

Source: Ibec Technical Services Corporation (1952: 38)

The report went on to offer both broad critique and specific suggestion. A pervasive pessimism and lack of confidence were identified as a fundamental Irish cultural malaise:

> The talk is of economic expansion, but the action of government, business and labor alike is too often along the lines of consolidating present positions rather than accepting the hazards inherent in changed practices upon which expansion depends. There are few evidences of boldness or assurance in economic behaviour to give substance to expressed economic aims. In fact, the declarations of expansive purpose are frequently qualified by expressions of a conflicting, anti-materialist philosophy, of an asceticism that opposes material aspirations to spiritual goals, and hence writes down the former as unworthy (Ibec Technical Services Corporation 1952: 80)

A banking system removing Irish savings to Britain rather than investing them productively at home, an incentive-stifling system of government regulation and taxation; an imbalance between productive and 'social welfare' public capital investment as well as an unequal exchange trading relationship with Britain all came in for criticism. A cattle industry organised to add value domestically rather than export live animals, mineral development, identification of imports that could be replaced by domestic products and the use of TA to promote the efficiency in manufacturing that would make exporting feasible were all suggested as lines of expansion to be pursued. The critique of excessive linkage with Britain was also accompanied by the suggestion that:

> If Ireland were to establish a general economic climate favourable to private initiative, with institutions that provided strong incentives for investment in the modern capital equipment upon which high productivity depends, and equally attractive rewards for managerial and worker performance, development of the more promising lines of manufacture would follow almost automatically. Foreign capital likewise could be attracted in considerable volume to what would amount to a haven from state-imposed restrictions that are so widely prevalent in Europe (Ibec Technical Services Corporation 1952: 93)

This report completed the first of what had, as outlined above, been envisaged as a two-phase project. Here it was anticipated that 'at a later date (now undetermined) Phase 2 would show the IDA how to realise these [industrial] potentialities through detailed prospectuses designed to attract enterprises to develop specific industries'. The Ibec Corporation was not, however, at this point contracted to carry out Phase 2 and this second stage of the project duly fell foul of MSA's aid suspension.

USTAP after 1952: the opportunity cost of aid suspension

'Promising yet inconsequential at first', USTAP 'expanded dramatically after MSA absorbed ECA' (Machado 2007: 46). The 1951 Mutual Security Act contained the Benton Amendment which declared the policy of the US Congress to be:

> That this Act should be administered in such a way as (1) to eliminate the barriers to, and provide the incentives for, a steadily increased participation of

> free private enterprises in developing the resources of foreign countries . . . (2) to discourage the cartel and monopolistic business practices prevailing in certain countries receiving aid under this Act which result in restricting production and increasing prices and to encourage where suitable competition and productivity and (3) to encourage where suitable the development of the free labor union movements as the collective bargaining agencies of labor within such countries. (Quoted in Boel 2003: 31–2)

A year later the Moody amendment earmarked $100m in aid funding for carrying out programmes 'in furtherance of the objectives of [the Benton Amendment] with a view to stimulating free enterprise and the expansion of the economies of those countries with equitable sharing of the benefits of increased production and productivity between consumers, workers and owners'. The same amendment authorised the transfer of $2.5m to OEEC – which by this time was divided into a majority of members who were in good Mutual Security Act standing with the USA and a minority (including Ireland, Sweden and Switzerland) who were not – for the promotion of these objectives. The larger of the Moody Amendment's earmarked sums was doled out through a series of bilateral agreements between the USA and states that were in almost all cases its military allies. The smaller earmarked sum prompted the 1953 creation within the OEEC of an autonomous European Productivity Agency (EPA) of which all OEEC members, whether US military allies or not, were members. Ireland's membership of EPA will be discussed in subsequent chapters: here the bilateral allocations to 11 OEEC members of Moody aid are set out in table 2.7.

In the summer of 1952 the possibility that the second instalment of Mutual Security legislation containing the Moody Amendment might open the way for a resumption of US aid to Ireland without acceptance of the previously demanded conditions was discussed between Dublin departments. Acquiring weapons for the armed forces was the main concern on the Irish side but, because the requirements of NATO allies would take priority over Irish requests which 'might also set a precedent for other areas such as Burma, Indonesia etc.', Washington Embassy soundings held out no hope of success. They did, however, report that 'it seems there is a reasonable possibility of securing some aid on the lines of Technical Assistance if a strong presentation is made'. Back working for MSA in Washington, Harry Clement had drawn Irish diplomatic attention to the earmarked Moody funds, suggesting off the record that 'if we could produce suitable program we might be able to secure, say, $5,000,000 out of the total set aside'.[24] In Dublin, however, agreement prevailed that no approach to restart aid should be made. Within Industry and Commerce the view was taken that 'judging from our previous experience it would not be to our advantage to subject ourselves once more to American supervision in this [TA] field unless the sums in question and the probable results were very substantial indeed'.[25]

Table 2.7 **The uses of Moody and Moody-related aid in OEEC recipients as of the beginning of 1958**

Country	*Productivity grant programmes*	*Productivity loan programmes*	*EPA capital contributions*	*Total*
	$m	*$m*	*$m*	*$m*
Austria	4.74	6.73	0.80	12.27
Belgium	3.52	–	0.08	3.60
Denmark	8.18	0.59	0.24	9.01
France	26.10	–	2,40	28.50
Germany	3.62	23.80	0.80	28.22
Greece	0.14	1.18	0.08	1.40
Italy	13.81	10.52	1.76	26.09
Netherlands	10.63	0.41	0.24	11.28
Norway	4.26	1.52	0.32	6.10
Turkey	0.82	–	0.08	0.90
UK	5.48	2.80	0.72	9.00
TOTAL	81.30	47.55	7.52	136.37

Source: Boel (2003: Appendices table A–1)

How did the Irish experience of USTAP compare with that of other European states that received industrial technical assistance from the USA? The recurrent emphasis in the literature is on the huge scale of the interchange that took place.

> Under [USTAP] auspices more than six thousand European managers, workers, educators, and engineers visited the United States to learn production and construction methods by the end of 1951. They toured factories, conversed with businessmen and labor leaders, and attended management–labor seminars. The program traveled a two-way street, as hundreds of American specialists also

> went to Europe to teach and demonstrate the American System and know-how to Marshall Plan recipients . . . In 1953, with the creation of a European Productivity Agency, the number of technical missions visiting the United States soared. (Machado 2007: 46).

Britain led the way in this field, with the establishment of the Anglo-American Council on Productivity (AACP). Under AACP auspices 66 joint employer–trade union teams visited the USA 'to investigate specific sectors or particular practices (for example production engineering)' between 1948 and 1952. At the same time the London ECA mission was running a parallel programme of industry missions – taken together with those of AACP, the total number was about one hundred – and of study placement for British managers in USA. These missions were followed up by intensive efforts to disseminate their findings throughout British industry (Tiratsoo and Tomlinson 1998: 36).

Under Harry Clement's influence, the Irish TA programme had acquired a strong Type B orientation. An influx of between 70 and 80 US experts was expected to arrive in the country during the first six months of 1952 but, with the aid suspension coming into effect, scarcely a handful actually did so. Type A TA, which the IDA favoured and claimed to be the preference of the vast majority of Irish industrialists, was relegated to a minor role in the Irish programme by ECA's Type B emphasis. Nonetheless, 18 Irish industrial associations were either contacted by the IDA or took the initiative themselves in relation to sending a team to the USA under the TA scheme. Almost two thirds of these groups made some active form of application or inquiry but only two – Flake Oatmeal Millers and Paper Mills – actually succeeded in sending teams to USA. The number of team visits is brought up to four if to these specifically industrial ones are added a team from the Congress of Irish Unions (CIU) and some Federated Union of Employers (FUE) nominees who were attached to a huge 1951 European employer's mission.

The predominance of small firms in Irish industry was noted by the Dublin Mission at the outset of ECA TA promotion as a structural obstacle to securing a high level of industrial participation. The IDA in March 1951 reiterated this point to External Affairs:

> In the case of practically all the Groups concerned, it was evident that the industry was organised on the basis of small units where there was no substitute immediately available for the key personnel that would normally be selected to represent the management interest. This key personnel (often a working

> Managing Director) could not be spared away from the business for the eight to ten weeks normally required for a Technical Assistance Scheme.

At this particular time 'the precarious position which had developed in relation to raw material supplies generally had made it more difficult for representative Irish firms to contemplate leaving their businesses without top expert management capable of taking immediate decisions on raw material supply questions.'[26] Special pleading might be suspected here, but good grounds for discounting such a view is provided by the general acceptance among economists of the serious problems Ireland experienced in relations to raw material prices and supplies as a result of the Korean War (Kennedy and Dowling 1975: 207–8).

It is striking that in more than half the cases where positive interest was expressed but no Type A mission materialised, a significant obstacle is traceable to the US supply side of the TA programme. The most commonly encountered obstacle was intimation from ECA in Washington or Paris that a visiting Irish team would not be welcomed by its industrial counterpart in the USA. The concentration of Irish industrial activity in easy-to-enter areas lacking technological or other barriers seems the most plausible explanation for such negativity. In these areas US producers were likely to have felt particularly exposed to threats from external competitors and reluctant to facilitate the imitative upgrading of their operations. Another obstructive factor was the increased emphasis on relevance to military preparedness which marked ECA evaluation of TA project proposals in the 18-month period between the outbreak of the Korean War and the agency's replacement by MSA. Against this background, the Dublin ECA Mission killed off some Irish project proposals that patently lacked any claim to this relevance without sending them out of the country (Murray 2008: 25–9).

Much energy was invested in building up the industrial side of the Irish TA programme, which measured in authorised dollars had become 'proportionately much larger than that of any other country' by late 1951, yet the numbers of those involved in industry who actually participated in TA projects was actually very small in the comparative European context. Obviously the shorter duration period during which aid flowed, together with the terms and timing of the aid suspension which resulted in all but three per cent of the authorised funding being lost, played a large part in this. But it is also noticeable that, even while the TA programme was in place, the level of contact between the aid providers and manufacturing industry or trade union leaders was much less than that prevailing in relation to equivalent figures in the agriculture or tourism sectors. This absence of personal network links was compounded by the failure to establish a national productivity centre in Ireland.

A national productivity centre for Ireland?

To derive maximum benefit from TA, ECA urged participating countries to set up national productivity centres. The concept of these centres built on the British AACP experience and envisaged giving technical assistance and productivity activities an enduring institutional framework that would be efficient, national (as opposed to American) and – with government, management and trade union input – tripartite. When the issue was raised with the Dublin ECA Mission early in 1950, its response was to point out that ECA's ideas 'seem for Ireland to be on a rather pretentious scale'. Mission activities were focused on agriculture, tourism, minerals and fuel rather than manufacturing industry. In the Irish industrial field it observed that the IDA 'approximates in many respects the Productivity Center' – 'it seems likely that the Authority would view itself as responsible for the general functions of such a center and would regard the establishment of another as redundant'.[27]

A luncheon in External Affairs on 12 June 1950 attended by two Paris-based ECA officials introduced the concept to a high-level Irish ministerial and official audience. Here 'it was agreed that the proper body for the implementation of a productivity scheme in Ireland was the IDA and the vital importance of the promotional aspect of this activity was emphasised'. A memorandum for the government on the issue was quickly circulated by External Affairs. This envisaged a productivity committee composed of three nominees each of labour, management and government, established on a permanent basis and funded by a government grant-in-aid. By the end of June, government approval for the proposal was forthcoming on the understanding that specific proposals would be submitted by Industry and Commerce after consultation with the IDA.[28] Such proposals were not be forthcoming for reasons set out in a letter from the IDA on 9 April 1951:

> We had discussion with Paris representatives of ECA as to what would be involved in the setting up of such a centre. They worked out a scheme of organisation based upon eight major functions. This involved a staff of approximately forty and an annual expenditure on salaries of about £23,000, to which would be added approximately £7,000 per annum for other expenses, making a total annual expenditure of £30,000.

The Minister for Industry and Commerce 'took the view that we [IDA] should defer putting up definite proposals until a stage had been reached at which our own staff difficulties . . . had been dealt with'. The IDA letter went on to attribute the 'far too ambitious' character of the proposals to the fact that 'the ECA people themselves had little or experience of the actual working of a Productivity Centre'.[29]

In June, following a change of government, an External Affairs memorandum revisited the issue. It was noted that 'while the ECA people from Paris were very enthusiastic about the establishment of a full-scale Productivity Centre in this country this enthusiasm has not been shared by either Mr Miller or Mr Clement of the local Mission'. To Clement, 'who is primarily and enthusiastically interested in our industrial development programme', was attributed the view that 'the Productivity Programme being operated by Paris was geared to heavy industry and designed primarily to raise the marginal level of productivity in already highly industrialised countries'. In addition it was no longer clear in geopolitical conditions changed by the Korean War that the higher echelons of ECA attached the same priority to the productivity issue as they had previously done: 'there has been a decisive re-orientation of US Aid objectives – from Economic to Defence'. The recorded response of the new Minister for External Affairs, Frank Aiken, was 'that the desirability of letting the matter die a natural death might be considered'.[30]

The massive surge in military spending by the USA and its NATO allies that followed the outbreak of the Korean War changed the context for the productivity drive rather than diminishing its importance. If Communist armies had to be confronted, there was also a perceived imperative to protect living standards while diverting resources from civilian uses. Otherwise popular discontent could feed into increased support for the Communist parties of Western Europe, especially those of France and Italy. These considerations prompted ECA to launch a new Production Assistance Drive which aimed to provide Western Europe with both guns and butter.

At a meeting with Industry and Commerce officials on 8 August, Harry Clement intimated that:

> Now there was a fresh approach to the problem of productivity and ECA hoped to see in each Marshall Plan country, an agency on which would be represented, the Governments concerned, ECA, employers, labour and other sections of the community. ECA would enter into an agreement with each Government based on a definite programme of work, the assignment of

> definite powers and functions to the productivity organisation and a fundamental part of such agreements would be a proviso that the benefits resulting from assistance to industry would not be retained by employers but would be shared equally with labour and consumers.

ECA's insistence on benefit sharing was linked to its willingness to extend eligibility for TA to projects designed to benefit individual firms rather than whole industries. Industry and Commerce's Secretary responded that 'we could meet ECA requirements in regard to sharing with consumers but not with labour as otherwise wages and conditions in certain industries would get out of hand'. In response to a query as to whether 'the USA government were sponsoring the idea that labour should be given a share in the control of industry', Clement 'was emphatic that this was not US government policy and he pointed out that if this view were taken by manufacturers the whole productivity programme would fall to the ground'. However, 'he stressed that it was necessary to secure the full co-operation of labour interests as otherwise they would be opposed to any steps taken towards increasing productivity lest disemployment should follow'.[31]

Clement had told this meeting that 'the new ECA approach to productivity was based on the work of a Californian shoe manufacturer and a member of the American Federation of Labour' and it was from the shoe manufacturer turned senior ECA policymaker, William H. Joyce Jr, that the Washington Embassy received more information on 28 August:

> Mr Joyce told me candidly that . . . he thought that a new productivity board or agency . . . was not a suitable set-up for Ireland. He thought it would suffice if one or two top men in the Department of Industry and Commerce devoted themselves full-time to the question of productivity . . . It seems clear from my conversation with Mr Joyce that any method of operation or scheme of organisation which we may wish to establish to suit our own circumstances would meet with ECA's approval provided it was designed to secure their overall objective of increased productivity with the benefit of such productivity passed on to the community in general.[32]

In Dublin both Clement and Industry and Commerce had in the meantime concurred that the kind of productivity centre envisaged at ECA in Washington would not be suitable to Irish circumstances. Meeting Irish officials on 8 September Clement was said to have 'expressed the view that the existing series of Irish Technical Assistance projects constitutes in effect a productivity programme' and discussion now focused on arrangements for TA co-ordination between a short-staffed ECA Mission and Industry and Commerce, to which responsibility for all TA projects had passed in a post-election re-allocation of functions between itself and the IDA.[33]

In October, the close Washington ECA scrutiny now being attracted by the considerable scale that Ireland's authorised TA had attained prompted a third 'center' creation initiative. Here the proposal was for a 'TA Center' that would not simply co-ordinate the rolling out of the projects, but would arrange for the attachment of local personnel to visiting US experts in order to absorb useful experience and ensure that the experts' recommendations were subsequently followed up and implemented. Transmitting these proposals, Clement added his own suggestion that 'the "TA Center" would have the general responsibility for developing workable relations with the business community concerning those TA projects that depend for success upon the full understanding and co-operation of Irish industrialists and businessmen'. Here he envisaged creating 'a TA Advisory committee composed of progressive, influential business leaders'. But at a meeting on 2 November with Clement and Scott Behoteguy, the Assistant Director of the TA Division of OSR Paris, the Interdepartmental ERP Committee resisted the TA Center proposal on cost grounds. The furthest it would go was to support the seeking of sanction from Finance for an additional officer to co-ordinate all technical assistance activities. A reply to such a request was still awaited when the expected large influx of experts was all but obliterated by aid suspension.[34]

Conclusion

During 1950 and 1951 the ECA TA programme for Ireland expanded rapidly, with industry emerging – somewhat accidentally – as its main focal point. US aid suspension in 1952 prevented this programme moving from conception to execution. Although the possibility of seeking to have aid restored was subsequently considered on the Irish side, no action was taken and the suspension became permanent. Ireland therefore missed out on the later 1950s heyday of substantial earmarked USTAP funding under the Benton and Moody amendments. In 1950–1 three separate proposals for the creation of an Irish national productivity or TA centre were discussed. But because broad, if conditional, government approval for the concept was not translated into the creation of a concrete structure, the US aid period ended without an Irish productivity organisation in which government, management and trade unions were participants. Much official time and energy went into the conception of the Irish industrial TA programme, but neither businessmen nor trade unionists had any involvement in a process which left the cultural pattern of Irish industry untouched.

CHAPTER THREE

US Innovations After US Aid: Technical Assistance and Irish Industry, 1952–73

Introduction

How did the US-introduced innovations of technical assistance and productivity promotion fare in Ireland after US personnel and US funds ceased to be available to support them? This chapter looks first at what the Irish government salvaged from the wreckage of the authorised TA programme after the January 1952 aid suspension. It then examines the extent to which during the first half of the 1950s TA was conceived by Industry and Commerce as a tool for promoting greater efficiency and lessening the reliance of industry on very high levels of protection. The difficulty encountered in attempting to implement a TA-driven upgrading policy on the ground is illustrated by a case study of the electric lamp manufacturer, Solus Teoranta. How the eventual conclusion of agreements with the US government for the spending of the Grant Counterpart Fund and the Irish move to play an active role within EPA gave a major fillip to TA and productivity projects in the later 1950s is then documented. The 1961 disbandment of EPA coincided with the Irish government's decision to apply for membership of the EEC. For Ireland to continue to access external sources of TA would involve accepting the status of being 'in the process of development'. This might have undermined the state's claim to able to fulfil the obligations of full – as opposed to associate – membership of the EEC. At the same time, the massive task of adapting protected Irish industries to give them a chance of surviving in free trade conditions was being spelt out by the reports of the Committee on Industrial Organisation. This set the stage for the simultaneous domestication and expansion of the Irish industrial technical assistance and productivity promotion drive that would be pursued throughout the 1960s.

Technical assistance in Ireland after Marshall Aid

In the immediate aftermath of US aid suspension the Interdepartmental ERP Committee reviewed the future of TA in Ireland. There was agreement that `the idea of state contribution to the provision of technical assistance was too valuable to be abandoned'. On 15 February 1952 the government agreed a basis upon which TA would continue to operate in the post-aid situation. The key elements of this were:

- That the principle of a state-sponsored technical assistance programme should be maintained notwithstanding that any dollar expenditure involved will no longer be defrayed by the United States Government;
- That for this purpose, the present Vote for Technical Assistance (which is at present limited to projects put forward with the approval of the Economic Cooperation Administration) should be expanded in such a manner as to enable funds to be made available for technical assistance projects of any kind, including visits of Irish technicians to any country abroad and visits by foreign technicians to Ireland;
- That the standard State contribution to a technical assistance project should be 50% of the total cost of the project, with discretion for a larger proportionate state contribution in exceptional cases, each project to be recommended by the appropriate Department and approved by the Department of Finance;
- That when the proposals for the utilisation of the Grant Counterpart moneys are submitted to the United States authorities, the amount proposed in respect of technical assistance should be raised from that already approved by the Government, namely £250,000, to £350,000, so as to provide for that part of the expenses, which under the Economic Cooperation Administration programme were met by the United States authorities.[1]

Given the prevailing policy thrust of sharp deflation aimed at rectifying a large balance of payments deficit, the decision to retain the TA Vote is remarkable. The context of Grant Counterpart Fund availability was crucial to this outcome. As noted in chapter 2, the creation of equivalent value local currency funds as a counterpart to dollar aid was a standard requirement whether US aid came in the forms of loans or grants. If loan aid was received, the recipient country's government was effectively free to decide how the counterpart funds should be spent and the Inter-Party government had largely used up Irish loan counterpart money on agricultural projects by the time it lost office. In the case of grant aid, the expenditure of counterpart funds had to be agreed between the recipient government and the US authorities. Discussion on how this would be done was under way by late 1951 with the Irish government tabling a set of proposals that would devote the great bulk of the funds to agricultural development. The skewing of TA towards industry had been unintentional – a largely fortuitous outcome of the micropolitics of the agriculture and tourism policy fields that began to be reversed with the displacement of James Dillon as Minister for Agriculture. Increasing militarisation of the ERP after the start of the Korean War also placed renewed stress on Ireland's role as a food producer. Laboratory facilities for the Institute for Industrial Research and Standards (IIRS) and an unspecified share of the allocation for TA made up the minor industrial components of the proposed distribution of the Grant Counterpart Fund.

When aid was suspended, the general expectation among Irish civil servants was that a Grant Counterpart agreement could fairly quickly be reached and that the funds would be available for spending in the near future. When the Technical Assistance Vote was first created in 1950 to facilitate greater participation in the ECA TA programme, one third of the £150,000 fund consisted of a transfer from the Grant Counterpart Fund agreed between the Irish and US governments. Citing this precedent, Frank Aiken informed the US Ambassador on 4 June 1952 that 'the Irish Government proposes to create a special fund of £350,000 by a transfer of this amount to the Vote for Technical Assistance from the Grant Counterpart special Account, with the agreement of the US Government'.[2] But under US law the approval of the US Congress as well as that of the relevant US executive agencies was needed before unused counterpart funds could be released where suspension of aid had been imposed. The agreed release of funds for TA would not precede the conclusion of a comprehensive agreement for spending the Grant Counterpart money. It was to be August 1954 before an overall framework agreement for a series of specific sub-agreements was in place. The TA sub-agreement was not to be signed until July 1957 – five and a half years after the aid suspension took effect. As will be seen later in this chapter, this timescale contributed to a breakdown in the inter-department consensus supporting continued TA spending.

Salvaging TA from the aid suspension wreckage

What to do with the existing TA programme that had been developed in collaboration with ECA was the other issue facing the Interdepartmental ERP Committee in January 1952. Here it was agreed that 'the projects with which it had already been decided to proceed should be re-examined on their merits, special advertence being had to the influence of ECA pressure when the original decision was taken in a particular case, and also to the relative value of American technical assistance and assistance available from other sources'. Responsible for almost all the suspended projects, Industry and Commerce undertook a review whose recommendations were approved at the departmental conference held on 10 March.[3] As shown in table 3.1, of the projects deprived of any dollar support about half were continued to a greater or lesser extent by Irish government funding while half were entirely discontinued.

Table 3.1 **Action by Irish government after aid suspension in relation to ECA-authorised TA projects for which no dollars were provided**

Project Continued	*Project Dropped*
Peat gasification	Analysis of power potential
Sulphuric acid production	IDA: Special industrial problems†
Industrial minerals exploration	IDA: Direct productivity assistance
Dollar export projects (Córas Tráchtála)	Phase two of industrial survey
CIE projects: maintenance, engineering and hotels*	

* Continued in part: the hotels project was completely dropped

† One sub-project was almost spared. At Industry and Commerce's Departmental Conference on 10 March 1952 the recommendation that 'the project for fuel conservation in industrial and other undertakings should be proceeded with, the cost of the services of two British experts for six months being defrayed by the State' was approved. Opposition from the Department of Finance later led to its being dropped

All of the continued projects were in the semi-state sector and virtually all had a history preceding the advent of ECA TA. Peat gasification fitted into a pattern of Irish industrial research concerned to find economic industrial uses for Ireland's endowment with an abundance of peat and seaweed. Supported by very small amounts of state funding since the early 1930s, this activity gained impetus from the expansion of turf production and utilisation that occurred in the fuel crises of the war years and during the coal supply difficulties that persisted into the 1950s. Its external engagement now returned to the peat-producing countries of Europe. Mianrai Teoranta was engaged in mineral exploration before ECA TA and turned to a British consultant when it ended. A proposal developed in conjunction with Britain's Imperial Chemical Industries (ICI) by Ceimicí Teoranta – the industrial alcohol producer – for sulphate of ammonia production based on gypsum had been under consideration when US TA came on stream. ICI resumed its involvement when US TA was withdrawn. CTT, by contrast, was a creation of the Marshall Plan period which was only beginning to function as aid was suspended. Its negotiations with two US firms on projects that had been designed to launch it into operation were at an advanced stage by the end of 1951 when the MSA axe fell. With a remit to develop dollar exports, 'it was felt that it was vital for the success of Córas Tráchtála, Teo. to get technical assistance from the United States'.[4]

The consultants to CTT were given the brief of exploring the potential for exporting specified products to the USA. Their three month study, which CTT published in 1953, involved visits to 108 separate plants most of which were involved in food processing or textiles. Their report began with a blunt discussion of business attitudes in which it was stated that 'we have discovered no inclination among Irish producers to take any sort of risk'. The predominantly family-owned businesses were accused of 'smugness' and a catalogue of illusions which obstructed their proprietors from approaching issues of export marketing in a realistic way were enumerated, including the illusion that the Irish product was of superior quality and that it would be possible to successfully sell in the USA 'on the basis of sentiment, nationality or friendship towards Ireland and the Irish'. None of the products examined was considered worth recommending for market research. The consultants commented on the 'deplorable physical condition' of many of the factory buildings they visited and, like the Ibec Technical Services Corporation report, attributed this to insufficient tax allowances for depreciation. Ireland, they considered, 'has few advantages in costs of manufactured products, except foods':

> Most raw materials have to be imported . . . most machinery and tools are imported. Labour costs are relatively low, but lack of high speed production line methods restricts the output per worker. This is largely due to the policy of making so many varieties of goods, to meet the Irish market (Córas Tráchtála 1953: 28)[5]

Of the discontinued projects, the power potential one related to a semi-state company – the ESB – which had never wanted to have it and took the opportunity presented by aid suspension to kill it off. Apart from the second phase of the industrial survey, the rest of the discontinued projects category was made up of the IDA projects dealing with horizontal and vertical industrial problems. Of the two, the horizontal problems project had made least progress prior to aid suspension. In late October 1951, draft letters seeking bids from consultants for studies of the five horizontal problems were sent to the Washington Embassy. However, the project appears to have become stuck towards the back of the projects queue with no finalisation or circulation of these letters taking place. The vertical industrial problems project had moved further forward, with suitably qualified specialists being identified for the furniture, industrial alcohol and pharmaceutical industries, but firm contracts were not in place on 8 January 1952. Sigurd Johnson, an Associate Professor of Furniture Manufacture and Management in South Carolina, subsequently made a cut-price offer to do the Irish project for a fee plus local expenses 'as he would be doing another overseas Consulting job in Germany this Summer with overseas transportation paid for'. A similar offer was received from Edgar Carter, recently retired Executive Director of Research at Abbot Laboratories in Chicago who wrote to the Washington Embassy 'indicating that in the new situation of the suspension of aid, and as he was being retained on a Consultant's salary by Abbot Laboratories, it might be possible for him to undertake the project . . . for the cost of first-class expenses of the trip for himself and Mrs Carter, without any salary or fee'. These offers were relayed to Dublin but not taken up.[6]

The TA Vote was initially attached to Finance, but in October 1952 that department communicated its intention to discontinue it while leaving any other department free to propose making provision for TA in its overall Vote. Industry and Commerce took up this option and, as table 3.2 shows, the pattern of its subsequent TA spending mirrored the one that had emerged from its post-suspension review of projects. Almost all the funds went to semi-state companies and only one substantial grant was made to a private sector firm. Expenditure stopped in August 1956 when Finance, 'citing the urgent need for stringent economy' with balance of payments problems again to the fore, called a halt to any further Industry and Commerce commitments until the TA allocation of £350,000 from the Grant Counterpart Fund actually became available.

Table 3.2 **Expenditure under technical assistance sub-head of Department of Industry and Commerce Vote in the years 1953–4, 1954–5 and 1955–6**

Year	*Project*	£
1953–4	Peat gasification	6,226.0.0
	Drying of milled peat	41.0.0
	Minerals exploration	12,678.0.0
	Meat by-products	118.0.0
	Total	19,063.0.0
1954–5	Minerals exploration	8,801.0.0
	Nitrogenous fertilisers	10,888.0.0
	Fish meal production	1,266.0.0
	European Productivity Council [EPA project no. 229]	370.0.0
	Printing of report of Labour delegation to USA	61.0.0
	Total	21,386.0.0
1955–6	Minerals exploration	168.8.7
	Nitrogenous fertilisers	182.0.0
	Business management [EPA project no. 229]	13.0.0
	Peaceful use of atomic energy	232.18.6
	Fuel conservation study	48.17.8
	Gateaux Ltd.	1,750.0.0
	RRGDATA (Mission to Sweden)	
	Total	2,495.4.9
Total for Three years		42,944.4.9

Source: NAI DIC R303/13/11/1

Nonetheless, a connection continued to be made between providing technical assistance and lessening the private sector's reliance on high levels of protection. Indeed, approval of the proposals that killed off the ECA-authorised Direct Productivity Assistance project that had sought to develop this link was immediately followed at Industry and Commerce's 10 March 1952 departmental conference by a discussion of technical assistance for industries that set out a perspective whereby:

> There was a community interest in having these firms, especially when they enjoyed protection, as efficient as possible. There was evidence that many of

> the firms were anxious to secure technical advice and to pay for it; it was pointed out that if the State did not contribute to the cost, the Government would not be entitled to get a copy of the report. Moreover, one of the main objects of the new Vote for Technical Assistance now before the Dáil was to provide funds to assist private firms in obtaining specialised advice from abroad. It was proposed to re-examine the cases in which it had been decided not to make a state contribution, with a view to the preparation of a list of industries (especially protected industries) which appeared to be in need of technical assistance; it was further proposed to induce these industries to secure technical assistance in consultation with the Department.[7]

Responsibility for both tariffs and technical assistance to private industry had been functions quickly brought back into Industry and Commerce from the IDA after Lemass returned to office in June 1951. This did not disrupt the ongoing development of the ECA TA programme of which Lemass and the Department Secretary, John Leydon, were strong supporters. However, the strong deflationary measures of the April 1952 budget and their damaging effect on industry prompted Lemass to temporarily row back on his emphasis on the need for greater efficiency in protected industries. Shortly after returning from an extended absence owing to ill health, he issued a new instruction at the 9 June departmental conference. Although 'since the end of the war tariff applications . . . were searchingly examined in the Department before any recommendations were put forward', current recessionary conditions warranted a change in approach. 'Where a prima facie case existed – and he was disposed to accept that such a case existed in many instances', Lemass directed his officials that 'the tariff might be imposed preparatory to any detailed examination of the extent and nature of that now carried out before applications were submitted to him for a decision'.[8]

This return to the spirit of 1932 was, however, to give way to a renewed concern for greater industrial efficiency in the later part of the government's lifetime. With a new relationship between the IDA and Industry and Commerce established, the department embarked over more than two years on a series of nearly 70 'industrial surveys'. The purpose of an industrial survey, according to Lemass, was 'to ascertain gaps in production with a view to stimulating manufacturers to make good any deficiencies disclosed'. Tariff reviews that would commence when the programme of surveys was completed were intended 'to ascertain whether existing protection was inadequate or whether some reduction might be considered'.[9] As the programme of surveys drew towards completion, official attention reverted to the difficulties of evaluating efficiency levels and taking action to remedy those judged to be deficient. At a departmental conference on 28 April 1953 'mention was made of the difficulty created by the absence of comparative manufacturing costs and it was suggested that the Board of Trade might be asked to supply confidentially costings of British manufacturers'. Lemass, however, was chary of any departure from an arm's length relationship with a body that played an important role in negotiating and monitoring Anglo-Irish trade agreements.[10]

In return for protection, whether new or increased, the firms that benefited were usually required to give Industry and Commerce undertakings in relation to the prices they would charge. But at a departmental conference on 23 February it was admitted that 'there was no machinery in the Department for ensuring that these undertakings were honoured' and that, where they were not, 'the penal action open to the Minister of reducing or abolishing the protection could scarcely be taken because the result might be the closing down of the industry':

> The Minister recalled that the Industrial Efficiency and Prices Bill, 1947 provided for taking other sanctions against such firms. It was stated that the IDA, when they had responsibility for this matter, had it in mind that tariffs generally should be reviewed in the light of changed conditions since they were imposed, but that because of shortage of staff they had been unable to undertake this work.[11]

On 30 November the departmental conference was told of the Minister's intention to promote new legislation 'relating to industrial efficiency, prices etc. under which the IDA would be charged with specific functions in relation to the efficiency of industrial production'. In line with this approach, responsibility for tariff reviews – to be carried out in an order of priority set out by the Minister – was to be transferred back out of the department to the IDA, a move that could be made without waiting for the new legislation to be passed.[12] A prioritised list was submitted for approval in April 1954 when Lemass directed that the matter be deferred because it was 'inappropriate to initiate such fundamental work as reviews of tariffs at a time when a General Election was in progress'.[13] With the election producing a change in government the transfer of tariff review responsibility went ahead, but the proposed new industrial efficiency legislation was dropped. How the project of reducing required protection levels through TA-stimulated increases in efficiency fared amidst these twists and turns in protection policy emphasis will be now be examined through a case study of one firm, Solus Teoranta.

Solus

A Bray-based manufacturer of electric lamps and glassware, Solus had an annual output of 2,250,000 lamps and was the beneficiary of a quota that allowed only 100,000 lamps to be imported each year. It was the initiator of the lone Type B project proposal put forward by the IDA for TA Budget inclusion in August 1950 (see chapter 2). ECA favoured Type B over Type A TA in Ireland, but because this proposal was treated as firm-specific (although Solus, as a virtual monopoly, was in effect a one-firm industry) it made no progress over the next year. The Production Assistance Drive presided over by William Joyce Jr created a more favourable climate for firm-specific projects in late 1951, but with a larger TA programme in place than the available staff on both the Irish and US side could cope with, and uncertainty arising from the proposed replacement of ECA by MSA, the Solus proposal was not pushed forward by Industry and Commerce although the firm continued to be interested in obtaining US advice.[14] At the key 10 March 1952 departmental conference discussion which decided to discontinue the ECA project that would have addressed selected areas of private sector manufacturing inefficiency while supporting a general policy of inducing protected firms to take up TA, Solus was one of two firms to which specific reference was made.

Industry and Commerce officials subsequently raised the TA issue with the company, only to be informed 'that the Directors take a different view in this matter now that the scheme will not be operating under ECA'. A very dim view was taken of this response, although the weakness of the department's position was also acknowledged:

> Some persuasion should be put on the firm, as the matter does not rest entirely with them. The whole community is paying for inefficiency, if it exists, and there is no competition with Solus. We are completely in the firm's hands in all vital matters such as the possibility of extended manufacture, possibility of obtaining machinery and its cost, costs at which articles can be produced at any given output, and so on. If the firm could be induced to take technical assistance with State help, we could have resolved independently many things which are now obscure, as we could include in experts' terms of reference such queries as we wished.[15]

Solus were invite 'to amplify your reply' as it appeared to the Minister 'that if the necessity for technical assistance existed under ECA auspices the necessity for it has not disappeared merely because ECA funds are no longer available'. The company maintained that it had wanted US expert advice on the production of fluorescent lamps but, as its plans for this had been deferred, 'we cannot avail of your offer at the moment to provide alternate Technical Assistance to that provided under ECA auspices'. Pointing to the absence of reference to fluorescent lamps in the correspondence and notes on file from 1950, Industry and Commerce officials considered the firm's letter as 'not at all frank' and 'endeavouring to draw "red herrings" across the issue'. They shrank, however, from taking action to secure compliance with their wishes. Their considerations happened to coincide with a Dáil complaint by James Dillon that the firm's products were sub-standard. In June it was decided to wait and see whether the results of tests the IIRS had been asked to carry out on Solus lamps would strengthen the department's hand.[16]

This wait was to last more than a year. In the meantime Industry and Commerce had covered the electric lamps industry in its programme of surveys. At a meeting between department officials and Solus directors to discuss the findings on 30 April 1953 the issue of TA was again broached:

> Mr O'Reilly [Chairman of Solus Teoranta] stated that his firm would not consider the question of obtaining Technical Assistance from Britain as in his opinion any Technical Assistance obtained from that quarter would be influenced by the attitude of his firm's competitors in Britain. When questioned by Mr Murray as to the possibility of obtaining Technical Assistance from the USA, Mr O'Reilly stated that he did not think any Technical Assistance whatever is necessary. In his opinion the staff in the Bray factory are fully skilled and competent in the manufacture of electric lamps. After further discussion Mr O'Reilly added that his firm might consider the question of Technical Assistance after they are installed in their new factory in August next.

At the meeting the firm also let it be known that installation of new machinery in the new factory would result in between 75 and 100 women out of a current workforce of about 300 losing their jobs. Civil servants subsequently minuted the fear that the company would try to offload the blame for letting workers go on to the Minister who had pressed them to adopt new methods and a suspicion that it might be 'more a matter of tactics than necessity' as 'if they retain workers after claiming that they are unnecessary, the lowering of prices can obviously be deferred rather than forced'. Coincidentally, in April 1953 Finance linked offering no objection to the renewal of the current import quota to the completion by Industry and Commerce of 'the promised inquiries into the price and quality of the Irish-produced lamps'.[17]

On 1 June 1953 the Industry and Commerce departmental conference discussed an approach received from 'certain French interests who were contemplating the manufacture of electric lamps for the Irish and export markets'. The French proposal involved the 'formation of a company with a capital of £100,000 complying with the Control of Manufactures Acts, capable of producing in Dublin approximately twice the quantity of electric lamps needed for the Irish market'. The promoters hoped to export half the output to South Africa, Israel and other countries. It was noted that:

> If the proposal materialised there would be serious repercussions on Solus Teoranta who were already producing electric lamps at Bray under protection and who were being officially pressed to improve their production methods etc. The Minister felt that there was a certain degree of obligation on his part to safeguard Solus Teoranta as it was they who had commenced the manufacture of electric lamps etc. in this country. While he would not have any power to prevent a new company from engaging in the manufacture of similar goods as long as it complied with the Control of Manufactures Acts, he could possibly discourage them by informing them that existing productive capacity appeared to him to be adequate. The fact that Solus Teoranta were the sole manufacturer might, however, give rise to objections to such a course.[18]

In this instance Lemass was to be rescued from his difficulties by the failure of the proposal to proceed. In October the IIRS reported only some minor failures of Solus lamps to comply with the approved standard. The basis of James Dillon's complaint appeared to be that 'the imported lamps with which the Deputy had compared the Solus lamps were of the coiled coil variety which was more expensive than the single coiled lamp made in this country and which gave a greater output'. However, Solus 'had already decided not to produce coiled coil lamps because the Irish market would not justify the expense'. Industry and Commerce responded to the IIRS report by deciding 'to press Solus Teoranta to improve production methods' and, when renewal of the lamp import quota order came up for consideration in March 1954, 'it was mentioned that it was understood that Solus Teoranta were negotiating with an external firm with a view to obtaining certain technical services'. In May, a group of Industry and Commerce officers visited the Solus factory, but had neither the time nor the qualifications to appraise its arrangements properly. It was noted that 'the company does not wish for technical assistance', with the observation that 'if technical assistance were provided, with some grant of state funds, it would settle, once and for all, the doubts that this company's manufactures seem to inspire'.[19]

Early in 1955, Industry and Commerce considered a proposal from Philips Radio Manufacturing, an Irish satellite of the large Dutch company, to broaden its product range and move into manufacturing electric lamps. The department decided to discourage the move as 'it was clear that if the production of electric filament lamps were to be undertaken by Philips their production would duplicate the production of Solus Teoranta and any employment which would be given by Philips would be at the expense of employment given by Solus Teo. at Bray'. A Philips representative was subsequently informed that they could legally manufacture lamps as the law stood 'but that in face of the Minister's views it would seem unwise for them to do so'. Subsequently the Philips factory did produce coiled coil lamps and fluorescent lamps. Solus, for its part, 'entered into financial and production arrangements with the GEC of England and associate companies'.[20]

Examination of the 1955 Philips' proposal had the effect of drawing attention to the fact that 'flash lamp bulbs were being extensively imported, although Solus Teoranta had intimated some time ago that they were planning to produce them'. On enquiry it was learned that Solus 'have facilities available to meet the entire market for flash lamp bulbs and that a similar position obtained for miniature decorative bulbs'. The company 'has submitted an application for quota protection for these and other types of bulbs which are outside the scope of the present quota; and Solus Teo. are at present compiling information in support of the application'.[21]

The policy of inducing protected industries to secure technical assistance in consultation with Industry and Commerce was certainly not a success in the Solus case. Unsure of what they could and should do, department officials retreated when faced with company's unwillingness to co-operate. In spite of its apparent shortcomings, Solus could rely on the department's support to preserve its monopoly position in the Irish market – and even to consider extending the scope of the import quotas upon which this monopoly rested – without being required to deliver price or quality improvements in return.

The Grant Counterpart Technical Assistance sub-agreement

By the summer of 1955 – three and a half years after aid suspension – an Irish draft of a Grant Counterpart TA sub-agreement had been sent to Washington for consideration while Finance's power to refuse sanction to any TA proposal was being employed to stop Irish TA. Nearly two years would be consumed before a draft that satisfied the US demand for clearly specified and costed proposals was agreed. In the process Industry and Commerce would whittle down a series of lists containing around 25 potential projects that its various divisions, branches and satellite agencies had put forward to just three project headings. These were a programme of coalfield exploration, a small grant to the Irish Management Institute (discussed in chapter 6 below), and a heading that combined 'employment of consultants by industrial firms; participation in European Productivity Agency (EPA) projects; possible establishment of a national productivity centre'.[22]

A mixture of pessimism and optimism underpinned the Leinster and Arigna coalfields project proposal. Security of fuel supplies remained a major official concern well into the 1950s after the experience of the Emergency years and a post-war British delivery record that had at various times been unsatisfactory as regards both quantity and quality. The Director of the Geological Survey who believed that Ireland's own coal reserves 'were likely to be far more extensive than was at present thought' supplied the optimism. The coalfield proposal attracted unfavourable US comment, as it had done in Ireland within Finance, but ultimately the objection was not pressed and the project was allowed to proceed.[23]

In proposing a second project which provided a framework within which a wide range of specific technical assistance and productivity initiatives could be accommodated, Industry and Commerce referred to revived discussion of a national productivity centre that would actively link Ireland to the work of the EPA – an issue that will be considered below – and offered a retrospective view of TA take-up by private industrial firms. While ECA TA was on offer, an effort to interest private enterprises had been made 'without much success'. After aid ceased and TA was continued under Irish government auspices, 'the response was still disappointing'. But a recent shift from a whole industry focus towards 'projects involving the engagement by individual firms of Industrial Consultants for the purpose of advising on industrial plant and organisation' resulted in an upsurge of applications from the middle of 1955. As Irish funding for TA was sharply cut back and then stopped, only one such project (Gateaux) had actually gone ahead. Close to a dozen more were approved but left in limbo, awaiting the release of funds by the completion of the Grant Counterpart TA sub-agreement in July 1957.[24]

Irish–US disagreements were not the only reason for the long delay in concluding this TA sub-agreement. Internal disputes between Irish departments also played a part. At stake here were two issues: how the £350,000 allocation would be divided up and whether TA would continue to be funded after this allocation had been exhausted. In December 1955 Industry and Commerce sought 'the maximum possible allocation' for its projects. Agriculture responded in January 1956 with a proposal that it and Industry and Commerce should each get £150,000 with the balance divided between any other interested departments. In its reply Industry and Commerce widened the issue by stating that its 'Minister . . . would wish to have the principle firmly established that state funds will continue to be available for suitable Technical assistance projects, irrespective of whether the State contribution is to be recouped from the Counterpart Fund provision or not. Should this principle be assented to . . . the question of allocating the £350,000 . . . should not present undue difficulty'.

Table 3.3 **Industry and Commerce projects in Grant Counterpart Fund Technical Assistance sub-agreement**

Project	*Amount (£)*
Grant to Irish Management Institute towards establishment of a Management Development Unit	6,000
Employment of consultants by industrial firms; participation in European Productivity Agency projects; possible establishment of National Productivity Centre	54,000
Exploration and evaluation of resources in Leinster and Arigna coalfields	80,000
TOTAL	140,000

To this, Agriculture's Secretary responded that 'we are quite prepare to support departmentally the thesis that Technical Assistance should not be limited to the funds provided by the Grant Counterpart, though I doubt the wisdom of making a big issue of this with Finance at this early stage: it might only lead to a long delay'. The line taken by Finance representatives on the Interdepartmental ERP Committee was that it could not be assumed that any source of financing other than the sum set aside in the Counterpart Fund would be available for Technical Assistance projects. This Industry and Commerce claimed to be 'at variance with the terms of the Government decision of 15 Feabhra 1952, on the subject of technical assistance'. Obliged in the end to accept £140,000 (see table 3.3), attempts by Industry and Commerce to trade a reduced claim on the Grant Counterpart TA allocation for a commitment to continued financing for TA when this source was exhausted failed to achieve anything other than delaying the conclusion of the sub-agreement.[25]

Technical assistance, productivity and the advent of EPA

With the suspension of US aid, discussion of an Irish productivity centre lapsed. However, the US Mutual Security legislation passed in 1952 provided for the transfer of funds earmarked for productivity promotion to the OEEC. This US funding prompted the 1953 creation within the OEEC of an autonomous European Productivity Agency (EPA).

As discussion of setting up a productivity agency began, the main Irish concerns expressed were that it should not add substantially to the cost of Ireland's OEEC membership and that it should not interfere with the workings of the existing OEEC Ministerial Committee for Agriculture and Food. Industry and Commerce expected Ireland to derive no significant benefit and was inclined to have nothing to do with the new body. External Affairs, on the other hand, felt that it would be impolitic of Ireland to appear reluctant to co-operate with its establishment and argued that it would be 'difficult having regard to our membership of OEEC to disassociate ourselves from the proposed agency' – a view that prevailed once cost and agricultural fears were dispelled.[26]

Since EPA was intended 'to federate and guide the national productivity centers, as well as to service them' (Boel 2003: 136), its advent revived the issue of setting up an Irish productivity centre. In February 1954, a few months before a general election that would replace Fianna Fáil with a second Inter-Party Government, an Industry and Commerce Departmental Conference discussed liaison with the EPA and 'concluded that it was not necessary to establish a National Productivity Agency and it was proposed that such an Agency should not be established'.[27] This was to be the last time that discussion of a productivity centre was to be restricted to ministers and state officials. When the subject was broached with William Norton, the Minister for Industry and Commerce, in October 1954 by OEEC's Alexander King, IIRS was asked to convene an informal committee on which business, labour and other interests were represented to conduct an examination. In 1957 the Irish Management Institute (IMI) would be asked by Norton's successor, Seán Lemass, to play a similar role related to a more limited remit. These later phases of productivity centre discussion will be discussed in chapter 4 below.

In the absence of a national productivity centre, Industry and Commerce served as the EPA's Irish point of contact. This department circulated information it received regarding EPA projects to organisations that it considered likely to be interested but 'no special measures have been taken to publicise or advocate support for such projects and the question of participating is left entirely to the Irish interests themselves'. Any participating interest had 'as a general rule' to pay out of its own resources any costs incurred through its involvement that EPA did not cover. Industry and Commerce did not support EPA project participation from its technical assistance funds on the grounds:

> That the Projects are not initiated in this country; that they are not tailored to our particular needs; that even where there is Irish participation, it is by no means certain that any national as distinct from individual advantage is gained and that, as a general principle, it seems preferable that State funds should be applied towards the cost of technical assistance projects which are initiated in this country and which are designed to deal with specific Irish problems and conditions rather than that such funds should be used to contribute towards the cost of schemes organised by the Agency and designed to deal with more general problems of countries industrially more advanced.[28]

No Industry and Commerce representatives attended any level of EPA meeting in Paris. Nor, in the absence of interest on Industry and Commerce's part, were these covered by the one-man-band Irish delegation to the OEEC. With no Irish input into formative project design discussions at headquarters, the assertion that EPA projects were unsuited to Irish industrial needs became something of a self-fulfilling prophecy. The lack of an active engagement with Paris also meant that any Irish organisation potentially interested in participating in a particular project was likely to learn about it late in the day. Many of the features of Ireland's mode of minimal involvement in the EPA between 1953 and 1958 are illustrated by the case of EPA project no. 312. On 15 August 1955 an official in the Industries Division of Industry and Commerce forwarded documents regarding this project to a colleague in the Labour Division and sought her views on the possible participation of Irish trade unionists. The reply began by noting that:

> Stage A of this project appears to have passed us by unnoticed as it consisted of a meeting held in Florence last April of professors of psychology and industrial sociology and directors of research institutes from both the US and Europe to hold discussions on human relations.[29]

A further, Stage B, conference was now to be held in Rome in January or February 1956 and it was envisaged by the EPA that 'tripartite' national delegations of up to nine members consisting of employer or worker representatives and national productivity centre nominees (including human relations experts) would attend. Industry and Commerce circulated information to IMI, CIU and ITUC. CIU and IMI decided not to participate but ITUC expressed an interest in sending delegates. Industry and Commerce then found itself pressed to notify the EPA of its own intention to participate as, without employer/management or national productivity centre attendance, any trade union participants would not qualify to have half of their expenses paid by the EPA and would only be given the status of observers without speaking rights rather than that of delegates. Technical assistance funding was also sought from the department to cover the other half of the union delegates' expenses.

A memorandum prepared for the departmental conference on 25 November to which the matter was referred for a direction stated that 'it was not considered that there was any case for sending a delegation from the Department as we had no positive contribution to make'. This memorandum recommended that no technical assistance grant be given and that ITUC 'be informed that the report of the Rome Conference will be forwarded to it when it comes to hand'. The reply sent to the ITUC on 9 January 1956 made use of the EPA's stated requirement that delegates should carry out preparatory work under specified headings that would facilitate the pooling of knowledge and experience at the conference to argue that representation of the Department could not be justified: 'in view of the short notice which was given of the holding of this conference there was no time to prepare the necessary data for it.' On 26 October copies of a report on the conference were sent by the Labour Division of Industry and Commerce to both ITUC and CIU.[30]

In the agency's early years only two exceptions were made to the general rule that Irish TA funds would not be made available to support EPA project participants. A grant was made to cover the full cost of the participation of an IMI nominee – UCD Lecturer Michael MacCormac – in a 1955 management mission to the USA (see table 3.2, p. 52 and chapter 6). In 1956 a grant of £300 was given to three consulting engineers partly to defray their expenses as members of another Mission to the USA.[31] There were, as a result, very few Irish participants. Unlike most EPA members, Ireland did not have US aid dollars with which to subsidise participation. But Sweden and Switzerland were in the same position and their governments actively provided financial support to their nominees in the case of projects they deemed relevant to their interests.[32]

With EPA's future under review as its initial three years drew to a close, Irish departments recorded their views on the agency's value in the summer of 1956. Agriculture, which had been involved in 15 EPA projects, gave a positive assessment – 'the Department would be anxious to continue its association with the work of EPA the value of which will probably be even more significant as time goes on'. Industry and Commerce was much cooler – there had been little participation in a mass of projects whose value to Ireland was debatable. In terms of industrial benefits, continued participation would be difficult to justify. But 'wider considerations' that led it to accept the External Affairs view that participation should continue included 'the fact that the US Government attaches particular importance to productivity and that if Ireland did not continue its membership of EPA it might affect the present negotiations with the US Government regarding the Technical Assistance Sub-Agreement'.[33]

References to EPA in Sub-Agreement drafts from Ireland were certainly received warmly in the USA with the Washington Embassy reporting in August 1955 that the Industrial Division of MSA's successor, the International Cooperation Administration (ICA), 'had viewed with particular pleasure the reference to the activities of the European Productivity Agency in Article 1 . . . schemes of this sort would preclude any possibility of undesirable projects creeping in'.[34] Industry and Commerce was prepared to frame projects in ways that pandered to such US enthusiasm while allowing its own priorities to prevail in the actual use of money. Thus a review within the department of the final sub-agreement draft in May 1957 noted:

> In connection with the second of our heads of expenditure . . . it is stated there that the provision . . . may possibly provide for grants towards the cost of establishing a National Productivity Centre. It may seem a little odd to leave this in the Annex in view of the Minister's decision at Departmental Conference on 6th May, 1957, that no further action need be taken in the matter of the establishment of a National Productivity Centre. The possibility, however, was originally included in the head because the U.S. authorities are keen on the setting up of National Productivity Centres, and I think that it would be impolitic to propose to them now that it should be deleted. The wording was

> deliberately left vague so that we will not be in any way committed to the establishment of a Productivity Centre.[35]

Of the £54,000 allocated to the head 'employment of consultants by industrial firms; participation in EPA projects; possible establishment of National Productivity Centre' only about £1,000 was to be expended on EPA-related activities The speech delivered by Seán Lemass in September 1957 at the official opening of the new premises of the IMI's Management Development Unit provoked an outburst of exasperation in the Paris Embassy at the manner in which Industry and Commerce was calling for increased productivity while ignoring EPA – 'if we do not participate in its activities . . . our subscription is largely money down the drain'. The following year a change in attitude was finally signalled when *Economic Development* stated that:

> So far, this country, unlike the majority of OEEC countries, has not a national productivity centre, activity in this sphere being carried on under the aegis of the Department of Industry and Commerce. The work of that Department will, it is hoped, be augmented shortly by a committee under the auspices of the Irish Management Institute. Ireland is the only OEEC country which is not an active member of the governing body of the European Productivity Agency or of the Agency's Productivity Committee. If we played a greater part in the Agency's activities, we could reasonably hope to receive, at comparatively little cost, an increased share of its technical assistance allocations . . . We should participate more fully in the European Productivity Agency of the OEEC. (Department of Finance 1958: 164 and 219)

By the time an Irish productivity centre finally materialised in 1959 all of the Grant Counterpart Fund's TA allocation to the heading that encompassed it had been committed if not actually spent. Indeed this money was almost all gone by end of 1957. Unresolved in Interdepartmental ERP Committee discussions, the issue of whether any further funding should be provided for TA came before the government on Industry and Commerce's initiative in January 1958. Provision for TA in Industry and Commerce's Vote was restored for 1958–9 and subsequently repeated although Finance continued to maintain that 'it could not properly be assumed that funds will continue to be voted indefinitely in the future or that, if voted, they would equal the current year's provision'.[36] The Irish National Productivity Committee, which had no budget of its own, initially drew on these TA funds in order to meet the costs incurred in liaising with EPA.

Technical assistance from EPA

Although Ireland stood out within OEEC in not having a national productivity centre, its low level of involvement with EPA was less unusual. As Boel (2003: 119) notes: 'early on it had become obvious that the poorer member states, namely Greece, Portugal and Turkey were also those that participated the least in the EPA's projects'. To address this problem a programme for underdeveloped areas was instituted from 1955. This 'dealt with economic development in general rather than restricting itself to the narrow field of productivity enhancement', as well as having more flexible (effectively country-specific) rules and more favourable financial conditions than EPA activities generally. Half a dozen member or associated states – Italy, Greece, Turkey, Yugoslavia, Spain and Iceland – took part in the programme which USA strongly supported (Boel 2003: 202–3). One of its most distinctive features was the creation of trial and demonstrations zones. Thus in Sardinia 'industries such as weaving or basket-making were created, more productive methods in agriculture were introduced, adult education was developed and the hygiene and the nutrition provided for school children was improved' (Boel 1997: 117).

Shortly after its inauguration the Irish National Productivity Committee (INPC) recommended that the government should consider having Ireland 'in whole or in part' classified as 'an area in the process of development'. Industry and Commerce, however, opposed this. External Affairs generally sought to keep Ireland's options open, supporting, for instance, Iceland's application to join the programme because 'Icelandic participation would broaden the criterion of eligibility and it would thus be to this country's advantage in any demarches that may be made at a later date concerning Irish participation'.[37] Discussion within the Interdepartmental ERP Committee in October 1959 indicated that INPC continued to favour the idea that at least western parts of the country might be designated in the same way as Southern Italy. However, by the end of the year INPC was concentrating on garnering resources from flexibility within the administration of mainstream programmes and wished to defer action in relation to 'area in the process of development' status. Before the February 1960 meeting of EPA's governing body a note from the Irish delegate and INPC chairman Denis Hegarty was circulated:

> Ireland is not an undeveloped country in the sense in which this expression has been applied by the Agency. The standard of education is high and progress has been made in agriculture. Industrialisation is, however, of comparatively recent

> growth and though the Employers' organisations and the Trade Unions are well organized and there is a fairly good relationship between them on the negative side of industrial relations (absence of serious strikes etc.) it was only very recently that a climate of opinion was created which made possible the kind of joint action necessary to support a productivity drive. This accounts for the fact that Ireland has made comparatively little use of EPA's services until very recently.
>
> Management and labour were, in fact, brought together last year and there is now considerable joint interest in the subject but certain promotional work is necessary to support the propaganda effort. This promotional work should take the form of EPA sending over experts to conduct seminars etc. calculated to create interest in the new techniques. This work has already been done in the more industrialised European countries. To this extent, therefore, it would be necessary to authorise continuation of management services to Ireland for a limited period, say three to five years, on the same basis as they were available heretofore to European countries generally.[38]

The minutes of this EPA Governing Body meeting record that:

> The Governing Body agreed that Ireland should still be able to take part in certain virtually terminated types of projects for which certain funds were still available. The Delegate from Ireland would get in touch with the Secretariat on this matter.[39]

However, arrangements for Ireland to eschew 'area in process of development' status while being facilitated in playing catch up with the mainstream of developed member states by accommodating EPA officials were about to be derailed. At the end of 1959 a process of transforming OEEC into a body that would have Canada and USA as members was under way. A Group of Four appointed to draw up proposals for this reinvention reported in the spring of 1960 and in the autumn a Preparatory Committee got down to detailed work on a convention. Before it, the Irish delegate reported, were proposals from the OEEC Secretary General to abolish EPA, 'to transfer its activities on behalf of the less developed countries to the new Technical Assistance Committee and to distribute amongst other bodies such of its activities on behalf of the advanced countries as it was agreed to retain in OECD'. On the abolition of EPA she commented:

> This proposal came as no surprise. The elimination of EPA was advocated in the Group of Four report . . . and its activities on behalf of the advanced countries have been under fire for the past few years by the USA and by other OEEC delegations, who wished to have them curtailed in favour of the scientific and technical personnel programme and the programme for less developed countries.[40]

Discussions involving External Affairs, Industry and Commerce and INPC were under way in November 1960 after the Taoiseach had seen the reports from Paris on the Preparatory Committee's proceedings and 'the proposals under discussion affecting the European Productivity Agency had attracted his special attention'.[41] In January 1961 the Paris Embassy Counsellor serving as the Irish delegate to the Preparatory Committee offered the following assessment on the emerging situation:

> As matters stand, we seem to be in danger of falling between two stools. On the one hand it seems practically certain that some of the projects on behalf of the more advanced countries (in which Ireland is particularly interested) will be dropped . . . Even if the USA and the other members of the Preparatory Committee were prepared to continue the special arrangements for Ireland . . . – and this can by no means be assumed – it is clear that we will have to pay a great deal more for considerably reduced benefits. On the other hand the majority of projects at present operated in the EPA for areas in process of development are not appropriate to a country at our stage of economic development. In these circumstances it is inconceivable that our fellow members would not be prepared to agree that Ireland, which they recognise to be a country in process of industrial development, should be provided in the Technical Assistance Committee with the type of project best suited to her needs . . . It seems to me quite probable that our request in Preparatory Committee to be allowed to continue the special arrangement agreed to by the Governing Body of the EPA – obviously accorded to us because of our less developed status – may lead to queries as to why we do not contemplate participation in the technical assistance programmes. Would it not be more dignified for us to make the proposal ourselves?[42]

Industry and Commerce's stated position was now that 'on the supposition that this country can obtain from the Technical Assistance Committee the kind of services which she needs, there would no objection to Irish participation in the programme of that Committee'. But what the briefs that department prepared and transmitted to Paris sought was continuation under the new regime of the existing special arrangement. Fellow member states were to be told that 'Ireland now requires the productivity services which other countries needed earlier . . . the continuance of such services even for a further two to three years is very important from this country's point of view'.[43] Irish diplomats pursued this line while the Preparatory Committee was wound up and the question of what EPA services would be retained was left to various new committees of the OECD in the Autumn of 1961. With weeks to go before all EPA activities were to be wound up, it was reported from the Industry and Manpower Committees in May 1962 that 'we have put in a plea for the maintenance of several management projects but we are getting very little support from the other delegations'. By then INPC's secretary was expressing the view that there was 'nothing worthwhile' left of the EPA activities and that 'in these circumstances the National Productivity Committee intend to seek through the OECD, the United Nations and the ILO the services of a productivity expert for a couple of years'.[44] While committees had procrastinated, EPA had effectively dissolved.

Technical assistance secured and domesticated

Why was Ireland so reluctant to take on 'area in the process of development' status even when access to TA resources was lost by failing to do so? National pride or prestige was certainly a consideration for some. Chairing a session at INPC's first labour-management conference at Red Island in September 1959 Todd Andrews told the delegates:

> You are going to hear now representatives of the trade unions and of management in a country which is euphemistically known to be in the process of development. To my mind it always horrifies me to hear my country described in those terms. It really means we are a backward country.[45]

As Minister for Industry of Commerce, Jack Lynch seems to have felt a similar aversion, with the delegate to OECD's Preparatory Committee noting in January 1961 that the Industry and Commerce officials she was working with 'seem to be rather fearful of reopening the question with their Minister, though the INPC would warmly welcome permission to seek the services we need in the Technical Assistance Committee'.[46] The crucial factor during 1961–2, however, was the decision to apply for full membership of the EEC once it had become clear that Britain would also take this step. When the proposal for an OEEC free trade area had to be faced early in 1957 the government had decided that 'no commitment to join the proposed free trade area should be entered into until every possibility had been explored of securing adequate safeguards as a country in process of development' (Maher 1986: 65). In the months that followed common cause was made with Greece and Turkey in seeking very lengthy deferral of the obligations to remove tariffs and the provision of developmental investment funding by the richer OEEC states. By mid-1961, however, the Irish government 'sought to convey a picture of a dynamic and rapidly growing economy' and 'to neutralise any impression the Six might have as a result of the OEEC negotiations of 1957–8 for a Free Trade Area, that the Irish economy should be ranked with those of Greece and Turkey' – states seen as suitable for association with rather than membership of the EEC (Maher 1986: 126). Draft Minutes of an October 1962 Interdepartmental ERP Committee meeting indicate that, while complex Irish interests entailed ambiguity, OECD was a forum in which a developed image was to be projected:

> The representatives of the Department of External Affairs explained that they had been advised by the Department of Finance that it is essential for us to accept [less-developed] status in such documentation (both UN and OECD) in order to safeguard our position on tax incentives for foreign companies investing in Ireland. On the other hand the Committee of Secretaries had recently decided that that it would not be advisable for us to participate in the OECD Technical Co-operation Programme for less-developed countries in view of our application for full membership of the EEC. Our position was therefore rather ambiguous but it did seem wiser not to highlight our industrially less-developed status in the OECD at the present juncture.[47]

A motion for the approval of the Convention creating OECD in OEEC's stead was the occasion on which Ireland's 1961 application for EEC membership was first debated by the Dáil. Here 'the Taoiseach emphasised the many radical and painful adjustments and adaptations which membership of the Community would entail and went on to outline the action which the Government planned to take to ease the transition to a new economic environment' (Maher 1986: 129). In industry a Committee on Industrial Organisation (CIO) was set up to carry out a comprehensive programme of surveys in order to identify problems in coping with free trade conditions and to promote adaptation to the coming economic order. Referring to TA and marketing grants, a CIO interim report recommended that Industry and Commerce and CTT 'should review the developing needs of Irish industry in regard to production standards and export marketing so as to ensure that the grants are adequate in amount and coverage' (CIO 1962: para 19).

In response the government announced in July 1962 that grants of 25 per cent of the cost involved would be made available towards expenditure on buildings, plant and equipment incurred in adapting industry towards conditions of freer trade. This was followed in October 1962 by extension of the existing scope of TA grants which would henceforth meet half the cost of consultancy, training and study visits abroad. Consultants could now be engaged with grant aid 'to advise on matters directed to the improvement of productive efficiency (including examination of the management organisation and/or financial structure of such firms)' or 'to examine aspects of the distribution and sale of goods on the home market'. Grants for training courses and study visits would cover 'attendance at wholetime courses of training of managerial and supervisory (including work study) personnel engaged in industry', 'the attendance at wholetime courses of training on productivity techniques and procedures of trade union officials and trade union representatives (including officials and trade union representatives of employers' unions)' and 'visits abroad by representatives (management and management and labour jointly) of firms and industries to study aspects of industrial organisation'.[48] Within Finance, great hopes were entertained with regard to what consultants might achieve in Irish industrial firms:

> [CIO survey] figures show that only a very small percentage of Irish firms availed of the scheme of technical assistance grants. What is even more depressing is that many firms are not aware of the existence of the scheme. Few people would argue that this indifference is a reflection of the fact that that Irish industry in general could not with profit avail of the services of industrial consultants. In a recent paper read to the Royal Statistical Society, Professor Johnston of Manchester University estimated that industrial consultants in Britain have succeeded in raising by 50% the productivity of firms which they visited; he also estimated – on a conservative basis – that industrial consultants have in recent years been responsible for one-third of the increase in total industrial productivity in Britain. These figures indicate the extent to which, without any or very little capital expenditure, industrial productivity can be

> raised. It is hardly necessary to underline the significance of these figures for Irish industry which is faced with a massive task of adaptation (Murray 1963: 89).[49]

Table 3.4 shows the sums voted to Industry and Commerce and, at the end of the period, to Labour for TA during the 1960s.

Table 3.4 **Industry and Commerce and Labour technical assistance funds, 1960–70**

Year	*Industry and Commerce TA*	*Labour TA*
1960–1	205,000	-
1961–2	200,000	-
1962–3	150,000	-
1963–4	270,000*	-
1964–5	350,000	-
1965–6	350,000	-
1966–7	300,000	-
1967–8	360,000	-
1968–8	312,000	60,000
1969–70	260,000	90,000

* From 1963–4, a separate grant-in-aid to the Irish National Productivity Committee was also paid. This was initially £40,000: for grant-in-aid amounts in later years see table 8.3 (p. 174 below).
Source: Industry and Commerce estimates, Labour estimates, various years.

Conclusion

Technical assistance was retained as a sub-head of Irish government department Votes after US aid ended in 1952, but Finance's power to withhold the sanction that every individual project required meant that very little funding filtered through to industry until the late 1950s. By then, a shift in Finance policy from deflation to development and pressure from Irish non-government actors that will be discussed in chapter 4 was creating a less chilly climate for TA and productivity initiatives. In the early 1960s Industry and Commerce succeeded in having TA funding made an ongoing part of government expenditure. But although it had won a battle against Finance it had also lost a war. The application to join the EEC as a full member was the culmination of a shift between 1957 and 1961 away from a continuation of protectionism to the greatest degree possible and towards the exposure to the rigours of free trade of industries that would, it was hoped, have adapted themselves in order to survive (Whitaker 2006). Secured in this strategic context, domestically resourced TA was a consolation prize for a defeated department.

CHAPTER FOUR

Partners in Adaptation? Government, Business and Trade Unions

Introduction

From its initiation in 1950, discussion of organisational arrangements to promote technical assistance activity and preach the gospel of productivity in Ireland took it for granted that government, business and trade union support would be essential to achieve success. However, the circle of those actually involved in addressing the question of whether an Irish national productivity centre should be set up was for several years restricted to ministers and state officials. This chapter describes how Irish non-government actors became engaged in bipartite and tripartite bodies promoting first a productivity drive and later a wider process of planning for economic expansion within a European free trade context. Yet industry level joint action did not root itself successfully in Irish soil. By the late 1960s a series of industrial policy initiatives were filling the vacuum left by this failure – a reinvention of the Industrial Development Authority (IDA), an unsuccessful attempt to integrate the state 'field' services supporting adaptation and a governmental turn towards mergers as the most feasible means of rationalising Irish industry for free trade survival.

Discussion of an Irish productivity centre convened by the Institute for Industrial Research and Standards

This circle of those involved in discussing the setting up of an Irish productivity centre widened beyond civil servants and ministers early in 1955 when Tanaiste William Norton, prompted by a visiting senior OEEC official, Alexander King, asked King's host, the IIRS, to convene an informal committee to examine the issue on which business, labour and other interests were represented. Making up this committee, which met for the first time on 8 March

1955, were two statutory agencies with industrial development remits (IDA and IIRS), two business representative bodies (the Federated Union of Employers (FUE) and the Federation of Irish Manufacturers (FIM)), two rival trade union congresses (the CIU and ITUC), and a new organisation with a non-aligned view of itself, the Irish Management Institute (IMI).

IIRS grew out of an Industrial Research Committee set up in 1933 and supported by a modest amount of piecemeal government funding. By the end of the 1930s it was channelling about £6,000 annually to the three National University colleges for research that was mostly concerned with trying to identify industrial uses for Ireland's abundance of peat and seaweed. Moves to place the committee on a more secure footing were under way in Industry and Commerce by the early 1940s when these were put to one side to create the Emergency Scientific Research Bureau, whose staff sought to improvise solutions to the problems thrown up by the wartime interruption of the flow of vital imports. With the end of the war, the project of a permanent industrial research institute was revived and an Industrial Research and Standards Act was passed in 1946.[1] A change in status left its access to resources largely unchanged, however, with Lemass telling a departmental conference in September 1952 'that he was of opinion that expenditure on industrial research on the present limited scale was unproductive and wasteful because the research was too confined to be effective'.[2]

First within OEEC, and then within EPA, the European productivity drive had a 'hard' technological as well as a 'soft' socio-political side. Alongside other European national applied science institutes, the IIRS had an involvement with 'hard' side activities but its approach to the 'soft' side was dutiful rather than enthusiastic – 'the factors affecting productivity may be economic, political, fiscal, sociological, psychological as well as technological and it is only in connection with the technological aspects in the main that the Institute could concern itself'.[3]

IDA, as we have seen, had been involved in discussions with ECA after broad, if conditional, government approval for setting up an Irish productivity centre was given in July 1950. When the proposals produced by ECA were deemed to be 'far too ambitious' in the Irish context, IDA put forward as a realistic alternative that 'the objectives of the Productivity Programme should be achieved through the combined machinery of the IDA, the Institute for Industrial Research and Standards and the Central Statistics Office, aided by a small special staff either in the form of a separate organisation or within one of the above-mentioned Bodies, which would have the job of supplementing or co-ordinating activities in this particular field'.[4] While IDA's main subsequent concern had been to ensure that it should no longer be the Irish recipient of correspondence from OEEC addressed to national productivity centres, this did not necessarily involve the rejection of the idea that an Irish productivity centre could make a useful contribution. Thus at an early meeting of the informal committee in July 1955, the IDA representative 'referred to the fact that it had been necessary for the Minister . . . to appeal recently to Associations of Manufacturers to formulate technical assistance projects for the industries they represent . . . it was rather disheartening to learn that the Minister had to make such an appeal. . .the question of a productivity centre would be worth looking into'.[5]

While non-government organisations were not involved in the productivity centre discussions of the US aid period, there has been an attempt to get CIU, FUE and ITUC to jointly participate in a mission to the USA under the TA programme. The refusal of CIU to join a team which included ITUC nominees stymied this effort. A plan was next hatched between Industry and Commerce and ECA to have two missions visit simultaneously. The FUE representatives would officially form a team with CIU nominees but would also, it was planned, take part in joint activities with the members of an ITUC team that would travel to the USA separately. This plan unravelled completely. In the Autumn of 1951 a CIU team went to the USA on its own. Shortly afterwards some FUE nominees participated in a huge pan-OEEC employers' mission and the organisation appeared to lose interest in any future Irish joint mission. The possibility that FIM might go instead of FUE with ITUC was raised in November 1951 but 'the Minister [Lemass] said he did not favour the idea of regarding the Federation of Irish Manufacturers as being representative of the employers'. With US aid suspended, an ITUC team visit in the summer of 1952 was supported by Irish TA funds. Prior to its departure, reports reached Dublin of the CIU using its US trade union contacts to try and queer the ITUC team's pitch.[6]

The background to this behaviour was the 1940s splitting of both the Irish Labour Party and the Irish Trade Union Congress into warring factions. Politically, Labour in Ireland had found itself disabled by the centrality of constitutional issues with most organised workers voting not on class lines but for nationalist or unionist parties. Industrially, trade union membership grew dramatically in the period during and after the First World War with a spectacular period of grassroots syndicalist-style militancy in the south coming to an end only when the Free State army was freed to confront it by civil war victory (O'Connor 1988). On a partitioned island, the Irish Trade Union

Congress established in 1894 continued to operate on an all-Ireland basis. But, with its affiliated unions organised on divergent local, Irish or British Isles lines, it experienced growing internal tensions.

While the strongly nationalist Irish Transport and General Workers Union (ITGWU) was the main beneficiary of explosive membership growth after the First World War, a significant British Isles general workers union presence was also established around this time in the shape of the Amalgamated Transport and General Workers Union (ATGWU). The situation regarding large general unions was further complicated when James Larkin, the ITGWU leader in its early years, returned to Ireland in 1923 after a decade in the USA where he clashed with the new leadership dominated by William O'Brien and formed the breakaway Workers Union of Ireland (WUI). Among the smaller and/or more specialised unions the struggle for political independence was accompanied by a wave of Irish breakaways from amalgamated unions with British headquarters. The proportion of the membership breaking away varied, but in most cases the breakaway and the original organisation were to be found co-existing in a less than amicable fashion, although the investment in enmity appears to have been considerably greater among union officials than among the rank and file (Hannigan 1981). Union membership plummeted in the later 1920s but, as it recovered against the backdrop of industrialisation behind high tariff walls in the 1930s, the trade unions' perceived state of irrational fragmentation, internecine conflict and unresolved national belonging came to the fore as a policy concern. By 1936, government intent to legislate if internal reform measures were not forthcoming had been signalled to the ITUC. Trade union legislation passed in 1941 reserved the negotiating licences unions would require to organisations that had their headquarters within the southern state (McCarthy 1977, O'Connor 1992).

In 1946 the Supreme Court held that this requirement breached the constitutional right to freedom of association. By then splits had occurred within both the Labour Party, which had experienced a sharp rise in support thanks to the hardship and inequity of the Emergency regime, and the ITUC. In January 1944 the ITGWU disaffiliated from the Labour Party and most of the TDs it sponsored formed a rival National Labour Party. One of the two grounds for this move was specific: the admission to the Labour Party of the 'disruptive' James Larkin, the detested enemy of the ITGWU's O'Brien for more than two decades, and of his son 'Young Jim'. The second, which overlapped with the first given the political history of the Larkins (O'Connor 2002), was that communists had been permitted to join the party. Stalemate on the issue of reorganisation had left the ITUC on the brink of a split in 1939 when an 'advisory' Council of Irish Unions was formed. Early in 1945 the congress finally divided over attendance at a world trade union conference being hosted in London by the British TUC. The ITGWU and a number of smaller Irish unions took the position that attendance was incompatible with Ireland's neutrality and withdrew to form the Congress of Irish Unions (CIU) when the sending of a delegation was approved (McCarthy 1977, Milotte 1984, O'Connor 1992, Allen 1997).

The Fianna Fáil government's reaction to the split in congress was that 'generally speaking, it will be our policy to build up the prestige of the Congress of Irish Unions and to treat it as the more representative organ of Trade Union opinion'.[7] The CIU attempted to reciprocate by keeping Fianna Fáil in office after it had lost its overall majority in the 1948 general election but this was frustrated when National Labour TDs revolted, citing their voters' social welfare interests as grounds for joining four other opposition parties to form an alternative government rather than backing the unpopular outgoing one (Allen 1997, Dunphy 1995, McCullagh 1998) The presence of both Labour parties within the new government paved the way for reunification in 1950, but the split between the Congresses proved far less tractable and did not finally end until 1959.

The debilitating division between the two rival union congresses produced by the 1945 split was very much in evidence in 1955 when the IIRS-convened committee started meeting, with the CIU refusing to work alongside the ITUC. The country's largest union and the CIU's core member, the ITGWU, was prevailed upon to take the place on the committee vacated by the CIU but it then effectively withdrew from the work at an early stage. The committee's proceedings stretched over a period in which congress unity moves made significant progress, and by the time it disbanded towards the end of 1956 a Provisional United Trade Union Organisation (PUTUO) had been created. The participating ITUC adopted a broadly positive stance to productivity promotion provided conditions such as redundancy protection, benefit sharing and equal representation with management in the productivity centre were fulfilled. When PUTUO was formed it adopted a similar stance, recommending 'that both Congresses be requested to make representations to the Government that they should participate in European Productivity Agency projects and give sufficient notice of such meetings to the Congresses' (ITUC 1956: 148): if immediate decisions on appointing representatives were needed, these were to be left by the Congresses to PUTUO's officers.

'Merely partial representation of trade union organisations' had headed the list of objections to setting up a productivity centre advanced within the committee by FUE: its removal by PUTUO did not prompt any more positive appraisal by the employer body. Putting forward proposals rather than objections, FIM were more positively disposed. Through 'many and tedious meetings', the IIRS convened committee made tortuously slow progress. Finally, on 3 November 1956 Norton was sent a draft constitution for a productivity organisation, together with a letter which explained that:

> All the bodies invited subscribed to this document except the Federated Union of Employers. We expected that they would send us some communication saying why they were not willing to subscribe to the document but, as they have not seen fit to do so, we have thought it best to pass it on to you as an altogether unreasonable time has elapsed since you asked us to look into the matter. Whether there is any prospect of success for this organisation if the leading Employers' Association is not in favour of it, we must leave you to judge.[8]

The presentation of the informal committee's document coincided with the inauguration of an Industrial Advisory Council (IAC) to which its ministerial creator decided to refer further consideration of the question. A change in government in March 1957 led to Norton's departure from office and his replacement by Seán Lemass, who killed off the IAC by directing that no further meetings of the body be convened and also decided at a departmental conference on 6 May that no fresh action should be taken with regard to the setting up of a productivity centre.[9]

Despite the continuing absence of a national productivity centre, interaction between Irish non-governmental organisations and EPA increased over time and EPA officials proved eager to avail themselves of opportunities to encourage greater Irish participation in the agency's work. The trade union movement, IMI and the Retail, Grocery, Dairy and Allied Trades Association (RGDATA), a body that had not participated in the IIRS convened committee, were to the fore in this increasing interaction. With EPA paying travel and *per diem* expenses, and – on occasion – a more amenable attitude to providing small TA grants than was evident in the case of Project 312 on the part of Industry and Commerce, Irish businessmen and trade unionists were travelling to seminars in Europe from 1954 onwards.[10]

Applying the human sciences to industry: a specific EPA request for Irish action

The coalescence of a constituency of organisations favouring engagement with EPA was facilitated, and the option for productivity centre inaction chosen by Lemass on 6 May 1957 undermined, when EPA's Director, Roger Gregoire, made 'a personal request' to the Head of the Irish Delegation to OEEC on 3 May 'for your co-operation in putting into operation as quickly and efficiently as possible the Agency's programme for the human sciences and their application in industry', Project 405. The letter specifically requested 'your appropriate national authorities to constitute a joint committee in your country composed of management, trade union and government representatives as well as social scientists'. The national joint committees would collaborate with EPA in developing a European Research Plan and 'should also take part in the preparation and execution of each research undertaken in your country, as well as discuss ways and means to disseminate the results of research and to ensure their practical application'.

Although Industry and Commerce officials drafted a reply to External Affairs 'indicating that we do not propose to set up the Joint Committee', the Departmental Conference held on 1 July inclined towards a more positive response:

> While it was felt that there was need for such a body here, it was not clear to which existing Irish Organisation might best be assigned the task of examining and appraising the EPA suggestion with a view to formulating proposals for the establishment of a Joint Committee suitably adapted to Irish requirements . . . The Minister indicated that he favoured the idea of the establishment of such a Committee. He considered that the IMI would probably be best qualified to examine and appraise the EPA suggestion. He directed that the matter be discussed informally with Mr Hegarty, Vice Chairman of the Institute[11]

With leading IMI figures like Denis Hegarty positively committed to productivity promotion in a way the IIRS had not been, and with Industry and Commerce more actively supportive, the sounding out of potential participants continued over several months. In March 1958 a first preliminary meeting 'to consider the establishment of a Joint Committee to implement EPA Project 405' was convened by IMI. In addition to employer, manufacturer and trade union representatives, those invited comprised educational institutions (the two Dublin universities and the capital city's Vocational Education Committee) as well as a number of the larger semi-state companies (CIE, Bord na Mona, ESB and the Sugar Company)

Apart from their stated purpose, the preliminary meetings increased Irish contact with EPA, whose director came to Dublin to attend one in June, and provided a forum in which the national productivity centre issue was revisited. What emerged was in essence a resurrection of the 1956 IIRS-convened committee's constitution for a national productivity organisation. On this occasion the proposal did not encounter the stumbling block of obdurate FUE objection. It was, however, subjected to amendment when Hegarty headed a deputation that met Lemass on 11 July. Here the Minister took the view that 'the representation of the Industrial Development Authority on the Body was inappropriate in that it was made up of whole time Government nominees'. Originally conceived as a tripartite body with government, industry and unions equally represented, the Irish productivity centre was finally set up nearly a decade later as an essentially bipartite one in which educational and research institutions played a minor role alongside organised business and organised labour. This centre – the Irish National Productivity Committee (INPC) chaired by Denis Hegarty – operated alongside the National Joint Committee on the Human Sciences and their Application to Industry (usually known as the Human Sciences Committee (HSC)), chaired by UCD Professor E. F. O'Doherty.[12]

Setting out productivity principles

Both sides of the new productivity centre's remit – greatly increased collaboration with EPA and independent domestic initiatives – were to be in evidence over the INPC's first three years of existence (1959–61). Domestically, the initial focus of the new body's work was on defining a basis upon which the productivity drive could secure broad acceptance. To this end, work began, at the unions' prompting, on drafting a general Statement of Productivity Principles.

Agreed in September 1961, the principles associated increased productivity with improvement of living standards and the elimination of unemployment. Benefits from increased productivity 'should be enjoyed by all contributing thereto i.e. by the owners and the workers (as well as the consumer) having due regard to the necessity to strengthen the financial structure of industry and bearing in mind the interests of the community in general'. Employer–union consultation centred on safeguards for the worker should precede the introduction of productivity schemes. Such safeguards might take the form of 'assuring as far as possible the continuation of his present employment, developing a new job or finding suitable work for him'. Here 'the initial responsibility should rest with the Employer, the Trade Unions and the industry directly concerned, but where necessary, the help of the State should be sought for the provision of re-training and redeployment schemes or special compensation'. The principles also stated that a separation should be maintained between productivity co-operation in the common interest and 'normal industrial negotiations with regard to wages and conditions of employment'.[13]

Agreement on the principles was not easily reached and the events leading up to its achievement illustrates how the INPC operated in a tripartite way even though it was formally bipartite. When a draft circulated in November 1960 ran into FUE opposition, Lemass wrote to FUE supporting the concept of a principles statement on 29 December and suggesting that he meet an FUE deputation with Hegarty present to try to resolve the difficulties. FUE responded by seeking a private meeting and circulating a memorandum detailing its objections to the principles draft. These centred on the issues of benefit sharing and prior consultation. Both Hegarty and the Taoiseach's Department were unimpressed and both urged Lemass to press the FUE to accept the principles. The latter pointed out that practical work such as joint missions abroad was being held up by the dispute and that failure to agree 'would almost certainly contribute to a worsening of industrial relations and to mutual recrimination between employers and workers'. The former commented: 'so many of them [FUE members] are unenlightened as to the value of this new approach'. At his meeting with the FUE deputation on 23 January 1961 Lemass followed the line suggested. With regard to sharing, 'I said that in view of my own public statements in the matter I could not press unions to drop their insistence on this word'. The difficulty with consultation, construed by FUE as 'a written-in right of veto', Lemass characterised as 'a very theoretical objection' querying whether productivity change would actually be attempted in the absence of agreement.

The FUE appeared unmoved and subsequently sent Hegarty amendments to the draft that were based upon the January memorandum. When Hegarty in April tabled his own revised draft, rather than the FUE amendments, for discussion by INPC, the protest that followed also referred to 'instances which have occurred at factory level which reinforce very clearly the misgivings which have been expressed by many concerning the possibilities for contention inherent in the publication of any document of this nature'. A continuation of these occurrences might, it was threatened, force FUE to review its participation in INPC. The standoff was eventually resolved by the INPC setting up a sub-committee of its FUE and Irish Congress of Trade Unions (ICTU) members that had hammered out an agreed document by late 1961. The rebuff from Lemass to the FUE's attempt to enlist his support for the watering down of the productivity principles did not settle the issue but it set the parameters within which accommodation between FUE and ICTU was subsequently reached.[14]

In 1961 EPA was disbanded as OEEC became OECD and Ireland applied to become a full member of the EEC. The first of these developments led to the productivity drive becoming a domestic rather an international concern. The second led to the creation of an important new body with a tripartite constitution, the Committee on Industrial Organisation (CIO).

Tripartite structures and industrial adaptation

A mix of EPA funding support and a more liberal provision of departmental technical assistance grants had been the basis upon which Irish interaction with the agency had expanded since 1959. Both INPC and HSC were provided with secretarial support by Industry and Commerce, but neither body had a budget of its own. Technical assistance funding had to be sought on a project-by-project basis. Against the background of the changes taking place in Paris, Hegarty embarked on a campaign in late 1961 to establish a national productivity body with a greatly widened range of activities supported by a secure source of Irish state funding. The revamped INPC, it was proposed, would operate an advisory service targeted at small and medium enterprises, provide general information services, engage in promotional activities through a network of productivity committees organised on both an industrial and a regional basis, support educational activities and promote research. Over the next two years, the continuing support of Lemass was drawn upon by Hegarty and by his successor as INPC Chairman, ICTU General Secretary Ruaidhrí Roberts, to have a multi-faceted INPC established as an independent company limited by guarantee in receipt of an annual grant-in-aid from Industry and Commerce's budget.[15]

The CIO was initially conceived as a collaboration between Finance, Industry and Commerce and the Federation of Irish Industries (FII – the changed name of the FIM[16]) but it was subsequently reconstituted to provide representation to ICTU, FUE and the IDA. This committee oversaw the work of a series of survey teams 'each comprising as a minimum an economist (drawn from inside or outside the civil service) and an officer of the Department of Industry and Commerce, with a secretary also provided by this department'. An industry being surveyed had the choice of appointing a full member to the team or of appointing an associate or liaison officer. Also:

> The industries being surveyed were invited, indeed pressed, to nominate a technical expert to the team but no industry agreed to this step . . . The cost of the teams was borne entirely by the state, although if any technical experts had been appointed, the industry concerned would have been required to pay half the cost of these experts' services (FitzGerald 1968: 57)

In all some 55 industries, which accounted for 78 per cent of manufacturing employment, were surveyed. An extensive catalogue was compiled of serious shortcomings that would have to be addressed if company collapses and job losses were to be kept to a minimum as trade was freed. Recommendations for increased state aid to and support for industry, including a widened range of TA, were put forward. Industry and Commerce was to be restructured with the creation within it of an Industrial Reorganisation Branch (IRB). Within individual industries Adaptation Councils were to be set up. 'Comprising a relatively small number of industrialists elected by their colleagues, together with an independent member from outside the industry who might normally be chairman', these councils were envisaged as agencies to foster co-operative action between the firms within an industry. This was to be carried on in consultation with each industry's Trade Union Advisory Body (TUAB).

Much of the process of securing agreement for the proposals to revamp INPC involved waiting for the shape of the CIO proposals for carrying on adaptation work to emerge and then securing acceptance from Industry and Commerce that INPC activities would not duplicate or cut across those of a reorganised IIRS, an expanding IMI or the department's own newly created IRB. During 1962 and 1963 CIO itself sought to promote communication and liaison between 'organisations which have as an objective the improvement of efficiency in industry' through luncheon discussions to which the Chairmen and Chief Executives of eight bodies were invited.[17]

Incomes policy, economic planning and consultation with industry

Early in 1963 a spanner was thrown in the works of expanding tripartite consultation by government action. Lemass had initially sought to counter expressed disquiet about a rising wage trend by pointing to increased productivity as the counteracting means by which economic expansion should be sustained. However, the tone of his speeches sharpened noticeably as the economic situated deteriorated during 1962, producing a substantial visible trade deficit. On 28 September 1961 he had favourably contrasted wage rises accompanied by increased productivity with Britain's resort to a wages freeze and also made reference to the role of FUE and ICTU in framing the productivity principles. By contrast, while his speech to an FUE dinner on 27 February 1962 again referred to the productivity principles, this was accompanied by a riposte to a union leader's claim that an output rise could absorb the round of wage increases which observed: 'but as faith without good works will not avail, so also must principles be backed up with action. We need the action – and we need it soon'. In another speech, to a Dublin Fianna Fáil Comhairle Ceanntair dinner, on 29 December 1962 Lemass declared: 'there is a need in 1963 to "close the gap" between incomes and productivity . . . during 1963 "close the gap" must be our purpose and slogan'. A White Paper on Incomes and Output entitled *Closing the Gap* was published in February 1963. Accompanied by a pay standstill for all government departments and the state-sponsored bodies, this led to a hostile union response expressed through the withdrawal of representatives from a range of bodies that included the Committee on Industrial Organisation and the National Employer–Labour Conference.[18]

This disruption proved short term, however, and by the end of 1963 the revamped INPC had been unveiled and a new tripartite National Industrial Economic Council (NIEC) had also been launched. NIEC was initially proposed as a body that would examine issues relating to incomes policy but, with emergence of a 'tacit agreement' to avoid this 'tricky issue', its focus was put on reviewing the progress of the Second Programme for Economic Expansion which was to run from 1963 to 1970 (FitzGerald 1968: 156–7). The industrial side of the programme dovetailed with the required measures of adaptation to free trade conditions laid out in the CIO reports. The at best uncertain prospect of early EEC entry had vanished with General De Gaulle's veto on the British application in January 1963, but the government determined to press on with tariff reductions. By 1965 it had negotiated an Anglo-Irish Free Trade Agreement which would expose Irish industry to serious competitive pressure by the end of decade, a date by which it was hoped that early EEC entry might also be in prospect. With the die firmly cast in favour of free trade, INPC and NIEC appeared to provide the means of mobilising a broad base of support for a sustained efficiency drive at the level of individual industries. Thus Garret FitzGerald wrote of the CIO:

> The work of the committee showed that if the difficult field of industrial relations is by-passed, management and labour in Ireland can co-operate effectively in the public interest. There had already been signs of this in the work of the Irish National Productivity Committee but the CIO firmly established mutual confidence between the two sides of industry in matters of common concern. (FitzGerald 1968: 67)

But, either on a bipartite (INPC) or a tripartite (NIEC) basis, industry-level joint action was to prove ineffectual and was given up for dead by 1968. In the case of INPC, problems were exacerbated by a long running field service turf war with IMI.

The advisory service conflicts

That INPC should run an advisory service targeted at the smaller firms which, even with the availability of TA grants, remained least likely to use the services of consultants was first proposed by Denis Hegarty in January 1960. A Dutch scheme provided a model and it was envisaged that Irish advisers would initially be trained in Holland. The union members of INPC responded by suggested that an initiative be deferred until INPC 'should make it clear by means of a public statement that the interests of the workers would be safe-guarded in a productivity drive'. Almost two years elapsed before the Statement of Productivity Principles satisfied this condition. The advisory service then formed part of the blueprint for a post-EPA INPC. At this point the question of duplication with IMI activity arose. In discussion Industry and Commerce were slow to accept Hegarty's assurances that the INPC plan was acceptable to IMI, with Jack Lynch writing to Lemass in March 1962 that he was 'aware informally that some people at any rate in the Management Institute feel very strongly about Mr Hegarty's proposals'.[19] While an INPC advisory service eventually secured departmental approval, there was increasing tension between IMI and INPC which came into the open when, with a new term of office for INPC members beginning in January 1965, IMI decided that its two representatives would be the Chairman and the Director *ex-officio*, thus excluding Hegarty from an organisation in which he had served as Chairman and Vice-Chairman and which was to a very considerable extent his personal creation (Cox 2002: 101–5).

The advisers trained to run INPC's service 'returned from Holland in December 1963 with the impression that the diagnostic survey was not working there and the feeling that it would not be useful here'. Those operating the service subsequently lobbied to have restrictions on their role removed so that they could operate professionally along the lines of commercial industrial consultants. One criticised restriction arose from the separation made by the Statement of Productivity Principles between productivity co-operation in the common interest and 'normal industrial negotiations with regard to wages and conditions of employment'. This, it was claimed, led to the advisers being 'debarred from the work study/remuneration/personnel area'.

Joining the nature and scope of the advisory service that should be provided as a bone of contention was the issue of whether the service should continue to be attached to INPC or located elsewhere. The employers' side of INPC favoured transferring the service and supported a proposal made by IMI in 1967 to have the service integrated into its structure, arguing that through such a move a synthesis of management advice and management development could be achieved. The unions opposed such a transfer because it would remove the advisory service from the sphere of joint management–union action in pursuit of productivity. Complex organisational and reporting schemes were devised but failed to provide a basis for resolving an impasse that dragged on into the 1970s. Amid the protracted disagreement, the service unsurprisingly experienced serious problems with staff recruitment and retention.[20]

Activating joint approach bodies at industry level

The industry-level engagement of NIEC took the form of reviewing progress towards the attainment of the detailed targets set out in the Second Programme. In 1964 civil servants from Finance's Development Division held separate discussions with the Adaptation Councils and Trade Union Advisory Bodies or – in their absence – with other representative groups 'to elicit the reasons for any deviation from expectations' (NIEC 1964: 10). Finance (in consultation with the other departments involved) drew together the results of these reviews to form the basis of a report that NIEC published. This envisaged moving from separate to joint discussion with business and unions at the next review but, before this could take place, the whole question of joint action structures had become a controversial issue.

Development of industry-level or 'vertical' productivity committees formed a central part of the programme of the post-EPA INPC. The first committees were established for printing and footwear in 1963 and a committee covering the distribution sector was set up the following year. Two further committees were being formed when the movement came under fire. The source of the attack was a group of nine Independent Chairmen of Adaptation Councils. The April 1965 statement from these Independent Chairmen claimed that 'improvement of co-operation between management and trade unions should be undertaken jointly by the Adaptation Councils and the TUAB instead of by Productivity Committees which tend to cut across the joint activities of the Adaptation Councils and the TUAB'. and that 'the work of the INPC is at present having a disruptive effect on a number of industries'.[21]

FII – which held the chair of the INPC – supported the Adaptation Councils it serviced while ICTU, which was highly critical of the Adaptation Councils' failure to communicate with TUABs, supported the establishment of further productivity committees. The two sides agreed that the current situation would remain frozen while the NIEC served as a forum for further discussion of industry-level structures. The move later in the year to joint discussion for the second annual review of industry within the Second Programme was not 'completely successful' with the NIEC concluding that the value of the review meetings 'would be greatly enhanced if they were linked with regular meetings during the year of adaptation councils (or industrial associations) and trade union representatives' (NIEC 1966b: 20–1). In April 1966 Lemass took up this theme in a speech that made specific reference to the review's findings:

> The preparing of Irish industry for the test of free trade, and to achieve the maximum rate of growth which is feasible, must be seen as a joint responsibility of management and workers . . . regular consultation between managements and Unions, to discuss development plans in a constructive way, and not only to cope with particular difficulties as they emerge, is essential to the process of building Irish industry . . . the recasting of Irish industry is not only a matter of new production procedures, better machines or larger factories: it is, more particularly, a matter of developing new attitudes to the problems of human relations in industry and to the functioning of the industrial partnership.[22]

In May NIEC published its *Report on Arrangements for Planning at Industry Level* (NIEC 1966c). This underlined the limited extent to which the arrangements envisaged by CIO had been realised. Twenty-four adaptation councils had been set up but many had experienced difficulty in getting independent members or independent chairmen from other industries. This had been compounded by the failure of 23 of the 24 councils to appoint a full-time executive to work under the chairman as recommended by the CIO. There was a lack of communication between the adaptation councils and both the TUABs and government planning and development agencies. Co-operation between all the firms within an industry, the foundation on which the adaptation structures rested, was an innovation requiring a 'revolution in existing attitudes' which had failed to take root.

The NIEC report backed the idea of establishing development councils that, depending on the circumstances of particular industries, would either take vertical productivity committees as their base or would bring adaptation councils together with TUABs. The development councils would undertake the annual review of progress under the Second Programme and the INPC would bring to them 'proposals for joint activities relating to productivity'. But, met 'on the side of industry with a reluctance to embark on a further experiment and by doubts about the wisdom of participating in joint bodies which would concern themselves with the future of each industry and in which industrialists would face both trade unionists and officials' (FitzGerald 1968: 66), NIEC's proposals were never to be translated into practice. Admittedly unsatisfactory adaptation bodies were left to their own devices while, stranded in limbo by the ongoing impasse, the early vertical productivity committees withered away outside the distribution sector.

The 'unavoidable impressions' the 1966 review of industrial progress conveyed to NIEC were 'an insufficient concern by industry with the problems likely to face it in the years ahead, an incapacity to recognise – or at any rate articulate – the problems looming in the immediate future and an overestimation of the State's influence on the course of economic affairs'. 'Some confusion' was acknowledged to surround the Development Council proposals and a further examination by NIEC of matters that 'require a fuller treatment than we have previously given them' was promised (NIEC 1967: 16–17). By the middle of 1967 the Second Programme had been effectively abandoned by the government. A further review of industrial progress was carried out in that year, although in this instance it was Industry and Commerce IRB rather than Finance Development civil servants that participated on the government side in order to redress 'an undue emphasis on statistics at review meetings to the detriment of discussion of matters of more practical concern to the industries represented' (Department of Finance 1968: 24).

By the autumn of 1968 a 'CIO II' exercise – in which a tripartite committee supervised a series of team surveys – was under way and the annual reviews of industrial progress begun in 1964 were at an end. At the same time NIEC commented on the experience of the Second Programme years:

> We recommended the establishment of Development Councils . . . but little or no progress has been made in that direction. If such bodies are to be established they may have to operate at the level of the industry group (e.g. textiles, clothing, food) rather than at the level of the individual industry . . . since so little has been achieved on the institutional plane over the last four years, it may optimistic to expect that new bodies will be established and in effective operation within the next four years, the period of the Third Programme. New institutional arrangements take time – the more so when management and trade unions in many industries do not seem yet to appreciate that they are needed.

Reflecting on what was seen as at best passive acceptance of – rather than active involvement in – the planning process, NIEC signalled a shift away from a focus on industrial partnership by suggesting that 'the next programme must be explicitly social as well as economic in its contents and objectives' (NIEC 1968: 13–15). While the focus of partnership building was turning from the industrial to the social, a set of significant industrial policy changes were taking shape that would fill the vacuum left by the failure to translate the CIO adaptation blueprint into practice. These involved the creation of a new IDA, the failure of Industry and Commerce to respond to Finance urgings to create an industrial efficiency service and agreement between the two departments on pursuing adaptation through that the encouragement of mergers.

Reinventing the IDA

The IDA has up to this point been encountered as an agency to which a tariff review function was successively given, removed and restored. However, the agency's main focus after 1951 was on the attraction of new industry in the context of state grant aid. Initially this aid was available only in undeveloped areas of the west where labour was flooding out of agriculture and on to boats to England. By the mid-1950s it was available, with different levels for developed and undeveloped areas, across the state and had become linked to tax relief on profits earned from exports. Export-orientation was promoted both to ease the state's recurrent balance of payments problems and to protect the home market position of existing manufacturers from grant-aided industry competition – a generalisation of the particular considerations that chapter 3 documented in the case of Solus. These export-oriented new industries were mainly foreign-owned. In the early 1960s Britain and Europe were the predominant sources of investment projects although IDA promotional effort was greatest in the USA.[23]

Commenting on the Anglo-Irish Free Trade Agreement early in 1966, NIEC identified a need within the new context 'to ensure that the general attractiveness of the Republic of Ireland, as a location for new industries, is reasonably equivalent with that of Northern Ireland, the various regions in Britain and other relevant areas' (NIEC 1966a: 9). The IDA itself had a new Chairman with J. P. Beddy having stepped down after 16 years to be succeeded by J. J. Walsh. No doubt prompted by Walsh, the Minister for Industry and Commerce wrote to his Finance counterpart on 31 January 1966 that 'the time has come, I think, for a basic appraisal and probably a change in our attitudes towards industrial development'.[24]

The specific proposal contained in this letter was to bring in a US consulting firm, A. D. Little Inc. Finance initially opposed this on grounds of cost, suggesting a CIO-type survey as an alternative, but support for the proposal from the NIEC General Purposes Committee assisted its subsequent approval. Contact between Little and the IDA had been ongoing for almost a decade at this point. None of the ideas the firm had pitched to the agency had been taken up to date. Little had, however, done work for the Northern Ireland government, whose success in securing major US projects was much greater than that of its southern counterpart, and one of the possibilities for study raised by Little in 1962 with the IDA – the attraction of some electronics research and development activities – had aroused positive interest on the Development side of Finance. In 1966–7 Little reviewed Irish incentives in the context of what competitors were offering, examined Irish promotional agency structures and also conducted a review of the IIRS, whose performance was still considered to be unsatisfactory despite its reorganisation and expansion at the beginning of the 1960s. Alongside these studies, a team drawn from the IDA and the Finance Development Division carried out a survey of the grant-aided industries. By mid-1968 the government had approved a simplified incentive structure operated by a single agency that united the previously split promotional and grant-determining functions and had the freedom to recruit and remunerate its staff outside civil service procedures. With free trade seen to be rendering redundant the division between Irish firms operating in the home market and foreign ones servicing export ones, the new IDA was unveiled as a source of packaged incentives available to all new projects regardless of origin.[25]

An industrial efficiency service proposed and resisted

At the beginning of 1967, a revived prospect of negotiations in the near future for EEC entry led to renewed discussion between department secretaries of the state of Irish industry. On 14 April T. K. Whitaker suggested that, because of the transfer to it of the Second Programme's annual industrial reviews, Industry and Commerce's IRB was best placed to supply the analysis needed to formulate a negotiating position. But the material subsequently provided by IRB was judged to be seriously inadequate by Finance – 'there seems to be an unspoken implication that expenditure on adaptation is regarded as being tantamount to making industry internationally competitive'. When representatives of the two departments met on 28 September, 'it became clear early in the meeting that there was a fundamental divergence of opinion between the two Departments on the purpose of the exercise'.[26] Initiating correspondence at department secretary level, T. K. Whitaker suggested on 20 October the setting up of 'some kind of "industrial efficiency service"' in Industry and Commerce.

> [This] would get to grips on the economic, financial and technical plane with the problem areas i.e. prepare reports on the weaknesses which remain even after adaptation grants etc. have had their impact and the means by which as many firms as possible might win through to industrial efficiency . . . ([this] might be presented as a voluntary service but in effect be imposed upon any unenlightened firms). . . [this] would be a natural development even outside the EEC context: it is five years or more since the CIO surveys were made, a lot of adaptation money has been laid out since, and free trade has become formally inevitable under the Anglo-Irish Agreement. What would be more fitting than that the Department of Industry and Commerce (as a final service to industry, not to mention as a protection to itself) would now take positive steps to bring its knowledge of the industrial scene completely up-to-date and reassure itself that, financially and technically, everything possible was being done for industrial efficiency and progress?

In the light of J. C. B. McCarthy's eventual response that 'we do not think that this needs to be done since such a service is, as you may not have been aware, already provided by the IRB', Finance – while plainly lacking faith in the IRB's efficacy – did not think it worthwhile to pursue the matter further at this point.[27] During the course of the correspondence, McCarthy had fended off Whitaker's suggestion for industry studies to be jointly carried by Industry and Commerce and Finance, arguing that informal consultation between the departments was all that was required. Less than six months later, however, joint involvement in 'CIO 2' was proposed by the Minister for Industry and Commerce, George Colley, to his Finance counterpart, Charles Haughey. Progress with the adaptation recommendations of the original CIO and evaluation of 'the external marketability of industrial products with a view to ensuring that rationalisation and concentration of production are properly oriented' were proposed as the terms of reference of 'CIO 2'. In response, Haughey on 8 May expressed a preference 'for more direct action', pointing to 'the standard of expertise, especially technical expertise, not alone in industry but also in public service organisations dealing with industry' as an area ripe for such action. In a later letter Haughey was more specific about what he had in mind:

> Setting up in your Department an Industrial Advisory Service headed by the officer in charge of the IRB and including representatives of CTT, INPC, IIRS, IMI and ICC [Industrial Credit Company]. This Advisory Service would obviously have at its disposal a whole range of expertise – managerial, financial, technical, marketing – and could organise for any firm an expert team to study the firm's particular problems and advise on what it should do to ensure its progress in the free trade evolution of the industry to which it belongs. While this would be a service available on request, I see no reason why it should not be *offered* to particular firms by your Department or the Service, where this seems desirable. Apart from a diminished claim to future aids and incentives, one of the sanctions against rejecting the offer of the service would be publication of the rejection.

But Colley, while open to considering 'something . . . which will combine an advisory service with a special service for industries in difficulty so as to make sure we get early warnings and are not confronted with the kind of situation . . . where the industry was at its last gasp before we were called upon for help', was unyielding on the need for 'CIO II'. Haughey gave way and the Committee on Industrial Progress (CIP) was set up in September 1968.[28]

CIP published reports on twelve different industries between 1970 and 1973. These provided further evidence of the failure of the adaptation councils to fill the role that the CIO had envisaged for them. Adaptation expenditure had plainly resulted in a much-improved general standard of factory building and equipment. Changes to work practices – CIO had recommended incentive bonus schemes and more operator training – were, the reports suggest, much less in evidence. Technical assistance was perceived by its recipients as beneficial although the benefits eluded quantification. The overall impact of consultants was presented as being limited by the weakness of management structures – in women's outerwear, for example, 'the shortage of management personnel, or to put it another way, the excessive demands of multiple management functions on the existing management personnel, meant and continues to mean that the consultancy projects, however good in themselves, can often effect only a limited improvement in specific areas, while other areas of the company's management may be neglected and while follow-up action of a resolute and persistent kind may not be possible' (CIP 1970: 38–9). Only two changes to the existing range of incentives were recommended by CIP's final report – one 'to encourage firms to accept the special risks involved in market and product development' and the other 'to encourage mergers . . . by the provision of concessionary finance such as loan guarantee and/or interest subsidy' (CIP 1973: 33 and 36–7).

Mergers

Although mergers and amalgamations had been acknowledged by CIO as a potentially effective means to the end of industrial rationalisation, the emphasis of its recommendations was on industry-wide co-operation between firms which retained their separate identities and consulted with their industry's TUAB on an ongoing basis. The Wilson government's policy of aggressively engineering mergers in order to raise the technological level and export potential of British industry attracted Irish civil service attention although it was not the headline-grabbing Industrial Reorganisation Corporation (IRC) but the lower profile Industrial and Commercial Finance Corporation (ICFC) with its medium-sized enterprise orientation that appeared of most relevance to the Irish situation. Within the Irish system the Industrial Credit Company (ICC) played a broadly similar role to ICFC and this role came under scrutiny as the agency reorganisation proposals by A. D. Little were discussed in government departments.

Having already played a part in a number of important industrial mergers, ICC proposed in June 1968 to follow ICFC's example and set up a subsidiary which had the specific function of promoting and facilitating mergers.[29] At almost exactly the same time George Colley sent Charles Haughey – from whom he was still attempting to secure agreement to 'CIO II' – a proposal for a Commercial Mergers Council. He envisaged that this Council would be chaired by J. P. Beddy (who was Chairman of ICC) and would be an organisation 'established essentially in the private enterprise field' with no civil servant members. Whether the state should provide financial support – as well as 'benevolent encouragement' – for mergers Colley left open, proposing only that the Council's own activities might be supported by a grant from the Industry and Commerce TA Vote. Informed of the ICC initiative, he took the view that it would 'by and large meet what I had in mind' and envisaged that side by side with the ICC subsidiary would be 'the efforts of the Industrial Reorganisation Branch of my Department to seek out opportunities for mergers'.[30]

By September, however, Industry and Commerce were claiming that 'the rationalisation of industry through mergers and other measures is a very precise responsibility' of its Minister 'and is quite inseparable from the general re-adaptation of industry to newer conditions of trading'. It was therefore 'entirely unacceptable to the Minister' that the function should be assumed by an ICC subsidiary and he therefore revived his earlier Council proposal. A meeting on 19 December attended by Colley, officials of the two Departments and of ICC succeeded in assuaging the Minister's concerns.[31] By the time EEC entry prospects revived once again at the end of the decade a White Paper could observe in relation to industrial adaptation that 'it now seems to be generally accepted – at least by the more progressive firms – that financial linkages, mergers or takeovers, are the only really effective means of achieving structural re-organisation and rationalisation' (Department of Finance 1970: 122–3).[32]

Conclusion

Whether carried on under the banner of a productivity drive or that of planning for economic expansion under free trade conditions, neither bipartite (INPC) nor tripartite (NIEC) industry-level joint action could be considered successful. The lack of willingness of firms to collaborate with one another in industrial adaptation councils was a fatal stumbling block for hopes of effectively developing industry-level joint action bodies. Insofar as adaptive action was taken, concentration of capital through mergers rather than co-operation in associations of independent company units prevailed. Facilitating mergers became the officially favoured method of promoting rationalisation. Industrial adaptation was thus removed from the joint action sphere and placed in a discreetly hidden abode to which only bankers, factory owners and such civil servants as were taken into their confidence secured admittance.

Against this backdrop INPC and NIEC could at least claim to have contributed to one significant compensatory measure for employees. The Statement of Productivity Principles had in 1961 raised the issue of state compensation for redundant workers at a time when no coherent official policy had been formulated on how to handle what for the trade unions was a crucial aspect of adaptation:

> While supporting programmes aimed at increasing productivity, trade unions must nevertheless, because of the circumstances of the Irish economy, sound a note of warning which needs to be a raucous one at times if it is to command attention. Ours is not a full employment economy, as is the case in most other OEEC countries. It never has been and seems unlikely to be in the foreseeable future. Heavy unemployment here has been of long-standing and unyielding persistence. The harsh dilemma that this poses for trade unions is a dominant consideration in their approach to productivity questions (Nevin 1959: 208)

On the assumption that its recommended adaptation measures would be put into effect, CIO estimated that EEC membership would cause around 11,000 industrial job losses, while the Second Programme projected an industrial employment increase net of redundancies due to freeing of trade of 86,000 by 1970. Opponents of EEC entry, on the other hand, raised the spectre of 100,000 industrial jobs being lost in the process.[33] Both INPC and especially NIEC kept the redundancy compensation issue to the fore in the first half of the 1960s (NIEC 1965). In doing so they counteracted the slowness of government departments to face up to the problem.[34] Their action helped to lay the groundwork for a state manpower policy that in the mid-1960s established a new Department of Labour, an industrial training authority and statutory redundancy payment entitlements. From very restricted and ad hoc coverage under protectionism, state compensation for redundancy became a basic employment right in the course of adaptation to free trade.

CHAPTER FIVE

Educating Trade Unionists

Introduction

United States Technical Assistance and Productivity Program was an integral part of Cold War anti-communism. It explicitly aimed to foster 'free' trade unions and to undermine the strength of their 'red' rivals where these existed. After 1941 an open Communist Party political presence could only be found north of the Irish border. To the south, militant anti-communism was rampant. Huge demonstrations protested against persecution of the Catholic Church during the Spanish Civil War or in Communist-controlled parts of Europe in the late 1940s. Staunchly anti-communist as it was, Ireland nonetheless distressed European Productivity Area officialdom by its minimal involvement in the agency's activities. Irish trade union leaders were a group whose support for more positive engagement was cultivated by the EPA. When such engagement belatedly and briefly occurred, EPA 'laid the foundations for a trade union training system in Ireland' (Boel 2003: 174–5).

After very briefly considering Irish communism and anti-communism, this chapter examines the changing post-war context of Irish trade union education. From the late 1940s through the 1950s the education of Irish trade unionists was a bone of contention within a divided Labour movement with British-style secular provision struggling to survive in the face of initiatives that espoused the social teaching of the Catholic Church. The former was embodied in the People's College, the latter found expression in university extra-mural courses for trade unionists, in the foundation in Dublin of a Catholic Workers' College (CWC) run by Jesuits and in a variety of study circles. The Marshall Plan and the formation of EPA saw trade union leaders and their protégés exposed to new US and continental European influences. At the end of the 1950s proponents of the two educational approaches were represented on HSC and INPC, with the split between rival union congresses slowly coming to an end. During the 1960s first EPA, then OECD and finally INPC funding enabled the unified ICTU to run its own education programme. During the same decade the Catholic Workers' College, seeking to remain relevant in radically changing religious and social contexts, embarked upon an extended process of reinvention.

Communism in a cold climate

After James Larkin's return from the USA in 1923 Moscow turned to this legendary but highly idiosyncratic figure to lead its efforts to build an Irish branch of the international communist movement. Disillusioned with Larkin, it made overtures at the end of the decade to left-leaning elements of the Irish Republican Army. The Free State government's response was to enlist the support of the Catholic hierarchy to launch a red scare, passing new emergency legislation under which a wide range of republican and communist groups were proscribed in 1931. While communist activity had not provoked strong Church hostility in the 1920s, the early 1930s witnessed 'the rise of anti-communism which, following a relentless propaganda campaign in the popular Catholic press, had extended beyond its church- and state-inspired origins to become a widespread phenomenon' (McGarry 2005: 220) The reporting of atrocities against Catholic priests and nuns in Spain intensified popular anti-communist sentiment in the later part of the decade (MacGarry 1999). Press censorship in the Second World War years displayed marked anti-Soviet bias (O'Drisceoil 1996: 295–6).

With the party line swinging away from anti-fascism after the 1939 Nazi–Soviet non-aggression pact, communism's tiny southern Irish following found itself briefly in tune with the national political mainstream. But communist support for Irish neutrality ended once Germany invaded the Soviet Union in June 1941. The following month a decision was taken to dissolve the party's only southern branch in Dublin. Members were to join the Labour Party with the ultimate aim of promoting its participation in a coalition that would secure a parliamentary majority for entering the war on the Allied side.

Through active campaigning against the hardship and inequity of the Emergency regime, Labour's membership and electoral support grew strongly in the early 1940s, resulting in striking gains at the June 1943 general election. The new activism loosened the grip on the party's structures long held by the ITGWU enabling both James Larkin senior and James Larkin junior to join the party and stand successfully as Dáil candidates in 1943 (O'Drisceoil 2005). Larkin senior had dropped his links with communism at the end of the 1920s. But his son, who had studied at the International Lenin School in Moscow, was a leading Irish communist throughout the 1930s. His involvement thereafter is a matter on which conflicting claims have been made. Dominant figures in the WUI, both Larkins became members of a Labour Party Central Branch founded in 1942, to which a number of those active in the dissolved Dublin branch of the Communist Party had gravitated. Prominent figures in the Central Branch were also to the fore in a Dublin Executive of the Labour Party founded in 1943.

Irish neutrality denied communism the wartime popularity and respectability it enjoyed elsewhere, while the Soviet Union fought with Britain and the USA under a United Nations banner. The accusation that Communists had infiltrated the Labour Party had been made during the 1943 General Election campaign by Seán McEntee, a Fianna Fáil minister whose papers contain a number of Department of Justice reports from the period on Dublin Communist activities (Morrissey 2007: 334–5). Similar charges were repeated when, having failed to secure the expulsion of the Dublin Executive officers it held responsible for the unconstitutional nomination of Larkin senior as a general election candidate, the ITGWU disaffiliated from the Labour Party in January 1944. They were then amplified by a series of articles contributed to the weekly *Standard* by Alfred O'Rahilly, the President of University College Cork (UCC) and a leading proponent of Catholic social teaching. O'Rahilly's articles, some of which were subsequently reprinted in pamphlet form by the National Labour Party, contained extremely detailed accounts of activities and meetings which could scarcely have come from any other source than Garda informant and surveillance material of the kind to which McEntee was privy.

Forced on to the defensive, the Labour Party leader William Norton set up an internal party committee of inquiry before which 17 members were summoned to appear. Of these, six were expelled for the offence of having attended the October 1943 Congress held by the Communist Party in Belfast. With its altered line after June 1941, the party had prospered spectacularly north of the border. There it basked in the reflected glory of Red Army battlefield heroics, urged Labour–Unionist coalition at Stormont and demanded maximum factory output in support of the war effort. Indeed, a resolution on production passed at the 1943 Congress strangely prefigured the productivity drive and adaptation discussions in the south during the 1960s:

> Congress pledges all Communists to work to achieve maximum production for the war effort. It notes the powerful contribution that production committees have made to increase the war effort and pledges the members of the Party to work to create the effectiveness of these committees. In this connection Congress demands that greater authority be vested in production committees, and that members of the committees should be relieved of as much responsibility as possible in the workshops so that they can concentrate more attention on production problems. Congress also demands that there should be a frequent calling of conferences so that experiences are pooled and the best results obtained all round. Finally, in order to interest and mobilise effectively all workers, Congress demands that members of the production committees report regularly to meetings of the workers and seek their advice and assistance to further this all-important work of building up the weapons to defeat Hitler (Communist Party of Ireland 1943: 18)

Neither Larkin was implicated by attendance at the Belfast Congress and they remained Labour Party members. Writing in the *Standard* on 17 March 1944 O'Rahilly had accepted that Larkin senior was not to his knowledge now a member of any Communist organisation but claimed that Larkin junior certainly was. However, pouring scorn on the outcome of the committee of inquiry on 5 May, he wrote that 'the expulsion is too obviously a cloak for the Larkins, senior and junior' and that those expelled 'have been thrown to the wolves to take attention off these two'.[1] In the same month the Fianna Fáil government called a snap general election against the backdrop of the 'American Note', demanding the closure of the Axis legations in Dublin on the grounds that they facilitated espionage that might compromise Allied plans to invade Europe. The Labour share of the vote fell sharply from its 1943 level leaving the two rival parties with a combined total of 12 seats compared with the 17 won by the united party a year earlier. Larkin senior lost his seat but Larkin junior was returned. In 1948 'Young Jim' saw off fresh 'red scare' onslaughts from both McEntee and the *Standard*, continuing to sit in the Dáil until he stood down in 1957 to concentrate on trade union activity.

Within the trade union movement 'Young Jim' – who lacked his father's flamboyance but was widely recognised to be a man of formidable ability (Puirséil 2007: 114–16) – worked to restore a united trade union congress. He was strongly supportive of the bipartite and tripartite productivity and planning bodies created in the late 1950s and early 1960s, becoming as strongly identified with the NIEC as Ruaidhrí Roberts was with INPC. At the 1968 WUI conference, nine months before his death, he argued that 'it is vital to the future of this country and its working people that the Labour movement be increasingly active in supporting all forms of economic forecasting and programming not in an unthinking manner, but in a positive critical way, distinguishing between the NIEC and the Fianna Fáil party and government and striving continually to strengthen the whole concept of planned economic development and the leading role of the State in its realisation' (quoted in O'Riordan 2001: 35). The Larkins' 1944 antagonist, Alfred O'Rahilly, also exercised an ongoing influence on the Irish labour movement's development and it to this that we now turn.

Educating the worker

Before the Second World War southern Ireland had little or no provision of education for workers. The years after the war saw a number of new initiatives being taken in relation to trade union education against the background of labour movement division. Some originated within the movement with a view to advancing its cause: others came from Catholic sources within and without the National University colleges of Dublin (UCD), Cork (UCC) and Galway (UCG).

In November 1943 the Joint Council of the ITUC and Labour Party approved the setting up of 'an educational organisation which would be requested to formulate a scheme of adult education through regular tutorial classes'. With party and congress split, proponents of the scheme made contact with the two Dublin universities in 1945. Forging a link with Trinity's existing diploma in Social Science was suggested but, because this course was considered to be 'too elaborate and too technical', an experimental course in economics and social science delivered by UCD's Professor George O'Brien was pursued as an initial step (Roberts 1986: 7). In October 1945 this 'began very promisingly' but it 'collapsed in the following year' (McCarthy 1977: 389–90). A joint Labour Party and ITUC committee reviewed the situation in March 1947. By then a well-attended economics and social science diploma course had been launched in the Rathmines High School of Commerce but the committee concluded that, while this was worthy of support, 'it fell short of the aim of the two bodies, that is, the training of well informed propagandists for the movement'. The favoured option to emerge from these discussions was the establishment of adult education facilities in Ireland on the lines of either the Workers Educational

Association (WEA) or the National Council of Labour Colleges (NCLC) and an invitation to the Secretary of one of the organisations to visit Ireland for discussions was recommended (Roberts 1986: 9–11).

Ernest Green of WEA attended an ITUC special conference on adult education in January 1948 and returned to Dublin on a number of occasions later in the year. The setting up of a southern Irish WEA branch – both NCLC and WEA had operated for decades in the north (Boyd 1999, Nolan and Johnston 2003) – was endorsed although this was later altered to the foundation of the People's College Adult Education Association 'which, while it had good relations with the WEA, was not structurally connected with it' (McCarthy 1977: 389–90). Like WEA, the People's College sought to forge links with the universities. The idea of a joint university advisory committee ran into an objection to sitting on the same body as Trinity College from UCD's President, Michael Tierney. Separate advisory committee links with the two Dublin universities were then pursued. But, when UCD's decision to start an extra-mural programme of its own blocked a link with that college just before the October 1948 launching of the People's College, it was thought best for the fledgling to have no university relationship rather than to have one with Trinity College alone (Roberts 1986: 16–17)

As the Labour movement was turning its attention towards education in 1943, Alfred O'Rahilly became President of University College Cork. An inveterate controversialist, O'Rahilly had spent seven years studying to become a Jesuit before deciding not to take orders and embarking on an academic career in mathematics. Active in Sinn Féin and on the pro-treaty side of politics in the early 1920s, O'Rahilly had a longstanding interest in both adult education (O'Murchu 1989) and labour issues. When the ITGWU cited communist infiltration of the Labour Party as a ground for its disaffiliation, O'Rahilly, as we have seen, took up cudgels on its behalf in the *Standard* and also offered to write a constitution for the National Labour Party. To a Cork ITGWU official O'Rahilly observed: 'it is better to clear the air *now* . . . than when a crowd of communised emigrants return'.[2]

In October 1946 UCC inaugurated a two-year part-time Diploma in Social and Economic Science. The course 'was very highly regarded by trade union leaders in Cork, whether they supported the ITUC or the CIU' (McCarthy 1977: 389) and was run in collaboration with the City of Cork Vocational Education Committee whose officers were members of a union that was affiliated to ITUC. The Rathmines course that began in the following year was similar to the Cork one in both content and VEC involvement. The Archbishop of Dublin, who made available as a lecturer Fr James Kavanagh, a priest whom he had sent to study social and economic theory at Campion Hall, Oxford, for two years, also supported it. In 1948 UCC began extending its course to other centres in Munster while O'Rahilly repeatedly attacked in the *Standard* the ITUC moves to introduce education along WEA lines to southern Ireland. To a Jesuit he wrote privately:

> The position is exceedingly serious, and I want to speak frankly about it. The TUC – Miss Bennet, Larkin, Connolly, Swift etc. have got up a brand new scheme for adult education of Irish Catholic Workers. They are even going to ask the state to subsidise it. After all our struggle to have Catholic national schools is Dublin going to sit idly by and see the Catholic Workers of Ireland induced into secularism and Communism? I say Dublin because they are not putting a leg inside Cork. And I am planning to rescue Limerick and Waterford from them. I regard this as the most serious threat to the religion of the Irish worker since I reached the age of reason. If Dublin does not do something about it, things are going to be very serious. If a real protective Catholic Counter-movement is started I personally will get for you the backing of at least all the unions affiliated to the Congress of Irish unions and a number of the rank-and-file from the other Unions.[3]

At the general chapter of the Society of Jesus in Rome in 1946 'one of the major decisions taken was that Jesuits should, wherever appropriate, become involved in adult education and especially the teaching of social science throughout the world' (Gaughan 1992: 177). In Ireland this led to a decision to establish a Catholic Workers' College. O'Rahilly urged the Irish Jesuit provincial to link his order's provision of education for workers to UCD. That university's President, who was far from sharing O'Rahilly's enthusiasm for adult education courses, was eventually prevailed upon to appoint a Jesuit, Fr Edward Coyne, as director of extra-mural studies. The UCD programme began with a two-year diploma course in social and economic science in January 1949. A Jesuit-run Catholic Workers' College (CWC) operating independently of UCD was established under Fr Edmond Kent's direction in 1951 'when worker-students who had successfully completed the first diploma course at UCD indicated their desire to continue the study of economic and social questions' (Gaughan 1992: 184).

Fr James Kavanagh had been sent to Oxford by the Archbishop of Dublin 'with a view to the development of a diocesan structured plan for social education'. In 1951 he became Director of a Dublin Diocesan Study Centre – later renamed the Dublin Institute of Catholic Sociology – established to cater for a number of Catholic groups 'involved in social teaching' and a range of study circles. The approach of the institute was to conduct study and discussion classes for specific occupational groups. These included manual occupations such as bakers, busmen and dockers as well as bankers, civil servants, nurses and others. As with the UCC and UCD courses there was a tendency for the running of these classes to diffuse out of their original centre. J. Anthony Gaughan recalls his involvement as a curate in Bray at the end of the 1950s with a class drawn mainly from professional backgrounds:

> My input was a session every Friday evening from 8 to 10 at the Vocational School. I would lecture for three quarters of an hour, there would be a cup of tea and finally an open discussion. I ran the centre for the three years I was in Bray. In the first year we did a course on sociology based on Fr Jim Kavanagh's *Manual of social ethics*; in the second year we studied all aspects of communism; and in the third I attempted a more advanced treatment of ethics with reference to contemporary philosophy (Gaughan 2000: 40)

Faced with hostility from CIU unions that regarded it as an offshoot of the ITUC, lacking financial support from ITUC affiliated unions, competing with a variety of church-sponsored education initiatives and having a 'holy war' waged against it by the *Standard*, the People's College struggled to survive (Roberts 1986):

> The People's College . . . suffered only too clearly from the rather damaging charges that it was under British – or in any event external – influences, and also that it did not carry on its face the stamp of Catholic orthodoxy. . . Lurking behind a lot that was said on behalf of the ITUC official position was some idea that working class education must be the business of working class organisations, reflecting the almost tribal divisions in Britain between working class and middle class . . . In fact to both groups, to the ITUC leadership no less than to Coyne and O'Rahilly, education was not a neutral matter, but while in the ITUC proposal the emphasis was on the working class within society generally as against the privileged classes, the emphasis in the case of Coyne and O'Rahilly, was on the catholic nation, as against other nations, within which class had a minor meaning. The ITUC path, with its implication of a conflict within Irish society itself, was an ambiguous and uneasy one; while, on the

contrary, the catholic–nationalist path, enthusiastically followed, seemed within the horizons of southern society, to be calm, unifying and immensely plausible. Furthermore, in the climate of the time, it was inconceivable to many that education should be a matter of students picking and choosing subjects . . . particularly when the church in all such matters was not only the obvious but the essential guide (McCarthy 1977: 391–2)

There was, however, little that was 'calm and unifying' and much that was vindictively narrow-minded and anti-intellectual in the campaign waged against the library of the ITUC-affiliated Baker's Union, whose General Secretary, John Swift, was a founder of the People's College. This library was acquired for and housed in Four Provinces House, a new headquarters opened in 1946 where 'the hall was adorned with murals by Frances Kelly and Nano Reid; engraved plaques by Lawrence Campbell; paintings in the Executive Room by Frank McKelvey; and wooden busts in a splendid 8,000 volume library by Hilary Heron' (Devine 1990: 14). Allegations 'that the library contained irreligious books and was being hired to communistic bodies' led to Fr Edward Coyne being brought in to review the collection. Coyne's examination found nothing objectionable but controversy continued until the entire library was sold off to a Dublin bookshop behind Swift's back. The aspiration to provide the union's members with a social and educational as well as an administrative resource was stymied; much of the premises was leased to a commercial dancehall while the murals perished when a property developer later acquired and demolished the building (Swift 1991: 139–52)

With little financial support from even the ITUC affiliated unions, the People's College was to sustain itself by taking a cultural turn – moving away from the initial emphasis on economics and social science to offer courses on literature, music and the visual arts. This disappointed some of its founders such as John Swift – 'when advocating the establishment of the college he had had in mind an institution where workers would learn something about socialism' (Swift 1991: 131) Movement away from either economic and social content or from a trade union student body was also to be a feature of the development over time of the People's College's Catholic rivals. In UCC O'Rahilly's successor told the Ford Foundation in 1958 that 'when I was appointed to the Presidency of this College in 1954 I was intrigued by the courses which were given to young farmers' sons and decided that the limited income at our disposal would be better employed in giving courses to this group than to groups of workers living in towns throughout the province of Munster'.[4] In UCD 'what began with the purpose of arming trade unionists with a knowledge of the social encyclicals to ward off communism soon became a liberal, aesthetic education for adults' (McCartney 1999: 182).

In the case of the CWC, the original purpose – education and training of Catholic members of trade unions – almost immediately began to expand with courses being provided over its first decade for employers and managers, civil servants, primary schoolteachers and nurses. The college also ran pre-marriage courses and a course in 'political and social science for young politicians'. In time this eclectic mix got narrowed down and industrial relations came to be identified as its core field. Among the trade unionist students attracted by the relatively large social and economic content of its programmes was Paddy Cardiff. Cardiff's formal education owed as much to the British Army as to the Dublin Christian Brothers school he left at 13. But, far from being a member of the 'crowd of communised emigrants' whose possible return to Ireland worried O'Rahilly, Cardiff was 'repelled by communism', its 'restrictions and iron discipline being against my nature' (Devine 2002: 6). After his post-war return to Dublin, Cardiff, an (ITUC affiliated) WUI activist moving into officialdom, chose to attend the Jesuit college:

> I'd begun to get an idea in my head of the type of training that was required, partly from my practical experience, but also from things I had gleaned having read. There were a lot of misconceptions going around at the time [about the Catholic Workers' College] that it wasn't socialist and it wasn't this, that or the other. There was a lot of bull going on and it was seen as directly in opposition to the People's College . . . From my point of view, the Workers College dealt with industrial relations, civics, basic economics and sociology. As far as I was concerned national economics and sociology could have been the names of racehorses. I went up there for about six or seven years and gleaned a great deal from it. I took from it what I wanted and paid no attention to what didn't agree with my own political outlook, which was constitutional socialism. I had no time for the extreme Left and I never made any secret of it. I just stood up and made my point and that was that. The People's College were giving language lessons and subject matters which were divorced from the reality of what was required by trade unionists . . . Father Maloney was a great man altogether and very much on the workers' side of things and at that time we were faced with the inevitability of change and he had a whole paper about that and I was very much struck by what he had to say about the need to change, that if you stay still, you'll stagnate, like water (Devine 2002: 12–13)

Technical assistance, productivity and trade union education

Through the 1950s Marshall Plan aid, OEEC programmes and EPA projects hardly impinged on Irish trade union education. Technical assistance projects brought teams of senior figures from the rival congresses to the USA in 1951 and 1952 and occasionally provided sponsored individuals with opportunities to study at Harvard and other US universities. The question of support for broader trade union education provision was eventually raised in May 1957, concerning a grant made to the Irish Management Institute out of the Technical Assistance allocation from the Grant Counterpart Fund (discussed in chapter 3 above). On this occasion the CIU wrote to the US Ambassador and to Industry and Commerce seeking a 'share in the educational benefits arising from the agreement between the Government of Ireland and the Government of the United States of America' and enquiring 'whether any funds are available to enable this Congress to develop trade union education on similar lines to management education'. An Industry and Commerce memorandum reviewing the issue noted that CIU had supported a CWC application for Technical Assistance funding in 1956. This had been referred on to Education on the grounds that 'the courses of this college pertain rather to general social and economic studies than to technical matters'. Provision within the Technical Assistance Sub-Agreement for supporting participation in EPA projects was noted, and grants to CIU and ITUC to take part in a Paris conference on automation were referred to, before the conclusion was drawn that 'while participation in such projects is of educational value, it is unlikely that many suitable projects will arise in the future or that such projects would fulfil the plans of the Congress for trade union education'.[5]

The few 'suitable projects' were, however, sufficient for contact to be made between Irish trade union leaders and EPA officials that led to significant follow-up action such as the visit of Valerio Agostinone to Dublin in November 1957.[6] With the INPC established, and congress reunification almost in place, Agostinone revisited Ireland in June 1959 'to discuss possible suggestions for an extension of our programme to Ireland in the form of technical assistance in training activities of the Irish unions in the field of productivity . . . to examine with representatives of the Productivity Committee and the trade unions the possibility of establishing a programme for national activities.' ICTU informed EPA in September that due to 'the problems arising from the arrangements of the terminal conferences of the Congress of Irish Unions and the Irish Trade Union Congress, the subsequent termination of the CIU and the ITUC, and the reorganisation of the Irish Congress of Trade Unions it has not been found possible up to now to progress the proposed arrangements for trade union conferences'.[7] At the ICTU's inaugural conference in the same month a motion was passed calling on the Executive Committee 'to examine the needs of affiliated unions for educational and training schemes for officials and members within the trade union movement'. The following month a four man ICTU team that included Ruaidhrí Roberts visited Belgium and West Germany to study trade union education facilities as an EPA Intra-European Trade Union Mission.

The team subsequently produced two reports, the second and briefer of which was entitled 'Application to Ireland of Team's Study of Educational Establishments'. This began by noting a number of differences between continental and Irish conditions. In Belgium and West Germany unions tended to be fewer and larger, a statutory legal framework supported works committees and safety committees while a high degree of uniformity and standardisation of the role of shop stewards allowed for 'more or less uniform technical education in the performance of their functions'. Union subscriptions in these countries were high by Irish standards and the allocation of a substantial proportion of the unions' revenue to education provision appeared to enjoy general acceptance. The Irish situation nonetheless struck the team as presenting certain advantages. There was no need for provision to be made in two languages as in Belgium, 'we do not, as in the case of Germany when the trade union education services were being established, suffer from a grave shortage of either officials or members with previous long experience of trade unionism' and there was now a unified trade union centre:

> We believe that having regard to these advantages, and to the fact that extended assistance from the European Productivity Agency is available during the current year, it should be possible to commence at an early date to implement the ICTU conference resolutions on education

In terms of immediate action the team suggested the creation of an ICTU Education Committee and the relation of the programme of conferences agreed at the time of Agostinone's visit earlier in the year and then in the course of preparation with this Committee's proposals for trade union education. A union conference on education was also proposed. Concretely the organisation of night courses, day schools, non-residential one-week courses in Dublin and correspondence courses for country members did 'not appear to present insuperable difficulties'. A residential trade union school 'could be considered and an estimate of cost prepared' in the longer term – 'action on projects immediately possible should be undertaken concurrently with study of further projects' (ICTU 1960: Appendix 4).

In March 1960 the recently created ICTU Education Committee informed INPC that it was 'not yet in a position to submit a detailed programme' and enquired about 'the possibility of securing assistance for an Irish trade union educational programme on similar lines to the assistance received by the Belgian and other trade union centres, even though the detailed programme may take some further time for us to prepare.' In the following month Raymond Goosse of EPA came to Dublin for discussions. Out of these emerged the proposal that 'EPA would provide certain financial and technical assistance for: (a) an inquiry into training methods, techniques, and organisation used in other countries (b) the establishment of a pilot project in Ireland for a limited period'.[8]

By September the assistance had assumed the concrete form of the EPA covering the salary and expenses of an ICTU Education Officer appointed to conduct the enquiry and to administer the establishment of the pilot project. The appointee was Barry Desmond, an official seconded by ITGWU. Twelve months later the ICTU was offering to affiliated unions a varied educational programme ranging from week-long residential courses to One Day Information Conferences. Desmond's initial appointment was for three months but a succession of three or six-month extensions meant that his salary and expenses were still being paid by EPA when it was wound up in June 1962.[9] Meeting in the following month in Galway, the ICTU was informed by Ruaidhrí Roberts that:

> Congress, aware that the aid we have been receiving from the European Productivity Agency and later the Organisation for Economic Co-operation and Development would be reduced or would end this year, made application through the Irish National Productivity Committee for technical assistance grants so that these facilities would be continued. We were not alone in this, other bodies were also interested, for example, the Irish Management Institute. We have now within the last few days received word that the Minister for Finance has approved this application and sanction has been given for technical assistance grants to cover the activities that were previously undertaken through EPA assistance . . . These will cover such matters as trade union missions to other countries on the same level as that of last year and we will also be able to participate in other international activities to the same degree as we did last year. We will also be able to invite foreign experts if we require them

> and we will be able to continue our education programme. This is, of course, of very considerable benefit to us and enables us to carry on activities which otherwise would have had to come to a close (ICTU 1962: 328–30)

The extent to which ICTU came to benefit from technical assistance funding during the 1960s is shown in table 5.1. EPA funding of the Education Officer position from 1960 was followed three years later by half-funding by Industry and Commerce of an Industrial Officer post (whose first occupant was also Barry Desmond) and by INPC support for a work study and incentive payments advisory service introduced in 1966. By 1969–70, as table 5.1 shows, funding of this sort represented just over a quarter of ICTU's total income.

Table 5.1 **ICTU educational and related activities in receipt of technical assistance funding from international or Irish state organisations, 1960–70**

Financial Year	*Amount Refunded* £	*Refunding Agency*
31/3/1960	292-8-11	EPA
31/3/1961	314-15-7	EPA
31/3/1962	398-7-5	OECD
31/3/1963	1,403-1-7	OECD and INPC
31/3/1964	1,711-16-0	INPC, Industry & Commerce
31/3/1965	2,809-9-6	INPC, Industry & Commerce
31/3/1966	4,985-5-1	INPC, Industry & Commerce
31/3/1967	8,661-9-11	INPC, Industry & Commerce
31/3/1968	9,463-11-5	INPC, Industry & Commerce
31/3/1969	9,838-5-8	INPC, Industry & Commerce
31/3/1970	12,873-3-0	INPC

Source: ICTU Accounts, various years

The People's College and the Catholic Workers' College after Congress reunification

How were the colleges that had been closely identified with the rival congresses of the split period to relate to a new unified trade union centre that had itself moved into the educational field? The Report of the ICTU National Executive for 1962–3 records that body's approval of a set of recommendations made by the Education Committee about relations with the People's College. These stated that, as a matter of general principle, it was desirable that any expansion of trade union educational, training and cultural facilities should develop under trade union control. While extending the scope of the ICTU education and training programme 'would be long term and hardly possible within existing staff and accommodation facilities', Congress should not affiliate with the People's College but should encourage individual unions to do so. The unaffiliated ICTU should, however, 'be in a position to exercise guidance, and this can most suitably be done by continuing the arrangement entered into by the Irish Trade Union Congress' whereby an annual payment of £25 and the provision of secretarial assistance was reciprocated by two nominations to the Council of the People's College. This, the recommendations concluded, was not to be a precedent for establishing similar arrangements with other organisations.

Table 5.2 **Student enrolment in various CWC courses, 1951–62**

Year	*Trade union students (men)*	*Management students*	*Foremen students*	*Trade union students (women)*
1951–2	44	59		
1952–3	39	51		
1953–4	45	44		
1954–5	161	70		
1955–6	152	84	31	
1956–7	237	111	58	66
1957–8	312	172	59	107
1958–9	411	156	93	101
1959	414	136	92	112
1960	475	136	124	108
1961–2	513	148	104	121

Source: Irish Jesuit Archive CIR/20 1–55 Memorandum on the Catholics Workers' College 1947–62

The links established between CWC and the trade unions during the 1950s were extensive. With members drawn from twelve 'of the more important' unions, a Trade Union Advisory Committee was set up in January 1954. A quadrupling of trade union student numbers (see table 5.2) was attributed to its advice and efforts which encompassed drawing up the syllabus for trade union courses, recruiting students and winning the good-will of Union officials for the College. In 1957 eight trade union leaders were invited to form a Trade Union Board of Sponsors (a Management Board of Sponsors was formed at the same time) while a Trade Union General Purposes Committee was set up to engage in fundraising. The CWC Jesuits also cultivated more personal contacts – 'yearly visits are made to Trade Union Offices, Trade Union Officials are invited to College functions; factories are visited, etc.'[10]

The advent of ICTU was perceived as a negative development for CWC with Fr Kent writing to his Provincial in April 1960 that 'our position as a recognised Trade Union Educational Centre has been weakened, at least in the official trade union world':

> As a result of the amalgamation our friends found themselves in a minority of six to thirteen on the new Executive Council. This Council, moreover, for the first time in the history of Irish trade unionism has two members of the Communist party among its members and four fellow-travellers. This group has support from left-wing officials and socialist-minded members and is wielding in a short time strong influence at official level. They are ignoring the College and its work and trying to set up a Trade Union Educational Centre of their own. Our friends are dispirited and without a leader since the death of Walter Beirne . . . Recently also we lost through death three other friends in high places in the union officials world . . . We have, therefore, fewer friends in high places. In addition we have plenty of evidence of bolder communist activity in the city among the workers.[11]

In a long memorandum reviewing the college's past, present and future prepared by CWC's Jesuit teachers for a Provincial Consultation in November 1961, four factors were seen as underpinning the need for the kind of trade union education it offered. First, 'a situation of apathy and non-participation' prevailed within unions with branch meetings attended by a proportion of the members as low as five to ten per cent. For the CWC Jesuits 'this non-participation, with the apathy that causes it, is responsible for much of our industrial unrest. It means that workers are out of touch with their unions, ignorant of union policy, destructively critical of union officials, indisciplined.'

Second, out of apathy and non-participation arose 'a situation of danger' that 'gives easy opportunity to Communists if they wish to take over'. It was conceded that

> Communist influence, potentially a danger everywhere, is perhaps less likely in an Irish Catholic environment, but two factors aggravate the issue: one the mobility of labour between here and England, where a determined Communist attempt to win the Irish has some success . . . and two, the trade union movement is an all-Ireland one, united under an increasingly influential Irish Congress of Trade Unions in which the traditionally industrialised Presbyterian North is strongly represented. Belfast is the centre and main strength of Communism in Ireland . . .The chief danger in Ireland probably comes from attempts to gain full control of Trade Union education for the Irish Congress of Trade Unions, thereby excluding the Church from workers' education. We are in fact labelled as 'outsiders'. In such attempts, made intermittently, Socialists (there is still living a tradition of radical Socialism in Ireland), Communists, Northern Protestants and Presbyterians stand together.[12]

Third, a 'situation of ignorance of principles' also existed due to the early age at which most workers left school – 'the workers enter the industrial scene and an inter-denominational trade union movement without any specific knowledge and training in Catholic social principles'.[13] Finally, the 'absence of the Church from the world of the worker' meant that the clergy in general had little knowledge or understanding of trade union concerns:

> Our priests. . . .lack insight into industrial issues. They are unaware of the significance of industrial groups, of the place and function of trade unions in modern society. Their reactions to industrial problems are shallow and superficial . . . or they are no different from those of the typical middle-class and just as full of honest prejudice . . . If they do turn their . . . attention to industry, their hope seems to be to float a veil of piety over the industrial scene . . . priests are not socially interested. Priests' interests are very wide, the great majority are highly spiritual and philanthropic, but the vast field of industry is not included. They know nothing of job evaluation or redundancy agreements. A shop steward is as remote as a Baluba tribesman . . . They are not interested.[14]

Seeking to evaluate the work of CWC, the memorandum concluded that 'the existence of the college is one of the stronger influences working for a fuller understanding and a fuller appreciation of the nature of the Church's work in the field of social, industrial, political and family relations'. Offered as evidence of this influence was a story that when 'Young Jim' Larkin had disparaged the college within WUI, he 'was told by his own executive that no matter what he said or thought, the students of the college who are members of his union showed great improvement regarding interest in, responsibility towards and participation in the affairs of the union'. Considered for banning as a 'subversive' organisation in 1931 (Milotte 1984: 109), the WUI now had an executive committee 'a large number' of whose members were former CWC students.[15]

In the same month as the Provincial Consultation took place the conference on trade union education called for by the report of the ICTU EPA mission team that visited Belgium and West Germany was held in Lucan. This took the form of a weekend seminar attended by 58 delegates from 18 unions and one trades council where the speakers consisted of invited representatives from the Danish Confederation of Trade Unions and from OECD as well as one of ICTU's Joint General Secretaries (Ruaidhrí Roberts) and its Education Officer (Barry Desmond). Three appendices relating to this seminar that were not ready at the time of the Provincial Consultation were subsequently added to the long memorandum prepared for that event. One was a descriptive report, written at Fr Kent's request, by Jeremiah Fitzsimons, a member the WUI Executive and a former CWC student who remained actively associated with its trade union support bodies. Fitzsimons had been a delegate at the Lucan seminar and his report quoted Roberts as stating:

> He had been one of the founders of the People's College. He and others had been guilty of 'woolly' thinking in assuming that, since the autonomous body of the College had been made up entirely of trade unionists, they were therefore competent to teach trade union subjects. They had discovered their fault and were now concentrating on cultural subjects only[16]

A second appendix, 'prepared by Fr Liam McKenna SJ, as a Basis for a Staff Conference' sought to analyse the trend of the Lucan conference. This distinguished four attitudes towards CWC. The first was opposition (by Roberts and his leftist supporters). The second was a diffuse distrust of priests' involvement in trade union matters. The third was a pragmatism that would have specifically trade union subject matter taught by trade-union-provided courses but would leave broader adult education to other bodies including CWC. The fourth attitude was trust and support (combined in cases like that of Charles McCarthy with a desire to accommodate the pragmatic and the distrustful). Drawing a distinction between unformed and formed trade union students, Fr McKenna argued that a satisfactory division of labour would see CWC catering for the former while Congress 'developed advanced courses for applied technique, as is badly needed', for the latter. His analysis concluded that:

> The proposals of the first group (Rory Roberts & Co.) be ignored. The attitude of the second group should be met by human relations. The position of the third group should be discussed with them on the grounds that they have produced a paper plan drawing ink lines which ignore the fact that the student is one man who cannot, at least at the beginning, be carved into separate pieces. Quite the most undesirable consequence of the Lucan conference would be if the reasoned arguments of the third programme merely provided a weapon for the ideologists of the first programme. The fact that they have announced that their own institution the People's College was a mistake, suggest that this is now the tactic they intend to use.[17]

A third appendix – 'Some notes on the Lucan Conference by Fr T. Hamilton SJ for use in Staff Conference' – took a less sanguine view than Fr McKenna and laid the charge that 'the present moves, [are] being [made] under the inspiration of Continental Socialist "experts" and our own Socialist minority'. The Church cannot be excluded in principle from any section of Trade Union education, Fr Hamilton argued, and, if faced with this prospect, would have to consider withdrawing its acceptance in Ireland of an inter-denominational trade union *status quo*.[18]

In the early 1960s, as the Second Vatican Council began to change the Irish Catholic Church, the Irish societal value of 'bearing the stamp of Catholic orthodoxy' lessened. CWC's name came to 'occasion confusion and embarrassment in various ways and is thus detrimental to the work'. Within ICTU 'a number of our friends . . . indicated at various times that the term "Catholic" tends to alienate sympathy for the College among their non-Catholic colleagues and to gain support for the impression that the work of the College is exclusively and militantly Catholic'. Moreover, 'from being a College for trade union members it had by a natural process come to be a college for workers in the widest possible sense, so that the term embraced not only trade union members but employers, managers and supervisors equally well'. Both Boards of Sponsors unanimously supported a change of name. In addition 'objection to the designation Catholic has been voiced by no less than the Taoiseach, Mr. Seán Lemass, in conversation with one of the community'. CWC had been receiving a small grant from the Education Vote since 1961 but its Catholic label was perceived to be a handicap in relation to the Technical Assistance funding that other bodies engaged in 'promoting education in different aspects of industry and labour' – like IMI or INPC – were getting:

> As yet none of these has entered on the field of 'industrial relations' for which they have no special qualifications and for which it can be said that this College is singularly well-qualified. It would be quite possible, if not indeed probable, in default of the purpose and function of the college being made clear beyond doubt, these bodies should extend their scope to cover the field of 'industrial relations' or, failing that, a new body might be founded to take on this work. This would be a lamentable development in view of the fact that that the College can make a unique contribution in ensuring that the right principle and teaching will be applied, and that industrial relations will be influenced and moulded to a Christian pattern. All these considerations lend support to our conviction that it is a question at this stage of now or never.[19]

In March 1966 CWC announced the changing of its name to the College of Industrial Relations (CIR), presenting industrial relations as affording an opportunity 'for putting content into the spirit of ecumenism'.[20] The college is further discussed in chapter 6.

Conclusion

Anti-communism cast a long shadow over workers' education in southern Ireland. Even in its relatively moderate manifestations, the left was under constant pressure from suspicious religious conservatives from the early 1930s. Irish neutrality meant that it received no respite from this pressure during the war years. With the national trade union centre and the Labour Party both experiencing prolonged and debilitating splits, an educational extension to the labour movement was precariously placed. Priests and lay militants who were determined to save Irish trade unionists for their church provided better-supported alternative fare.

But in the 1960s the climate started to change and institutions that had proclaimed allegiance to Catholicism in their titles began to seek more neutral designations. CWC was not alone in this – the Dublin Institute of Catholic Sociology became the Dublin Institute of Adult Education in the mid 1960s. A reunited trade union congress with access to funding first from the EPA and later from the Irish government began to move cautiously into the direct provision of a fairly narrow range of education and training, taking care to keep its distance from the two colleges that the ideological battles of the 1940s and 1950s had raged around.

CHAPTER SIX

Developing Managers

Introduction

Although many European countries had long-established schools of commerce within or without their university systems, European managers were widely viewed as backward by the US counterparts in the post-1945 period (Engwall and Zamagni 1998, Gourvish and Tiratsoo 1998). If Europe's business leaders appeared technically deficient to US observers, those encountered in Ireland – where US consultants found 'significant antimaterialist cultural values, illusion-filled business attitudes and poor management practices' (Finnegan and Wiles 1995: 48) – were positively heroic in their shortcomings.

Bridging the education gap between European and US management came to be considered to be one of the principal ways in which the productivity gap could be closed – 'technical assistance programmes gradually began to incorporate elements that were essentially about selling Europeans the ideal of American business education, inevitably including the Masters of Business Administration (MBA)' (Gourvish and Tiratsoo 1998: 3). Transplantation was, however, a complex process in which some national systems (France, West Germany) were resistant to the import, and apparent adoption of the American model in the British case could mask 'the rather convoluted creation of a hybrid form' (Tiratsoo 1998: 140). Overall a complex picture emerges in which:

> There were American missionaries, certainly, though their agendas were eclectic and even contradictory. There were enthusiastic managers in Europe who often welcomed the importation of business school curricula from the United States and the suggestions which Americans advanced for the improvement of European productivity, particularly in production. At the same time . . . there were other actors in the play: politicians and government bureaucrats, with their own agendas; bodies representing the interests of employers: the

> trade unions; and the educational establishment, which was often more conservative and condescending in its attitude to business education than it was innovative and flexible (Gourvish and Tiratsoo 1998: 11)

The manner in which this play was staged in Ireland is the subject of this chapter. Working with the INPC, the EPA provided a channel through which American managerial techniques were introduced to Irish business organisations by the IMI and other educational bodies. After the demise of EPA, IMI was the leading beneficiary of the 1960s expansion of domestic technical assistance aimed at promoting adaptation to free trade conditions by Irish industry. Like communism, if to a very much lesser extent, US-style capitalism clashed with the precepts of Catholic social teaching. The Catholic Workers' College offered an alternative approach to management education that was critical of imported US ideas. But over time philosophical difference gave way to complementary functional specialisation as the college transformed itself into a College of Industrial Relations and sought entry into the circle of institutions supported by state technical assistance funding.

Ireland acquires a management movement

According to its historian, two separate initiatives converged to launch the IMI in December 1952. The first was taken independently by a group of Irish executives that straddled the semi-state and private sectors of the economy and included Michael Dargan, who had established contact with the US management movement while working in the New York office of Aer Lingus. The second originated at a meeting convened by Industry and Commerce with OEEC proposals to create a European Institute of Management as its background. In addition to a minister and senior civil servants, this was attended by executives from private and semi-state companies, a UCD professor and – at the suggestion of a Guinness's colleague – the chairman of the British Institute of Management (BIM), Sir Hugh Beaver (Cox 2002: 5–19).

A first national conference was held by IMI in Cork in September 1953 on the topic of training and the first issue of the journal *Irish Management* was published at the beginning of 1954. Early educational initiatives centred on courses for supervisors and foremen, with experimental courses being organised at the High School of Commerce in Rathmines and government introduction from Britain of the US-originated Training Within Industry scheme being advocated (Byrne 1954, O'Ceallaigh 1954). The running through its Irish subsidiary of an Esso course in conference leadership was an early example of provision for senior management, but a major initiative in this area did not come until the Joint Committee on Education and Training for Management formed in 1954 under IMI auspices reported early in 1956. This committee combined IMI activists with representatives from the universities and the Vocational Education system. Its proposal that aid from the Grant Counterpart funds be given to help establish a Management Development Unit (MDU) within IMI publicly posed an issue hitherto only discussed in private – government financial support for management education.

Politicians, bureaucrats and the development of Irish management

In Britain, the creation of BIM had been financially supported by the Labour government while, from the late 1940s to the late 1950s, US technical assistance was to inject an estimated £1m into British management education (Tiratsoo 1998: 142–5). In November 1952, shortly before IMI's inaugural meeting, government financial aid for the new body was privately broached by its chairman designate, Guinness's Sir Charles Harvey. Arguing that 'surely full support must include money', Harvey cited the British case where the government had increased its initial aid to BIM 'total of £150,000 spread over six years', in return for which 'the Government nominated the first Chairman and Council, but thereafter the BIM became independent'. For IMI, Harvey at this point unsuccessfully sought from Industry and Commerce 'a promise to double whatever we raise ourselves each year for say five years' up to an annual maximum of £5,000.[1]

A little over a year after this informal approach was rebuffed, the question was revisited at an Industry and Commerce departmental conference 'as the Institute was now firmly established and was acknowledged to be undertaking its work in a thorough and energetic way'. However, the Minister 'feared . . . a direct subsidy from the Vote might be held to involve responsibility for the policy of the Institute, for appointments made by it, and other matters' and it was decided instead to explore the possibility of channelling money from the Grant Counterpart Fund's proposed technical assistance allocation to IMI.[2] While agreement with the USA on the use of this allocation was awaited, IMI benefited from being made the first exception to Industry and Commerce's rule that technical assistance funds should not be made available for EPA projects when a grant was made to cover the full cost of the participation of an IMI nominee – UCD Lecturer Michael MacCormac – in a 1955 management mission to the USA (MacCormac 1955).

With the flow of US technical assistance to Ireland cut off at the beginning of 1952, the substantial funding flowing into management education in other European countries during the 1950s was absent in the Irish case. Encouragement and advice was, however, provided by the US Ambassador to Ireland from 1954 to 1957, William H. Taft III, who had previously served as a member of the Dublin ECA Mission staff from 1949 to 1951. Taft addressed IMI's first Annual General Meeting and in 1955 facilitated a meeting between IMI representatives and a senior official of ECA's successor, the International Co-operation Administration (ICA), Charles Warden. Warden told the IDA that 'although the Institute was very keen on going ahead with a drive for improved productivity they were not familiar with present-day activities in that direction'. Warden felt that 'it would be worth their while to get an expert from Paris to advise them on the best course of action' and was also favourably disposed to IMI receiving assistance from the Grant Counterpart Fund's technical assistance allocation. Taft subsequently organised a visit in April 1956 from Thomas McPhail, a Paris-based official in ICA's Productivity and Technical Assistance Division. McPhail told Industry and Commerce that he was favourably impressed by IMI and that 'he thought it would be useful if members of the Institute could visit Paris for the purpose of studying the operations of the European Productivity Agency on the spot'.[3]

By the time of the McPhail visit, IMI had already – in February 1956 – made a formal approach to Industry and Commerce 'applying for a total grant of £27,000, either through the ECA Counterpart Fund or alternatively through a direct Grant from the State' in order to implement a recommendation of the forthcoming Joint Committee report that a Management Development Unit be established within the Institute. This move came shortly after Industry and Commerce had signalled that, notwithstanding its broadly positive disposition towards providing funds to IMI, there was 'the question of inter-related activities which it would seem desirable to have sorted out before a Technical Assistance scheme would be ripe for decision'. Here the activities Industry and Commerce had in mind were the Training within Industry (TWI) scheme, the Catholic Workers' College and the possible establishment of a national productivity centre.[4]

At the time, the national productivity centre was being discussed by the IIRS-convened committee (see chapter 4 above) while the CWC had made an application for funding to Industry and Commerce just before IMI did so. TWI was developed under wartime conditions in the USA. Introduced in Britain during the war years, the British Ministry of Labour and National Service continued the scheme after 1945. Irish applications to participate prompted the British ministry to inform External Affairs in 1951 that, as 'our many home commitments allow only limited facilities for the training of representatives from overseas', its policy was 'to train only the representatives of subsidiary or associated companies of British firms or the representatives of the organisation nominated to develop the Scheme by the Government concerned'. No response was made at the time, but in 1954 an enquiry from the principal of the Cork Schools of Commerce and Domestic Science led to a restatement of the British position at a time when IMI was calling for the TWI scheme to be actively promoted in Ireland through the Vocational Education system. IMI's views were quoted when Industry and Commerce asked Education to consider taking up the British offer in July 1954.

A City of Dublin VEC teacher, Vincent Farrington, went to England for training in 1955 but, on his return and coinciding with IMI's own request for funding, disagreement arose about the context in which his newly acquired skills were to be utilised. On 10 January 1956 the Ministry of Education set out 'certain difficulties' that it perceived 'with a scheme that is almost purely an industrial one and rather removed from the sphere of education', arguing that 'since the firms participating in the scheme will be the gainers from the project, it seems only reasonable to expect that they should bear a large part of the organisation and expense and in this connection the Irish Management Institute may be of assistance'. Industry and Commerce, well aware of IMI's incapacity to assist, resisted a shift of responsibility in its direction until in late February the departments agreed a compromise whereby TWI, effectively no bureaucracy's child, would be launched in Dublin on a small-scale, experimental basis for a 12 to 18-month period by the city's VEC.[5]

The Industry and Commerce memorandum on the IMI funding application prepared for the departmental conference on 26 March 1956 took a line that was remarkably similar to that running through Education's 'difficulties' with TWI:

> While it is true that increasing productivity is a matter of national importance it is equally true that success in achieving it will confer definite financial benefits on private enterprise . . . it might well be asked why the Institute could not find the full cost of these courses from industry and business throughout

> the country instead of asking the State to defray a substantial part of the cost. This attitude is not surprising, however, as it appears to be the case that business firms adopt a parsimonious attitude towards the financial needs of the various Associations to which they belong. Trade Unions on the other hand build up their financial strength through contributions from their members which must involve an appreciable sacrifice to the individual member.

The memorandum went on to conclude that the project was 'entirely educational' and to recommend that it be referred to Education for consideration together with the previously referred CWC application.[6] When this was done, Education conceded that CWC 'would appear to be concerned with education of the University extra-mural type' but extracted quotations from the IMI's application to support its view that 'the Management Development Unit envisaged is primarily and directly concerned with the increasing of industrial productivity . . . the term "educational" could only be applied in an additional and incidental way to the activities envisaged by the proposed Unit'. Recognising that Education was unlikely to change its attitude and with a luncheon at which IMI was to present the Minister with a copy of the Joint Committee's Report being held the following day, a departmental conference on 10 April decided on a grant to the MDU of £5,000 (subsequently altered by the Minister to £6,000) out of the Grant Counterpart Fund technical assistance allocation when the relevant sub-agreement with the USA had been finalised.[7]

Employers, unions and the management movement

The launching of the IMI had the formal approval of the main umbrella private sector business organisations, FIM and FUE, but, as an Industry and Commerce official noted in response to Education's early 1956 suggestion that business assume responsibility for organising and funding the TWI scheme, 'the Irish Management Institute cannot be said to be representative of industry . . . the number of member firms does not exceed 250 whereas the number of industrial concerns included in the official Industrial Directory is approximately 3,500'.[8] Many of the executives active in promoting the development of management – such as C. S. Andrews (Bord na Mona and later CIE), Michael Dargan (Aer Lingus) and Denis Hegarty (Dublin Port and Docks Board) – worked in state-sponsored bodies rather than private companies. This led to management being publicly projected as much as a better way of transacting the business of the nation as of running private profit-making firms more efficiently. Although it was to identify itself subsequently with private entrepreneurial values and negotiate what proved to be abortive mergers with the umbrella private business lobbies (Cox 2002: 163–91), an IMI memorandum responding to a draft of the Statement of Productivity Principles in June 1960 was concerned that 'the statement should not contain anything inconsistent with the neutral stand IMI seeks to maintain between employer and worker'.[9]

IMI decided early on against formal links with the trade unions in spite of the precedent of union representation on a BIM advisory body. Fearful lest private companies be deterred by a union presence, IMI decided this did not apply to Ireland as union representation in Britain was at the request of the British government which had helped establish and finance the BIM. The two Irish union congresses did not seek any form of affiliation and were prepared to give IMI a broadly positive, if clearly qualified, response (Cox 2002: 39–41). The trade union leadership attitude to the IMI claim to be neutral between employer and worker is revealed in the response of Ruaidhrí Roberts to a proposal put in 1955 to the IIRS-convened committee that a national productivity centre's committee be made up of six trade union, three FIM, three FUE and two IMI nominees. With the unions seeking 50 per cent worker representation on the committee, Roberts wrote: 'no management an "employer" org. for this purpose. Even Inst. is rep. by employers & by courtesy recognised as "independent"'.[10] Around the same time the implications for unions of a diffusion of new management practices was placed in a broader context by the report of a Payment by Results Committee set up by ITUC:

> 'Incentive Bonus' systems based on 'work study' are more common in Northern Ireland, but there is a growing tendency to introduce such systems in the Republic, and the tendency has received an additional impetus since the establishment of the Irish Management Institute and, of course, the recent extension to the Republic of various Industrial Consultant services (ITUC 1955: 61)

The report differentiated the export-oriented industries of the north from those servicing the small home market in the south, stating that with the latter came 'greater preoccupation with the problem of redundancy'. Broadly progressive in the context of national economic development aspirations but deeply problematical in the context of unemployment, stagnation and emigration realities, developments in management education mainly highlighted to union leaders like Roberts the need to develop their own educational services in order to cope with the more sophisticated expertise becoming available to employers.

The education establishment and the management movement

Can the Irish educational establishment be charged with being 'more conservative and condescending in its attitude to business education than it was innovative and flexible'? At first sight higher education for business in Ireland would appear to have a quite innovative history. Table 6.1 adapts a chronology of European commerce school development before 1914 compiled by Engwall and Zamagni (1998) by inserting into it the principal southern Irish initiatives of the period. Utilising recently enacted agriculture and technical instruction legislation, the Rathmines institute was founded in 1901 with the aim 'ultimately to include a complete provision for higher commercial education for both the population of the Urban District itself and the neighbouring City of Dublin' and 'the township prided itself on the claim, whether true or false, that Rathmines had the only commercial college run by a local authority in the whole of the United Kingdom' (O'Maitiu 2003: 177). The provision made for Commerce degrees at the foundation of the National University of Ireland followed the recent examples of Birmingham and Manchester, aligning the new Irish colleges with the British '"red brick" tradition of civic, utilitarian, regional, non-residential universities' (McCartney 1999: 31).

But when one of the IMI's leading founders, C. S. Andrews, studied commerce at UCD after his release from internment following the end of the Civil War, the 'degree at that time had the lowest standing in academe, below even the BA pass degree in Trinity College which had an exceptionally poor reputation . . . commerce was derisively known as the "Dud's Degree"' (Andrews 2001: 37–8; see also Cox 2002: 7–8). In Cork, 'businessmen traditionally had little respect for university courses in commerce, and there were pathetic pleas for the poorly regarded Bachelor of Commerce degree to be given a chance' (Murphy 1995: 252).

Table 6.1 **Schools of commerce in Europe before the First World War**

1852	Institut Superieur de Commerce de l'Etat, Anvers, Belgium
	Institut Superieur de Commerce Saint Ignace, Anvers, Belgium
1854	Ecole Superieur de Commerce, Paris, France (1819)
1856	Wiener Handelsakademie, Austria
1866	Ecole Superieur de Commerce, Mulhouse, France
1867	Scuola Superiore di Commercio, Venice, Italy
1871	Le Havre, France
	Sciences Politiques, Paris, France
1872	Lyon, France
	Marseilles, France
1874	Bordeaux, France
1881	Ecole des Hautes Etudes Commerciales, Paris, France
1884	Genoa, Italy
1886	Bari, Italy
1892	Lille, France
1895	London School of Economics, England
	Rouen, France
1896	Nancy, France
1897	Montpelier, France
1898	Aachen, Germany
	Leipzig, Germany
	St Gallen, Switzerland
	Vienna, Austria
1900	Budapest, Hungary
	Dijon, France
	Nantes, France
1901	Cologne, Germany
	Academie für Sozial- und Handelswissenschaften, Frankfurt, Germany
	Municipal Technical Institute, Rathmines, Dublin
1902	Birmingham University, England (Commerce Degree)
	Bocconi, Milan, Italy
1903	Brussels, Belgium
1904	Manchester University, England (Commerce Degree)
1905	Toulouse, France
1906	Berlin, Germany
	Rome, Italy
	Turin, Italy

1908	Mannheim, Germany
1909	Stockholm School of Economic, Sweden
	National University of Ireland, Dublin Cork, Galway (Commerce Degree)
1910	Munich, Germany
1911	Finnish Business School, Helsinki, Finland
1913	Rotterdam, The Netherlands

Source: Adapted from Engwall and Zamagni (1998), Table 1.

A School of Commerce was set up in Trinity College in 1925 but seems to have been little more impressive than its longer established NUI counterparts – 'a fairly humdrum affair . . .[that] pottered along until 1962 . . . it did not add much lustre to the college, but at least it induced a few commercially minded fathers to give their sons a university education without feeling that they were completely wasting their time' (McDowell and Webb 1982: 449) The response to IMI's Education and Training for Management report made clear that, united for once across the religious divide, all the universities accorded business education a low priority. As Education informed Industry and Commerce in April 1956:

> The Minister's understanding is that the University institutions have difficulty in financing their present activities and he understands also from these institutions that their most urgent need, after their present activities are adequately catered for, is additional financial assistance for the development and modernising of their Medical, Science and Engineering Schools rather than their Commercial Faculties.[11]

Only in the 1960s did this situation start to change significantly with upgraded undergraduate courses in Commerce or Business Studies and new postgraduate courses including – at UCD in 1964 – the introduction of the Irish Republic's first MBA (Cox 2002: 131–54). Beyond the Pale upgrading proceeded more slowly with facility deficiencies prompting Industry and Commerce in 1968 to seek Finance sanction to donate £1,000 for books and other requisites to UCC where 'the course is the only one outside Dublin that caters for general management training at post-graduate and post-experience level'.[12]

In the case of the Rathmines Institute, 1930 was a year of significant change with the absorption of the Urban District into the Dublin city local authority area and the creation of a national vocational system administered by city or county Vocational Education Committees. Designated the High School of

Commerce in the 1930s, and renamed the College of Commerce in 1956, it had 'in the late 1950s up to 2,500 enrolled each year on higher level evening courses leading to examinations of professional and other examining bodies in advertising, cost and works accountancy, government accountancy, auditing, company secretaryship, banking, economics, law, languages, foreign trade, management studies, sales management, inland and air transport, commercial and secretarial studies and domestic science'. A specific School of Management Studies was set up in 1958. This 'specialised in part-time and short courses in co-operation with industry and commerce'. Work study was one of its principal areas of expertise and it served, among other things, as the base from which TWI was diffused into Irish industry. In the early 1960s Rathmines also initiated the first four-year full-time degree level course in business outside the universities (Duff et al. 2000: 22–3). Colleges broadly comparable to but operating on a much smaller and more restricted scale than Rathmines were maintained by VECs in Cork and Limerick (see Tomlin 1966: 313–15).

IMI as an education provider assisted by EPA

Having discussed provision for management education 'in the University, the technical college and the firm', the IMI Joint Committee report of 1956 'asked ourselves if any further facilities outside of those covered were needed in Ireland'. The further need it identified was for short, full-time courses with 'the task of broadening the vision of future top managers'. IMI should create within its organisation a unit to run such courses because:

> Unless the Institute provides itself with full-time educational and training facilities it will achieve, at best, a limited effectiveness in its general aims. The long-term survival of the Institute, supported entirely on the contributions of its business members, may depend to a large extent on the direct service which can be given to them in the educational and training sphere (IMI 1956: 64)

Having obtained the commitment of a modicum of Grant Counterpart Fund aid in April 1956, IMI turned to fund-raising from business and by the autumn had secured guarantees in excess of £4,000 a year for the next five years. An advertisement for a Director of Studies was issued and transmitted through External Affairs for circulation within EPA in September. In the spring of 1957 Norman Rimmer, who had been working for EPA on secondment from BIM, took up the post and in September a first two-week course for executives was held in IMI's newly acquired larger premises. The first Irish seminar conducted by EPA lecturers ('rather to the surprise of some who attended, neither of these was an American') was held in Rathmines in September 1956 and reliance on EPA to supplement its own modest resources in filling out an educational programme was a central feature of the activities of the IMI MDU's first five years (Cox 2002: 67–74). In addition to its own staff members, EPA had at its disposal participants in a 'pool of professors' programme which received funding from the Ford Foundation. This enabled US business school teachers to spend an extended period in Europe where EPA subsidised the availability of their services in member countries – when H. Lee Weber conducted a Dublin seminar on purchasing and stock control in February 1958 he was 'visiting his tenth country in eight months'. Table 6.2 illustrates the extent of IMI MDU reliance on EPA resources during the latter's final year of existence.

Reviewing management education in the early 1960s

In 1958, *Economic Development* stated that: 'if we are to progress, the general level of efficiency and productivity in industry must be raised . . . We should participate more fully in the European Productivity Agency of the OEEC. The work of the Irish Management Institute deserves the fullest support' (Department of Finance 1958: 218–19). The setting up of the Economic Development Branch (EDB) within Finance was, however, soon followed by conflict between this new actor and IMI.

The suggestion that EDB consider the state of Irish management education apparently originated with IDA Chairman J. P. Beddy. According to the EDB memorandum circulated in May 1960, 'Irish facilities for management education are not alone deficient but – making all allowances for differences in scale – fall far short of those available in other countries'. Lack of provision for the university graduate who was a potential manager was identified as the principal lacuna, with the bulk of Rathmines courses pitched too low for this person and the IMI MDU focusing on those seeking to make the transition from middle to top management. At the advanced management level, the two-week courses forming the domestically provided core of IMI's programme were unfavourably contrasted with the 'scope and depth' of the courses of 12 or 13 weeks' duration available on US programmes or at Britain's Administrative

Staff Colleges. The memorandum observed that only a small number of firms – and those the ones in least need of improving the quality of their management – had participated on the IMI courses. To EDB this indicated that the 'need for "selling" management education to Irish business' and 'the question of whether this could best be done by an extension of the present courses for middle and top management' required 'particular attention'.

Table 6.2 **IMI management development unit programme of courses 1961–2**

Date	*Subject*	*Days*	*Location*	*Lecturer*
1961 6–7 Sept.	Accident control	2	Dublin	Dr H. Pieters, EPA
12–13 Sept.	The Supervisor's Role in Management	2	Galway	H. MacNeill, Aer Lingus
15, 22, 29 Sept. and 6, 13 Oct.	Work Study and Productivity	6 x ½	Dublin	Guest lecturers
19–20 Sept.	The Supervisor's Role in Management	2	Waterford	H. MacNeill, Aer Lingus
2–3 Oct.	Self Service and Supermarkets	2	Dublin	M. Zimmerman, EPA
17–19 Oct.	Productivity Engineering	3	Dublin	Dr S. Eilon, EPA
24–25 Oct.	The Supervisor's Role in Management	2	Galway	H. MacNeill, Aer Lingus
2 Nov.	The Common Market	1	Dublin	Garret FitzGerald
7–8 Nov.	Personnel Policy	2	Dublin	R. Lahnhagen, EPA
14, 15, 28, 29 Nov.	Top Management Conference	1	Regional centres	Garret FitzGerald and I. E. Kenny
5–7 Dec.	Selling in the Common Market	3	Dublin	A. G. Joseph, EPA
12, 13 Dec.	Top Management Conference	1	Regional centres	Garret FitzGerald and I. E. Kenny
1962 22 Jan.–2 Feb.	Seventh Two-Week Management Course	12	Dublin	IMI Staff & guest lecturers
20–21 Feb.	Productivity measurement in small and medium-sized firms	2	Dublin	Dr F. Abb, EPA
6–8 March	Dynamic office management	3	Dublin	R. H. de G. Matley, EPA
19–30 March	Two-week marketing course	12	Dublin	Urwick Orr staff
9–14 April	Productivity engineering	2	Dublin	H. Branson, EPA
1–3 May	Effective management in small/medium business	3	Galway	IMI Staff and guest lecturers

Date	*Subject*	*Days*	*Location*	*Lecturer*
21 May–1 June	Seventh Two-Week Management Course	12	Dublin	IMI Staff and guest lecturers
12–16 June	Productivity engineering	2	Dublin	W. Rodgers, EPA
2–13 July	Residential University Course for Managers	12	UCG	Universities staff

Source: MDU Supplement Management 8 (8), August 1961.

This attention was to be paid in a wide-ranging assessment of management education needs carried out by a small expert group that 'should not exceed five or six in number and should not be "representative"':

> It should be composed of, say, three businessmen known to be interested in, and with some knowledge of, management education; a university man with experience in this field; and (possibly) a man from the Rathmines College of Commerce. The Economic Development Branch would be willing to collaborate with the working group if this were considered desirable. It would be most valuable if the services of the European Productivity Agency could be utilised; thanks to the efforts of the Irish National Productivity Committee, the Agency has recently shown quite a deal of interest in this country, and in this field their experience and special knowledge would be invaluable.[13]

The memorandum went in the first instance to Industry and Commerce, seeking its views and also clearance to bring Education into the discussion. Industry and Commerce replied that 'Education would be the key Department . . . in the event of a decision that State action in addition to the efforts, e.g. of the IMI and the IPA, is necessary to "sell" management education to Irish business'.[14] It also sought the views of IMI and INPC on the memorandum. During August both IMI and INPC reacted negatively to the kind of review group EDB had suggested. In the same month a meeting also took place between the Secretary of Industry and Commerce and the head of EDB at which the former complained at length about the confusion, overlapping, and unnecessary work EDB's initiatives were creating for his department while the latter professed a desire to maximise efficiency and minimise duplication, attributing difficulties that had arisen to the teething troubles of a novel type of activity. At a further meeting between the two departments in October, where the management education memorandum was specifically discussed, the position of Industry and Commerce was that 'the problem was one that came within the province of the Irish Management Institute' while EDB doubted whether IMI was the most appropriate body to review the issue. The two sides were agreed that discussions ought to be convened by Education, which was not present. When the three departments did come together in November it was on EDB's initiative and in response to IMI's decision to reconstitute its Joint Committee of the mid-1950s with a remit to review the current state of management education. Any joint departmental response to this pre-emptive move was forestalled by the attitude of Industry and Commerce that the IMI action was 'understandable'. Education considered seeking representation on the Joint Committee but, when it decided against doing so, an isolated EDB let its management education initiative lapse.[15]

With EDB sidelined, IMI resumed strategic control over the discussion of Irish management education needs for the next decade. What became known as the review committee produced an interim report in January 1962, recommending that the staff of the IMI MDU be expanded and that 'an investigation in depth into Irish managerial resources' be initiated. This investigation (Tomlin 1966) was carried out within IMI whose consultative board brought out a follow-up report assessing management education and training needs in the light of its findings in 1971.

The 1962 interim report recommendation that MDU's staff be expanded came at a time when EPA was in the process of being wound up. To finance this expansion, the Review Committee had left it to IMI itself to 'examine the question of further assistance from business, grants from foundations abroad and governmental support'. The Technical Assistance funds of Industry and Commerce proved to be far the most accessible of these sources. Table 6.3 shows the amounts granted to IMI out of voted monies between 1962 and 1972. In addition to the grants it received, IMI was further aided by the provision that 50 per cent of the fees charged to managers attending its courses could be recovered by their companies from Industry and Commerce. A hiatus between the Grant Counterpart Fund payments and domestic Technical Assistance when IMI received no grant aid occurred in 1961–2. Thereafter the amount of aid received rose steadily, although Industry and Commerce departmental conference records indicate that amounts paid fell substantially short of amounts sought in several years.

During this period it was the traditional supply, rather than the newer economic development, side of Finance that was exercised by management education. In 1966 Finance indicated concern at grant escalation and pressed for phased reductions to be made with grant aid ending in 1969 after six years of 'pump priming'. When aid was first sanctioned by Finance 'it was indicated that as a matter of principle, and also having regard to the state assistance afforded towards the cost of participation in the Institute's courses, the major part and ultimately, if possible, all of the expenses of the Institute should be borne by industry'. At Industry and Commerce, however, the Minister's response to the phased reduction call was that 'it was somewhat unrealistic to expect these bodies to carry on without State assistance the activities for which assistance is presently being given to them'. A year later when IMI, pointing to a proposed reorganisation of its structure and the acquisition of additional premises, sounded out the likely response to a request for an increase in its subvention to £90,000 in 1968-69, Industry and Commerce were 'sympathetically disposed' but anticipated that 'some difficulties might be put forward by the Department of Finance'.[16] Such difficulties, as table 6.3 shows, only delayed this figure being reached until the following year.

Table 6.3 **Irish state grant aid to IMI 1962–72**

Financial year	*Grant received (£)*
1962–3	4,000
1963–4	17,009
1964–5	21,562
1965–6	30,000
1966–7	51,000
1967–8	60,000
1968–9	60,000
1969–70	90,000
1970–1	120,000
1971–2	175,000

Source: Dáil Debates, vol. 259, 23 March 1972

Catholic perspectives and management philosophy

Financially and politically, IMI was the most successful provider of Irish management education but it was not the first institution to enter that field. As table 5.2 showed, the Catholic Workers' College (CWC) began running courses for management students in 1951–2 and courses for foremen in 1955–6. As IMI, after the creation of its MDU, focused on management's top brass, CWC, alongside Rathmines College of Commerce, continued to cater for its non-commissioned officers. Following a favourable report on its operation from an English expert in the spring of 1958, TWI moved from having the status of a short-term experiment based in Rathmines to being part of the mainstream of bigger city vocational education. TWI trainers had formed an association in 1957 and this was followed by the creation of the Irish Supervisors Institute (ISI), whose inaugural meeting was held at CWC in May 1960. During the early 1960s the Committee on Industrial Organisation took an active interest in education and training for both senior managers (where it tracked IMI's implementation of the Review Committee's recommendations) and supervisors.[17] On its recommendation an official Committee on Supervisors was established in January 1964 which reported two years later. This identified technical ability and human relations as the areas in which it was most important to raise standards among supervisors. With regard to education and training provided outside firms, the report advocated that TWI should be extended beyond its three current bases, that a two-year course devised by ISI should be promoted throughout the country with VEC co-operation and that ISI should get state grant aid.[18] Timing was, however, against the possibility that ISI might follow on a more modest scale a similar trajectory to IMI. By 1967 – as noted in chapter 4 above – the establishment of the state industrial training authority, AnCO, was in preparation and this body soon established its position as the predominant provider of courses for supervisors.

The 1960 EDB memorandum made no mention of CWC's role in management education, but the subsequent IMI study of Irish managerial resources included in its survey of providers what had by then become the College of Industrial Relations. This college, it was noted, 'differs both in its aims and in its methods from other organisations providing training for management'. Its aim was to help its management students 'to develop a social philosophy founded on reason and Christian principles' and because of this 'the College does not set out to train managers in the use of techniques, but does include sufficient discussion of techniques to allow participants to understand the human issues at stake in their use' (Tomlin 1966: 315–16). Capital, and private property more generally, had the Church's stamp of approval. But the kind of capitalism favoured by Catholic teaching was family-based, modestly scaled and properly subjected to overarching vocationalist regulation. Concentration of capital within large, powerful and unrestrained corporations on the US pattern was, however, to be deprecated. Hence the post-war adult education project of Alfred O'Rahilly in which 'all must be equipped, along prescribed lines, to fight against creeping statism at home and the spread of alien and subversive materialism, of the capitalist but more particularly of the communist variety' (Murphy 1995: 281).

Dubious as it seemed to Irish exponents of Catholic social principles, US-influenced management education was not subjected to anything comparable to the inquisition that British-style trade union education suffered in the 1940s and 1950s. It did, nonetheless, have an occasional shot publicly fired across its bow. In January 1960, Rev. Jeremiah Newman, Professor of Sociology at Maynooth, delivering an inaugural lecture to management students at the Catholic Workers' College, observed that 'while it is a cause for rejoicing that a number of Irish organisations are seeking to raise the standard of business efficiency, which we need so badly, a word of warning – however unpopular – must be interjected'. This warning was to the effect that 'any concern for the human side of the worker that does not take the higher aspects of his being into account is just as materialistic as the outlook of the era of "economic man"'. He specifically argued that 'a great deal of what goes by the name of psychology – particularly industrial psychology – is concerned with physiological and chemical reactions to stress' and that 'time and motion study that does not get beyond this aspect of man can only be regarded as materialistic behaviourism'. Irish managers and employers should avail themselves of courses of study on the nature of man which would help them 'to use discrimination with regard to contemporary literature on scientific management – and even regarding the views of visiting foreign experts on the subject'.[19]

The memorandum CWC's Jesuit teachers drew up for a provincial consultation in 1961 (see chapter 5 above) echoed in private Newman's reservations while placing them in a wider historical and social context. This memorandum identified a need for the kind of management education CWC was providing that arose out of both longstanding and new features of the Irish industrial situation. The features of longer standing were, first, 'a situation of hang-over from individualistic, selfish, non-Catholic outlook':

> Business in Ireland was long in the hands of non-Catholics. Its morality was that of the individualist school, the 'Protestant ethic'. At its best, it was animated by a high sense of duty, but narrow in its sense of class loyalty and propertied privilege. At its worst it was able to combine a private moral and religious code with a business and industrial practice divorced from morality or any standard of religious principle or of social or distributive justice. 'Business

is business' was the rationalisation of this schizophrenic approach. Catholics tended and tend to accept this business code or lack of it.

Second, 'too many employers continue to regard their firm or business as entirely a family concern with the upkeep of themselves and their families according to their station of life as the sole purpose and responsibility'. This absence of wider social responsibility was seen as 'part cause of the stagnation, frustration, emigration etc., that still plague us'. Third, prompted in part by the irresponsibility of business families, an 'attack on private enterprise' enjoyed significant support:

> The somnolence in the private sector has led some of our people who are dedicated to the cause of a modern and prosperous Irish economy to regard private enterprise as unsuitable for this purpose and to look to State enterprise for the solution. This tendency is reinforced by the doctrinaire Socialists, mostly Trade Unionists, and some management and public officials whose creed envisages the gradual decline and extinction of private enterprise and it's substitution by State enterprise.

A newly arising need, the memorandum argued, was 'to counterbalance narrow management training':

> With the increasing urgency of industrial expansion management training is seen to be essential. More than one institute has come to supply this need, e.g. the Irish Management Institute, the School of Management Studies, Rathmines. General approach, textbooks and many lecturers come from England and follow the secular concept of man and of industry prevalent there. Pavlov's dogs, neurosis in pigs, industrial unrest – there is a formula to cover them all. Added to this is the danger of the 'technological spirit' so penetratingly analysed by Pius XII. There is need to give a humanistic and Christian balance to these ideas

However, the sense of exclusion from the world of management expressed by CWC's Jesuits was even more pronounced than that felt by them in relation to the trade unions reunified in ICTU:

> The effectiveness of the College among members of management is, as can be noted from the low enrolments, limited. There is opposition in management

> circles because it is too easily assumed that while being well intentioned we are not sufficiently informed; in addition management institutes (which were founded only after the College) tend to suggest that they can supply more essential knowledge than we can and while we can't pin it down we have a feeling that they have a 'Keep Out' sign up as far as we are concerned. At these institutes they charge high fees while ours are very low by comparison. With the funds they have they can bring – as they have done – lecturers from the USA, England and most of the European countries, which is an impressive point with Irish Management. Likewise they send their personnel on all sorts of study tours again to strengthen their position. Further Irish Management has a high regard for University qualifications, though not many members have been through universities, and their assumptions regarding the College tend to have it classified as not sufficiently high in academic rating to satisfy their 'status-seeking'. Hence to gain greater influence among management the College needs a greater and highly qualified staff. It is essential that we mix more in the institutional activities of management.[20]

CWC did not attempt to consistently highlight the incompatibility with Catholic principles of 'narrow management thinking' but, as noted in chapter 5 above, sought instead to adapt to a changing environment in the early 1960s by laying claim to industrial relations expertise. Even before its 1966 name change, CWC moved into the ranks of organisations seeking TA funding when Fr Kent circulated a memorandum entitled 'Proposal to Establish an Industrial Relations Advisory and Research Centre' in May 1965. This argued that industrial relations was one of a range of functions whose integration within the firm was essential. But such integration 'cannot be successful without a joint commitment by employers and trade unions to a common set of supra-monetary values . . . such as the College is capable of providing'.

The initial response of Industry and Commerce's departmental conference on 21 June was that 'there was a need for greater attention to be given to industrial relations but it was questioned whether Fr Kent's proposal would meet that need'. Moreover, 'during the discussion on the matter it was suggested that close association of the proposed centre with a religious community might be inhibiting'. Nonetheless, prompted by Lemass, the Minister, Patrick Hillery, met Fr Kent and the proposal was subsequently discussed in detail between department officials and CWC representatives. One issue clarified in this discussion was the amount of grant sought – £20,000 a year for three years. Over this period the centre hoped to generate fee income and secure endowments sufficient 'to make further state subsidy unnecessary and possibly enable the centre to repay past State subsidies over a number of years'.

Industry and Commerce were not favourably impressed and a recommendation 'against getting involved in setting up this centre' went to its Secretary:

> I doubt very much whether such a centre would achieve anything worthwhile or that it would ever be financially self-supporting . . . I cannot see Irish employers engaging the centre for consultancy jobs at 200 guineas a week (half to be paid again by us as Technical Assistance?) It would be possible to contemplate, if a Centre were established at the instance of employers and workers, the Government showing its interest and approval by giving the centre a small annual grant, but, in fact, we are being asked to set up the centre & to be financially responsible for it for, it seems likely, an indefinite period

Fr Kent was informed by Hillery that, because of an ongoing review of the whole field of industrial relations that might lead to the introduction of new legislation, 'it would be premature for me to come to a decision on your proposal'.[21]

The College of Industrial Relations and the Department of Labour

In 1966, after the change in name had been implemented, Fr Kent broached the subject of having the College's annual subvention – then set at £2,000 – paid from the Vote of the newly established Department of Labour rather from that of Education.[22] When Labour's Secretary met Fr Kent at the latter's request in September 1968 the priest pointed out that 'the College continues to be run on a shoe string' contrasting the moderate fees charged for CIR courses with the 'excessive' ones charged by IMI, half of which were being paid as technical assistance grants by the government. His main concern, however, was to inform Labour that the Jesuits were reviewing their involvement in running the college – 'there were the pressures of the demands of educational and missionary work; there was the feeling that it was unwise to give the impression that an establishment of this kind was under clerical control; there was the general unsuitability of members of the Community for administering such an institution'.[23] The taking over of the CIR by a tripartite body of trade union, management and government nominees while Jesuits remained involved in teaching its courses was the alternative being canvassed.

By December, discussion of change at CIR assumed a more concrete form when the Taoiseach received a memorandum proposing the establishment of a new National College of Industrial Relations (NCIR). This envisaged a reorganised and largely lay-directed college recruiting a substantial salaried teaching staff and expanding the provision of industrial relations courses throughout the country in co-operation with other educational institutions. The Jesuits would waive rent from the NCIR on the premises owned by the order until such time as its Board of Trustees determined that the college had sufficient financial strength to pay. But even operating rent free, the financial projections of the memorandum indicated a deficit in region of £35,000–£40, 000 during in its initial years.[24]

After a range of departmental views had been expressed, an interdepartmental committee was set up to study the proposal further in February 1969. Reporting in September, this committee, anticipating an exclusive dependence on state funding, found it 'impossible to recommend the adoption of the proposals contained in the Memorandum as it stands'. While the committee was considering the Jesuit proposals, Education had independently initiated a national study of community needs for adult education and of the type of permanent organisation required to meet these needs. This was chaired by Con Murphy who was, coincidentally, an industrial relations specialist. Education's ongoing wider initiative enabled the interdepartmental committee to suggest that 'further consideration of the proposal made by the College of Industrial Relations should be deferred pending the results of the Murphy survey'.[25]

By the following April the Murphy enquiry had produced an interim report (Department of Education 1970) containing an appendix devoted to industrial relations. This began by accepting the view that 'better education services could make a significant contribution to improved industrial relations'. It recommended that 'an Institute of Industrial Relations be established as an independent corporate body' with a dual educational and research remit and that the 'possibility of enlarging the existing College of Industrial Relations as the nucleus of the proposed Institute should be examined'. Membership of the new Institute would be open to individual and corporate subscribers which would be financed by a mix of course fees, publications and subscription income. Corporate bodies, including the government, 'would pay an annual subscription of varying amounts to be agreed on'.

When Murphy's final report was published three years later (Department of Education 1973), the interim recommendation for this Institute was repeated, although it was admitted that 'the Committee did not receive much of a response to this proposal'. With the state taking its place in the ranks of the non-respondents, Jesuit successors to Fr Kent, who retired in 1969, developed through the 1970s a range of new programmes and expanded the college's paid lay staff within a context of continuing, but inflation ravaged, subvention by Education. At the end of the decade, as table 6.4 shows, some measure of financial relief was afforded when the switch in the college's source of government funding from Education to Labour, first sought by Fr Kent in the mid 1960s, took place.

Table 6.4 **Government subvention to the College of Industrial Relations, 1970–80**

Financial year	*Grant-in-aid*	*Department Vote*
1970–1	£5,000	Education
1971–2	£5,000	Education
1972–3	£6,000	Education
1973–4	£7,000	Education
1974 (nine months)	£6,000	Education
1975	£9,400	Education
1976	£10,000	Education
1977	£10,000	Education
1978	£10,000	Education
1979	£20,000	Labour
1980	£25,000	Labour

Source: Education Estimates, Labour Estimates various years.

Conclusion

From the early 1950s there were two distinctive approaches to management education in Ireland – the Catholic and the neo-American. As domestic state technical assistance funding came on stream in the 1960s, the IMI, which embodied the neo-American approach, secured an easy and lucrative access that the state long withheld from the CWC embodiment of the Catholic approach. During the 1960s IMI, for its part, moved closer to private entrepreneurial business values and away from a private sector/public sector balance that for a time underpinned a claim that management was neutral between employers and workers. From propounding a religious and philosophical critique of the mechanical impoverishment of mainstream management approaches, CWC moved to lay claim to a particular functional specialisation as it searched for relevance and survival.

CHAPTER SEVEN

Remoulding Mainstream Education and Inaugurating Science Policy

Introduction

Under its nineteenth-century union with Britain, Ireland acquired an education system which combined a measure of state funding, strict religious segregation and a high degree of control by clergy of the Catholic or Protestant churches. In the early twentieth century, Irish language revivalists began to exert significant pressure on this system. With partition and southern independence in the early 1920s, the new state channelled such educational activism as it displayed mainly into the enactment of compulsory Irish requirements. Apart from establishing a vocational education sector they neither developed nor dismantled,[1] independent Irish governments shied away from any interference with the Catholic Church's 'grip on education of unique strength' (Whyte 1980: 16–21). Unlike most other European states after the Second World War, Ireland did not actively pursue policies to expand educational participation, while for much of the 1950s deflationary economic policies accentuated the problems of an under-resourced system. Irish Education ministers generally adopted a stance of deferential passivity famously encapsulated in a 1955 Dáil speech by Richard Mulcahy:

> You have your teachers, your managers and your churches and I regard the position as Minister in the Department of Education as that of a kind of dungaree man, the plumber who will make satisfactory the communications and streamline the forces and potentialities of the educational workers and educational management of this country. He will take the knock out of the pipes and link up everything. (Quoted in O'Connor 1986: 1)

In this chapter, the focus is switched from the creation of separate specialist educational provision for managers and trade unionists to the transformation of Ireland's mainstream system of mass education. Gathering pace during the 1960s, the key aspects of this transformation were, first, greatly expanded levels of participation in secondary and higher education and, second, the rising emphasis on science and technology that diminished the predominant importance the Irish system attached to issues of denominational religious formation and language revival. Debate about the need for and organisation of an Irish national science policy proceeded in tandem with these new educational departures.

External influences, internal initiatives

The West is frequently presented as reacting to the launching of the first Sputnik satellite by the Soviet Union in October 1957 with a concerted drive to increase its own science and technology capacity that focused particularly on the availability of an adequate pool of qualified personnel (Geiger 1997, Krige 2000). In this vein the memoir of a key Irish educational policy maker of the period refers to Ireland experiencing 'the tremor that shook Western science when Sputnik One was hurled into space... and caused a feverish revision of the mathematic and science courses in Western education' and comments that 'it might well be claimed that the greatest single event in post-war education world-wide was the shooting into space of Sputnik One' (O'Connor 1986: 56 and 83).

In late 1957 the USA, as it had previously done to secure the setting up of EPA, offered funding, to be matched by an equivalent contribution from OEEC member states, for measures to address the scientific and technical (S&T) manpower shortage in Europe. This resulted in the 1958 creation within EPA of the Office of Scientific and Technical Personnel (OSTP). EPA did not survive the transition from OEEC to OECD but OSTP did, incorporated into a Directorate of Scientific Affairs headed by Alexander King who had previously headed OSTP while also holding the post of Deputy Director of EPA.

How OSTP and its OECD successor contributed to the process of transforming the Irish education system and helped to initiate consideration of an Irish national science policy are the main subject matter of this chapter. It should, however, be noted that the supply of S&T personnel was an issue that OEEC had been addressing prior to the creation of OSTP through the work of its Manpower Committee. Significant attention had also been paid to the issue by individual Western states such as the USA, Canada and the UK (Godin 2002).

Thus, while the issue's profile was certainly greatly raised by Sputnik, it also had a significant history preceding that satellite's sensational debut. Moreover, debates about scientific manpower shortage in Ireland – and about the role of science in Irish education and in the state's socio-economic development – had taken place in the 1950s apparently without either Eastern or Western external prompting. The chapter begins by examining these domestic exchanges.

Was there a shortage of scientific manpower in early 1950s Ireland?

The adequacy of Ireland's scientific manpower supply was first raised by the IIRS in a memorandum sent to Industry and Commerce in June1949. According to this memorandum, 'there is a serious shortage of in this country of "scientific man-power", that is, in the number of University graduates in Science and Engineering' that 'hampers the satisfactory conduct of Government Services and the growth of industries here and which calls for the application of remedial measures'. Specifically there should be 'an early and thorough inquiry under Government auspices'.[2] The urgency Industry and Commerce attached to the matter can be gauged from the two years it took to make a response. A Departmental Conference in June 1951 considered a memorandum setting out the findings of an informal investigation into the subject. These were that a shortage was experienced only in the cases of mechanical and electrical engineers (by government departments, local authorities and state-sponsored bodies like Bord na Mona, ESB and the Sugar Company) and of pure scientists (by the Department of Education's inspectorate and by secondary schools). Industry and Commerce had no information on the number of graduates employed in private industry but deduced that no shortages existed as no complaints had been made to itself or to the IDA: 'the lack of complaint may be due to the fact that University graduates in science and engineering are not employed to any considerable extent in private industry in this country.'[3]

This view of the situation was rejected by IIRS which reiterated its call for a full investigation. Industry and Commerce, however, took the view that any action required lay within the province of the Department of Education and the universities.[4] Almost two further years had elapsed by the time Education, after several reminders, produced its response which largely consisted of detailing the funding it was providing for the expansion of engineering and science courses at UCD and UCC.[5] Presented with this, IIRS again reiterated its enquiry call, citing initiatives being taken by OEEC (on whose Committee for Applied

Research the IIRS director was the Irish representative) to argue that it should encompass 'the whole field of Technological Manpower'.[6] An Industry and Commerce memorandum countered that:

> Apart from temporary fluctuations in the supply of and demand for scientific graduates, the real difficulty appears to be that there is not in this country either a tradition of industrial skill or the necessary reserve of skilled or semi-skilled labour. In the absence of this tradition of industrial skill and of reserve of skilled etc. labour no useful purpose would be served by the holding now of an inquiry or investigation on the lines of that suggested by the Institute.[7]

Exchanges on the subject continued into 1956 with Industry and Commerce and Education united in emphasising ongoing expansion of university facilities and rejecting the need for a manpower shortage inquiry. Faced with this, IIRS finally gave up repeating its call.[8]

Science in Irish education and society

In April 1957 two professors of Physics – Trinity's Nobel Laureate E. T. S. Walton and UCD's Thomas Nevin – wrote to the Taoiseach about the state of Irish science. Walton suggested that Ireland should have a scientific policy committee that would deal with education, research and the role of science in national development. Nevin concentrated on the desirability of increasing the number of science students and providing adequate facilities for their education. De Valera's reply invited the submission to him of memoranda from Trinity and UCD that he would then discuss with the Minister for Education.[9] Walton sent a further memorandum developing the argument of his initial letter while, from UCD, the Professor of Chemistry, T. S. Wheeler, took up the running with a variety of documents on science education deficiencies in the universities and secondary schools. One point Wheeler highlighted was that 'unfortunately in recent years religious taking science degrees in UCD are almost all destined for teaching abroad where a science degree is essential for official recognition'.[10] This left the Irish schools run by the orders to which these students belonged with unqualified teachers of the science subjects. When the Department of Education was brought into the discussion in June, its Chief Inspector argued that 'the position of science in our secondary schools is by no means as unsatisfactory as some would have us believe'.[11] The fact that the Council of Education had been engaged since 1955 in reviewing the entire secondary school programme provided the department with an argument for postponing any action until its recommendations were made.[12]

Early OEEC scientific manpower enquiries

In July 1957, several months before Sputnik One's launch and coinciding with discussion of the state of science in Ireland, the OEEC Council approved the setting up of a Working Party on Scientific and Highly Qualified Manpower. The Irish Delegation was approached by Alexander King of EPA to nominate a member:

> We should much appreciate the sending of a personality of authority in the scientific and education world. The type of person we envisage would be someone like Professor Wheeler but you have many other people of merit. On a number of scientific topics we already have contact with Dr. Donal Flood of the National Standards and Research Organisation [*sic*] in Dublin who would, of course, be acceptable.[13]

External Affairs circulated the request to Agriculture, Education, Industry and Commerce as well as the Taoiseach's Department but, in line with Ireland's prevailing mode of minimal EPA involvement, obtained no nominee for this working party. By early 1958, however, the Interdepartmental ERP Committee had emerged as a forum within which positive engagement with EPA/OEEC on S&T was beginning to develop. In the interim the conditional US offer of funds had set in motion the process of setting up within OEEC a new office dedicated to S&T manpower and a proposal to institute annual reviews by this office of national S&T manpower policies had been approved.

On 7 January 1958 the Interdepartmental ERP Committee agreed that Irish participation in the new S&T programme was desirable 'especially in the context of the Free Trade Area negotiations' and initiated a process of gathering material in anticipation of an annual review.[14] Reluctance to participate in matching the funds the USA had offered for the new office was expressed – 'the Minister for Industry and Commerce considers that, in accordance with our attitude in Working Party 23, we should take the line that Ireland, as an underdeveloped country, should not be asked to contribute'[15] – but later withdrawn in the light of the Paris Ambassador's response that 'in my view it wouldn't look too good for a country in the course of development to opt out of an exercise of this nature'.[16]

A changing context prompted some movement in Industry and Commerce's attitude to S&T questions. It informed External Affairs in August 1957 that it was 'unable to attempt an assessment of the scientific and manpower position in Irish industry',[17] but a year later its position was that:

> At the present level of industrialisation the supply of scientific personnel is equal to the demand. It is not unlikely, however, that if the industrial development it is hoped to stimulate by measures designed to attract external investment etc. materialises, the supply of scientific and technical manpower will become a live issue.[18]

Industry and Commerce continued, however, to disclaim responsibility for S&T manpower questions and to maintain that these were a matter for Education. Irish representation on OSTP's Governing Committee was assigned to the latter department. This was greatly to increase the exposure to international influence of a department whose 'approach to questions of interchange with other countries' had been characterised in 1955 by External Affairs officer Conor Cruise O'Brien as 'cautious to the point of being negative' (quoted in Whelan 2000: 309).

The Wilgress visit and the first OSTP annual review

The first concrete manifestation of the new international influence came when a former Canadian Ambassador to OEEC, L. D. Wilgress, was commissioned by the organisation in June 1959 to review the state of scientific co-operation in Europe. Prior to visiting Ireland in June, he discussed his mission with M. T. O'Flanagan, Education's nominee to the Governing Committee of OSTP. O'Flanagan subsequently noted that:

> Mr Wilgress will wish . . . in particular to find out if there is a proper understanding at the highest level of the link between scientific training and economic growth. . . he will wish to stir up interest at the highest policy level and stress the importance of scientific training and research to any national development programme.

Ireland would be 'the first of the "non-industrial countries" of OEEC which Mr Wilgress will visit'. In the industrialised ones he had 'had conversations at highest Government level', meeting in the United Kingdom with 'the Chancellor of the Exchequer, the Lord President of the Council, the Minister for Education and the Heads of Applied and Pure Research in Government and University institutions'.[19] In his two days in Dublin, Wilgress was to meet the Ministers of Education, Agriculture, Industry and Commerce, Lands (which had responsibility for fisheries) and External Affairs. He also saw the Secretary of Finance, the Directors of the Agricultural Institute and of the IIRS as well representatives of Trinity College and UCD.

An interim report Wilgress submitted to OEEC in July described Ireland as 'not so much an underdeveloped country as one seeking to arrest further underdevelopment'. The loss of a large proportion of science graduates to emigration was noted as were the inadequate and overcrowded facilities in which they received their education. 'There is not', the report commented, 'a widespread realisation in Ireland of the role of scientific research in the development of industry'. Ireland had sought – 'like so many other under-developed countries' – to develop industry by replacing imports. Little attention had been paid to developing industrial exports, where the requirement of high quality gave industrial research especial relevance.[20] The response to the report from Irish departments was broadly positive – as an External Affairs minute put it, 'considering Mr Wilgress was able to spend such a short time here, his report strikes me as remarkably sound'.[21]

Later in 1959 Ireland experienced for the first time the process of review by OSTP-nominated educational experts:

> The technique which was applied was to send to each country a small group of independent experts to discuss . . . with government officials and competent representatives of other interested circles. On the basis of these interviews they prepared a report which was then discussed at a 'confrontation meeting' at the headquarters of the Organisation, at which high ranking representatives of the examined country answered the various questions put to them by the 'examiners', and members of the Governing Committee (Papadopoulos 1994: 25)

The examiners who came to Ireland in October were H. W. Stowe, the President of Queen's College, New York and a professor of thermodynamics from the University of Grenoble's Institut Fourier, Louis Weil. Their report highlighted the low educational participation rates and the lack of integration between economic planning and educational development:

> This rate of progression from the primary grades to the secondary schools and to the level of the 'Leaving Certificate' appears to be unusually low. By modern standards of interpretation it must surely mean that a large proportion of the brain-power of the Irish people is not receiving its full potential development . . . It seems particularly unfortunate that in the new outline of plans for the economic development of Ireland, no provisions have been outlined for the part education must play

In the scientific field, they noted 'extreme overcrowding of the laboratory accommodation' in the universities, while at secondary level:

> Our study reveals a reasonably good mathematical training, at least for boys, but much less satisfactory training in physics or chemistry. Only a small proportion of secondary school pupils are so prepared as to be able to present themselves to a University science faculty for further training in physics, chemistry and engineering after leaving secondary school. The principal origin of this deficiency seems to be a lack of adequately prepared teachers of science.

One of the 'inquiries for further review at the confrontation meeting' contained in an appendix to the report posed the question: 'so far as teaching personnel are concerned, is the load of secondary education becoming too heavy for the church and private organisations to bear?'[22]

When the confrontation meeting took place on 17 November, the Irish delegation consisted of Education's Secretary, its nominee on the OSTP Governing Committee as well as Professor Wheeler and the Director of IIRS. The meeting itself threw up questions the Irish group would hardly have found themselves addressing in policy discussions at home. For example, 'one examiner said he had been told that there is no proper career structure for lay teachers in clerical schools – no promotion to headships or other positions of responsibility – and asked whether this hampers the supply of science teachers'. One of the Irish representatives sought to provide reassurance on this issue by arguing that 'Irish graduates go in for teaching as a last resort and once having fallen back on it are not much deterred by lack of promotion prospects'.[23]

The ban imposed by the Church hierarchy on Catholic students attending Trinity College (Burke 1990, Lydon 1992) was an issue subject to delicate and euphemistic handling in Dublin (Bowman 1993). In Paris, however, it was raised in a direct and critical way at the confrontation meeting:

> If the universities are crowded, why not with Irishmen? Why does Trinity College, Dublin, take one-third of its students from abroad? This college, replied the Irish representatives, is a special case. There is an ecclesiastical sanction upon it for Irish Catholics so heretofore it has not been filled to capacity, but in the current year owing to the British 'bulge', it has a full complement.[24]

Among their 'inquiries for further review at the confrontation meeting' the examiners had asked: 'what complexities emerge from the requirement that all students in Irish schools must learn the Irish language, and from requiring that much of the instruction in other subjects shall be given in that language?' Here the representatives responded with an assertion of the language's importance – 'one of the few surviving indications of our national identity' – and the argument that emphasis on its use in schools was not at science's expense – 'the schools that teach science through Irish are among the best at both science and Irish – and get the teachers they want'.[25]

The confrontation meeting ended with the examiners saying 'they had the impression things are stirring educationally in Ireland' while the Chairman observed that 'the relationship between education and economic growth is particularly important in Ireland and there are also problems arising from religion and history.'[26] But in some quarters the stirring was none too vigorous. Shortly before Lemass became Taoiseach, attention was drawn in April 1959 to the apparent lack of progress since the exchanges between de Valera and the science academics in 1957. As a result, Education was asked to prepare a comprehensive memorandum on science education in the light of the First Programme for Economic Expansion and other recent developments. An enquiry almost a year later elicited the response that such a memorandum was in preparation 'but it is not yet completed'.[27] At this date – March 1960 – the Council of Education's report on the secondary school programme was still awaited.

OEEC, OECD and the quickening pace of Irish educational change, 1959–61

On 8 November 1961, two years after the confrontation meeting, one of the Irish representatives – Education's Secretary, Terry Rafferty (O'Raifeartaigh) –

wrote a letter providing his Finance counterpart, T. K. Whitaker, with a highly positive account of the extent of Education's interaction with OEEC/OECD to date. According to this letter, 'perhaps the most useful item in the OSTP programme has proved to be the "Country Review"':

> These meetings have served three valuable purposes. Special national problems can be given international attention; the international 'confrontation' provides a strong stimulus for increased effort on the part of the national authorities concerned; and, finally, the comparison of various national situations is the best possible means for discovering those areas in which international action is needed, and in which OECD can be of greatest help . . . In addition to the 'confrontation', the Report of which found our Mathematics teaching to be soundly based, but our Science courses needing revision, this country has received assistance from OECD in organising a number of seminars for teachers of Science. A number of the suggestions in regard to Mathematics and Science which arose from the Confrontation would have already been adopted were it not for the fact that the final examination of them had to await consideration of the report of the Council of Education on the secondary school curriculum generally.

The letter then went on to refer to a suggestion that had been 'brought forward in an informal way' by Denis Hegarty but had not been acted on. This was that EPA 'should be allowed to send a number of experts to this country to carry out a study of our needs in the field of higher education'.[28] Inadequate university facilities had, as we have seen, forcibly struck OEEC observers in 1959. A limited enquiry into the accommodation needs of the National University of Ireland in 1957 and a scandal concerning the illegal manner in which academic appointments were being made in UCD were followed by the setting up in October 1960 of a Commission on Higher Education with very wide terms of reference (O'Connor 1986: 45–51 and 55). In December its Chairman Denis Hegarty informed a meeting of INPC:

> The Committee had an interest in improving scientific and technical education. He [the Chairman] thought the Committee could help the new Commission in its study of this matter. The Organisation for Scientific and Technical Personnel (OSTP), a sub-ordinate body of the OEEC, had at its service educationalists of the highest repute. He had discussed with Dr King of this Organisation the possibility that a team of experts of the highest level

> might be made available to the Irish Commission and Dr King had agreed with this proposal in principle. The idea was that an economist might be sent by the OSTP to study our educational system from the economic angle and collect data. He would then make a report and advise the Commission on the shape which the new efforts might take in education of a scientific and technical character.[29]

Although Hegarty told the INPC that he had 'discussed this idea with the Chairman and other members of the Education Commission who had expressed interest and approval', the Commission's discussion of the proposal produced an acceptance of the offer so qualified as to amount to a rejection – 'the experts would not act, or be designated, as agents of the Commission; the proceedings of the Commission could not be disclosed to the experts and the Commission would not be in any way bound by the report of the experts'.[30] Hegarty nonetheless persisted with the idea and in May 1961 approached the Minister for Education. A memorandum written by Terry Rafferty at this time contrasts strikingly with the letter he wrote to T. K. Whitaker less than six months later in its very negative attitude to OEEC/OECD.

Here Hegarty is depicted as a well-intentioned but tactless bull in the Irish educational china shop. The 1959 reviewers are disparaged with the charge that, having 'spent a short period here and discussed the teaching of science with all and sundry to their hearts' content', they submitted a draft report that 'contained so many errors of fact in regard to the structure of our system that it was necessary for the Department to re-draft most of it'. Further foreign experts would, it was claimed, fall into similar errors or else produce a report 'hedged in with so many qualifying reservations as scarcely to be worth the trouble'. Moreover, foreigners were not to be relied upon in relation to religion. The Commission on Higher Education's 'responsibility is to this country . . . its deliberations are bounded by the Irish constitution, particularly in regard to religion and to parents' rights generally' while 'no such responsibilities would attach to the EPA group':

> It is true that Mr Hegarty was able to assure the Minister that he had already pointed out to the EPA authorities concerned that the visitors must take into account that this State has an over 90% Catholic majority. In fact, however, the proposal as submitted to the Commission, spoke of the group's having due regard to the moral circumstances concerned, where obviously 'religious' and not 'moral', was the word needed, and doubtless intended. Where it was not

> felt desirable to use the plain word 'religious' in a communication to the Commission, it seems unlikely that the visiting group would take very seriously the religious side of things, although, as everyone knows, this is a vital issue in the sphere of higher education here.

Behind the proposal for outside involvement Rafferty detected an assumption that 'the standard of education in this country is in some way backward or undeveloped' to which he added the comment that 'one cannot see any European countries, except perhaps Greece, Italy or Portugal, where there is great poverty and a high percentage of illiteracy, allowing an outside body to examine collaterally with its own Commission its education or other position'.[31]

Perhaps because of the access to and support from Lemass that Hegarty enjoyed, this onslaught did not kill off his proposal. Instead the Minister for Education informed the Chairman of the Commission on Higher Education in July that 'he would be disposed to withdraw his previous reservations' if certain conditions were satisfied. The conditions stipulated derived mainly from Rafferty's memorandum. They were, first, 'that, as we have already been assured, the examination will be at OEEC's expense'. Second, that the examination 'be an instrument of the Commission, working within the terms of reference, constitutional and otherwise, of the Commission' and 'that it reports only to the Commission'. Third, that the assent of the University Colleges to being inspected be assured in advance either by the Commission or by the Department. Fourth, 'that there be no assumption that the educational system of this country is in some way backward in its standards or in the standard of is products' and, fifth, 'that the likely future of industry in relation to skilled man-power be also examined'.[32]

The Commission on Higher Education discussed the question again in September but rejected the idea that 'the experts should act as agents of the Commission' or that it should have any association with a survey of the universities. An expression of willingness to consider evidence submitted to it from any source was as supportive as it was prepared to be and the proposed involvement of OSTP went no further.[33]

But if the Commission was not for turning, Rafferty was on the point of switching from a very negative to a highly positive view of the contribution OECD expertise might make to Irish educational policy development. By November, the OSTP review he had derided in May was being viewed as 'most useful'. A study had been agreed in principle between Education and Finance in which OECD expert assistance 'would enable us to work out with reasonable accuracy' Irish educational targets and requirements. Rafferty was even proposing the active involvement alongside the experts in such of a study of those he had characterised in May as having 'very little feeling for the genesis and delicately interbalanced nature of our educational system':

> In the case of other countries that are carrying out such surveys it is the practice to have organised labour and employers' associations represented on the national team. Perhaps that position could be met here by including two representatives of the National Productivity Committee, one from the Labour and the other from the Employers' side of that Committee.[34]

The key development in the intervening period was government approval on 30 June of the proposals of a Finance Memorandum for the preparation of a successor to the programme for economic expansion that had now reached its mid-point. One sentence in this memorandum – 'Education will be covered in the new programme, special arrangements being made with the Department of Education for the preparation of material' – signalled a significant extension to the existing scope of the planning process in the direction that had been advocated by the OSTP reviewers. This held out the prospect of the Irish education system becoming better resourced – the point on which Rafferty had concluded his May memorandum:

> There are defects in the Irish system of graduate training, but probably none that could not be cured by one simple method, that is, better financial provision for more staffing, increased accommodation, and more and better equipment. This will be evident if it is considered that British universities receive about four times more than ours in the way of State grants.[35]

The economics of education

The major impact of OSTP on the Irish education system – and indeed on Western education systems as a whole – was to arise not out of the pursuit of the specific concerns that its title referred to but from a broadening out of its focus from scientific and technical education to embrace education as a whole and explore its role as a key factor in economic growth:

> The concentration of the initial OSTP programme . . . stemmed from the conviction that the rate of growth of the economy would be increasingly

> determined by the provision of education in science. But it was equally accepted from the beginning that the problem of producing an adequate supply of well qualified scientists, engineers and technicians was not one which could be examined independently from the output of the educational system as a whole, since such technical personnel represented only part of the apex of the educational structure. It was only logical, therefore, that a central objective of the programme would be to stimulate policies in Member countries for increased allocations of resources to education as part of their efforts to maintain an adequate rate of economic growth. Out of this simple idea emerged the 'Economics of Education' which was to play such a prominent part in the work of the Organisation and, more generally, in providing political support for the massive expansion of education over the next ten years (Papadopoulos 1994: 32)

Here the key developments were OSTP's fostering of the study group in the Economics of Education formed in 1960 and the conference on Economic Growth and Investment in Education held in Washington in October 1961. The study group developed a theoretical rationale for educational expansion while the Washington conference was a key moment in the dissemination of these ideas to a wider audience of senior policy makers (Papadopoulos 1994: 32–42, O'Connor 1986: 62–3, White 2001: 29–31).

No Irish economist was a member of the study group but it did include an Englishman who had significant Irish connections and a Dane who was to acquire such connections at a later date. John Vaizey began his career in industrial economics with a study of the British brewing industry. At Cambridge in the mid-1950s he became friendly with Patrick Lynch, who had previously acted as economic adviser to the Taoiseach and would subsequently combine an academic career at UCD with extensive external commitments. Vaizey's involvement with the brewing industry led to his co-authoring with Lynch of one of the volumes of the history of Guinness's brewery that were to mark its Dublin bicentenary (Lynch and Vaizey 1960). Time spent 'working with uncatalogued and unsorted archives' in Dublin meant that 'through the Irish book I got to know Ireland well' (Vaizey 1986: 123–4). Economic history had replaced industrial economics as Vaizey's main theoretical interest but it, too, was displaced when, prompted by the work of Richard Titmuss and Brian Abel-Smith on the National Health Service, he began to focus on the economics of education: 'I became an Expert on that somewhat esoteric but increasingly fashionable subject . . . [and] was drawn increasingly to Paris to work with international organisations' (Vaizey 1986: 123). Henning Friis, the Director of Denmark's National Institute of Economic and Social Research, who also chaired OSTP's Governing Committee, chaired the study group, to which Vaizey was a leading contributor. As discussed in chapter 8 below, Friis was to come to Ireland in 1965 as a UN consultant to study the country's social research needs. Moves to bring Friis to Ireland for this purpose were initiated by Patrick Lynch.

While great significance was later to be routinely attributed to Irish participation at the 1961 Washington conference, Irish preparations for it were disorganised to say the least. OEEC documentation had been circulated in the spring, with 15 June set as the deadline for nominations, but External Affairs seems only to have passed the information on to Education. Finance, whose participation was also sought by OEEC/OECD, did not become aware of the upcoming conference until mid-July. On 8 August the US Embassy sent External Affairs a minute stating that 'the United States Government attaches considerable importance to this conference and hopes that the delegation of each OECD member will include representatives of the departments of finance and education', before listing the members of the high-powered delegation that would represent the USA. At the end of August a US Embassy official told T. K. Whitaker that one of these delegates, Assistant Secretary of State for Educational and Cultural Affairs Philip H. Coombs, 'hoped that Dr Hillery, Minister for Education, and myself [Whitaker] would be present at this conference and that he would meet us there'.[36]

The Irish 'Investment in Education' report

Irish policy makers had accepted the significance of education for economic development prior to the Washington conference but a significant move to give this acceptance concrete and specific content was initiated at this event. In Washington Kjell Eide of OECD's Directorate of Scientific Affairs handed the Irish delegates – an Assistant Secretary from Finance and another from Education – a document entitled 'Pilot Studies on Long-Term Needs for Educational Resources in Economically Developed Country'. During the closing months of 1961, discussion on carrying out in Ireland the kind of pilot study OECD envisaged was under way, involving the departments of the Taoiseach, Agriculture, Industry and Commerce, External Affairs as well as the CSO. Support for the proposal was unanimous and planning for the study began in January 1962, with a meeting in Education which Alexander King came from Paris to attend.

At the next meeting on 7 March, with only Irish officials present, philosophical doubt made a brief appearance with the CSO Director M. D. McCarthy asking whether 'the question was perhaps being approached from the wrong point of view':

> We were asked to begin by saying what was needed in terms of manpower, etc., instead of taking as our point of departure the human resources available and what we can afford to give them. That is, the question was not being considered from the humanistic point of view.[37]

To this Education's Rafferty riposted that 'he was sure the human element would not be overlooked, but he felt that if we did in fact approach the question from the purely humanistic point of view, then little financial support would be forthcoming either from the Government or from OECD'. Irish perspectives were, if anything, more instrumental than those of OECD. One of the terms of reference suggested by OECD envisaged the making of 'alternative assessments of future social demand for educational facilities at different levels based on present trends and international experience'. At the March 7 meeting there were expressions of 'some disquiet about the implications of the word "social"'. By May, Finance had succeeded in getting 'social' removed and 'essential' inserted in its place. That the making of policy recommendations would not fall within the study team's terms of reference was also successfully stipulated by Finance.

Most discussion at the planning meetings centred on the question of the expertise needed to carry out the envisaged study. Initially, a necessity to source this from outside the country was perceived. The CSO Director told the 7 March meeting that 'the chances of finding in Ireland a suitable economist and statisticians for the study team were very slim indeed'. His suggested means by which the project leader might be recruited ranged from advertisements in the *Economist* and similar publications through his own contacts with the National Science Foundation in Washington to recommendations from John Vaizey or the OECD. Later at the same meeting, when the creation of a steering committee to work in tandem with the study team was being discussed, one of the participants remarked 'that as the members of the study team would be foreigners, it was desirable that the Steering Committee should consist of people who could give informed guidance to them'.[38]

By mid-April this perception was changing. At a meeting on 17 April with C. H. Murray of Finance, John Vaizey was unable to suggest anyone who might be available to fill the team leader position – 'economists were very scarce and economists qualified to undertake a study of educational needs and resources were doubly scarce'. The 'possibilities of a part-time assignment' were then turned to – 'for this to be at all workable the man in question would have to be resident in this country . . . he [Vaizey] suggested that we might consider the question of securing the release of a university academic from his university work'. A further project-planning meeting took place on the same day at which Irish officials were briefed on developments within OECD by Kjell Eide who stated that 'the Organisation would consider it vital that the project leader be a national of the country carrying out the study'.[39]

At the next meeting of Irish officials only on 23 May 'it was agreed that, both from the national and the OECD viewpoints, it would be preferable that the team leader should be an Irishman with a suitable academic background'. Patrick Lynch was identified as the preferred candidate for this role while an Irish statistician working for the United Nations in New York – W. J. Hyland – was to be sounded out on returning to join the study team by McCarthy. By 25 June Lynch's agreement had been secured, arrangements for Hyland's return were well advanced and – although a British candidate for a junior economist position within the team had been suggested by Vaizey – it was decided to seek the release of another Irish university lecturer, Martin O'Donoghue of Trinity College, to fill this role. A civil servant from Education – Padraig O'Nuallain, 'a secondary [school] inspector with a degree in mathematics' – completed the team.

With a purely Irish team taking shape, and 'informed guidance' for foreigners no longer required, the composition of the steering committee became a less salient issue. Successfully suggested for inclusion – 'though his experience of statistical exercises is limited, his presence on the Committee might be valuable' – was the Reverend Professor of Sociology at Maynooth, Jeremiah Newman. From Finance this suggestion drew the comment that: 'the idea of a church rep. may not be a bad one considering the traditional humanistic moral etc. bias of education here. A cleric might well be "educated" thro' membership of the Ctee. about the more materialistic manpower aspects.'[40]

How the new initiatives were viewed by clerics is not clear. In 1959 the OSTP examiners had 'learned from the Ministry of Education that the ecclesiastical authorities are no less concerned than state officials' about the shortcomings of Irish mathematical and scientific education. But when he had given evidence to Science Sub-Committee of the Council of Education in April 1956, Professor Wheeler was questioned on the effect the study of science 'might have on our way of life in giving us a material outlook'. His reply 'stated that science as such is amoral' but added that 'there is a Pontifical Academy of Sciences and the Holy Father, in some of his latest encyclicals, stresses the need for the study of Science'.[41]

During the period in which the educational study team was at work, the state of Irish education was one of the subjects considered by the priests on a Dublin Diocesan Committee to examine the Public Image of the Church set up by Archbishop John Charles McQuaid. The section dealing with education in the report the committee presented to the Archbishop in June 1964 depicted a system coming under severe criticism from the laity. Its suggestions included regular consultation between teachers and priests within parishes, encouragement of parents' committees or associations and the appointment of a chaplain for Catholic students in Trinity College. It also observed that 'if fees in secondary schools continue to rise, as many have recently, there is likely to be a growing body of articulate parents anxious for radical changes in our system of education'.[42]

Such recommendations were hardly congenial to McQuaid's authoritarian conservatism and were not implemented. A few years later, the extent to which state-initiated educational change was gathering pace, following the December 1965 publication of the study team's *Investment in Education* report, confronted the Archbishop. In July 1968 he received from the Jesuit editor of *Studies* an article written by Sean O'Connor, the Education Assistant Secretary heading the planning unit whose establishment had been called for in that report's one foray into policy recommendation. The editor's covering letter placed O'Connor at the centre of 'the sweeping changes introduced by the Department of Education', pointed out that it was unusual for a civil servant to write an article of this kind but that O'Connor – who 'is obviously deliberately provocative in some parts of his long article' – did so with his Minister's approval. Entitled 'Post-Primary Education: Now and in the Future', O'Connor's article concluded with a call for 'a dialogue at the highest level between church and state on the problems in education now surfacing':

> A change must be made: otherwise there will be an explosion, maybe sooner than later. No one wants to push the religious out of education; that would be disastrous in my opinion. But I want them in it as partners, not always as masters. (O'Connor 1968: 249)

The editor's purpose was to ask the Archbishop to nominate a contributor to a symposium on the article that *Studies* intended to publish. O'Connor was not 'provocative', the Archbishop wrote in a marginal comment on his article, 'he is erroneous – which is much more grave – on a moral issue'. While the note continued: 'I shall consider naming someone to comment', McQuaid was later to write to the Jesuit Provincial seeking to prevent publication of the article by *Studies*. In this he was to be unsuccessful. The Autumn 1968 *Studies* symposium led off by O'Connor's article clearly underlined the coming to an end of the 'dungaree man' state presence in Irish education.[43]

An earlier indication of this trend had come when, after seven years of deliberation, the Council of Education finally published its report on the secondary school curriculum in 1962. The prevalence in relation to policy of a different view to that of 'a body satisfied with the system as it then operated and unwilling to consider almost any amendment' (O'Connor 1986: 69) was asserted shortly afterwards in the Second Programme for Economic Expansion – 'a beginning has been made with the revision of the curricula in the primary and secondary schools so that they will accord more closely with present requirements, particularly in relation to mathematics, science and languages.'

The 'Science and Irish Economic Development' report

OECD's highlighting of the relationship between economic growth and education was a supplement to, rather than a substitute for, its continuing emphasis on the relationship between economic growth and science. In May 1962, as the Irish education study team and steering committee were taking concrete shape, the Directorate of Scientific Affairs circulated a document entitled 'Pilot Teams to Study the Needs for Scientific Research and Technology in relation to Economic Growth'. Irish participation was favoured by Industry and Commerce as well as by the recently revamped IIRS under its new Director, Martin Cranley. Finance was concerned about duplication of the work being done by the education study while Education took the position that the project should be deferred until the education study was completed ('in about two years hence').

Before two OECD officials came to Dublin in February 1963, an External Affairs official noted that 'the real purpose of the visit may be to have it confirmed in discussions with all concerned that a pilot scheme on scientific research may be a little premature'.[44] But, with Patrick Lynch expressing the view that the statistical work required by the two projects could be dovetailed and indicating the availability of some of the personnel of the education team (including himself) to contribute to the second study, these meetings produced the opposite effect to this predicted long-fingering. By the end of 1963, with 'hard' science expertise drafted in from the Agricultural Institute, Bord na Mona and UCC to join Lynch, Hyland and O'Donoghue, the new study's team had been formed. With a study team core in place at an early stage, the study's terms of reference was opened up to their input. In this instance these terms included within their scope the making of policy recommendations.

Organising meetings of the Ministers of Science of its member countries was another means adopted by OECD to advance its S&T agenda. Irish representation at these meetings, which began in 1963, was supplied by Education which set up an informal committee, drawing in some other departments, IIRS and the Agricultural Institute to carry out preparatory work for these meetings. In 1964 this committee was expanded to bring in engineering and science academics from the four universities. In addition to its original role in relation to OECD ministerial meetings, the committee thereafter became a forum in which the case for state provision of post-graduate and post-doctoral university research funding was pressed.[45]

These two parallel OECD initiatives to raise the salience of science policy issues were to have the unintended effect of bringing the Irish interests involved into head-on collision. In January 1965 the S&T Survey Team presented to a meeting of its National Advisory Committee a document entitled 'Proposals for a National Coordinating Body for Scientific Research and Development'.[46] The following month Education circulated for observations a draft Memorandum for the Government – 'Formulation of a National Science Policy'.[47] After redrafting, the former emerged as an interim report arguing for a National Science Council working to Finance's Development Division; the latter sought to formalise Education's control over science policy and enhance the status of the ad hoc advisory committee it had created. Objections by Finance and by Industry and Commerce forced Education to defer the submission of its Memorandum until the Survey Team's report was available to be considered at the same time by the Government.[48]

By the end of 1965, publication of the two volumes of the Survey Team's report (Department of Industry and Commerce 1966) had been rushed through government procedures. Finance then moved immediately to invite other departments to submit their views on the recommended attachment to it of a National Science Council.[49] A memorandum for the government proposing that this be done was issued from Finance in April 1967. This time Education was placed in the position of arguing for deferral.[50]

One Education argument was the need to consider alternative proposals for scientific and technological development structures that the Commission on Higher Education had produced. Coming nearly six years after it had turned away the offer of OSTP assistance, and more than two years after the reporting date indicated in the Second Programme for Economic Expansion had passed, the Commission's report was undermined by the inordinate delay in its completion. A multiplicity of reservations weakened its recommendations and its overall approach was out of tune with the policy thrust that had been generated by Irish state interaction with OEEC and OECD (White 2001: 42–50). In competition with the creation of a National Science Council linked to Finance were the Commission's proposals for a Technological Authority and for a National College of Agricultural and Veterinary Sciences which would integrate teaching and research activity within their respective fields. However, the Commission's report was to Education and 'institutions connected with other state departments to which the Commission made reference' – such as the Agricultural Institute and IIRS – 'did not feel any constraint on them to accept the recommendations, particularly when the proposals about education itself were a cause of dismay to many' (O'Connor 1986: 173).[51]

Remarkable in the light of the praise heaped upon the team headed by Lynch for its analysis of the education system (Department of Education 1965), a second argument adduced by Education against implementing the S&T Survey Team's National Science Council recommendation was that 'in scientific circles the Report is held in very low esteem'. Although not explicitly identified, the 'scientific circles' referred to here seem to have been the science and engineering academics brought on to Education's ad hoc advisory committee.[52]

In spite of this opposition, the proposal to create a National Science Council secured Government approval. Later in 1967, when Finance circulated a further memorandum dealing with the council's terms of reference and membership, Education returned to the fray seeking without success to split technology from science and keep the former outside the council's remit. To this Finance responded that 'it is through increasing the level and application of technology that the Council can best contribute to national development.'[53]

Conclusion

Unsuccessful domestic attempts to raise the profile of science and technology in Irish policy debate can be traced back to the end of the 1940s. By the late 1950s a combination of Soviet space-race achievement and Irish development strategy shift had created a more receptive environment internationally and nationally. Interaction with OSTP ended the isolation of the Irish Department of Education and the Second Programme for Economic Expansion did what international experts had been urging Irish policy makers to do by integrating education into economic planning. Writing privately to T. K. Whitaker in 1962, Terry Rafferty described the resultant change of context:

> It is only during the last four or five years that we have managed to struggle to our feet here and look around us at all. It was a sorry story – 25% of our primary teachers untrained, and that position getting steadily worse, the school building problem also getting steadily worse, no push forward in science teaching in the secondary schools, the universities neglected and losing heart, continual recriminations on all sides about salaries and what not . . . this situation is well on the way out and . . . now we can think in terms of planning.[54]

Both in education and in science and technology, the bridge between a general commitment to planning and a concrete programme of action was supplied by OECD-initiated pilot studies drawing upon Irish resources of expertise across a range of disciplines. In the case of the science and technology study, the context of alliance between Finance and Education was replaced by that of a struggle for control between the two departments, both of which were participating in OECD initiatives to promote the adoption of national science policies. Also relevant was a division between the S&T activities and interests of the education sector and those of research institutes like IIRS, whose sponsoring department, Industry and Commerce, backed the attachment of the National Science Council to Finance. This division the Commission on Higher Education proposed to abolish by establishing overarching integrative institutional structures. How the development of one specific field – that of the fledgling social sciences – was affected by the absence of such integration is examined in chapter 8.

CHAPTER EIGHT

Shaping Social Science Research

Introduction

In addition to its general promotion of science and technology, OEEC particularly influenced the institutional shape of Irish social science research. At the prompting of European Productivity Agency, the National Joint Committee on the Human Sciences and Their Application to Industry (HSC) was set up in tandem with Irish National Productivity Committee (INPC) in 1958. Through EPA it sponsored the training abroad of young research workers, promoted awareness of ergonomic issues and participated in the development of plans to construct a model industrial community at Shannon Free Airport. It also unsuccessfully sought funding for the setting up an occupational psychology research institute. As EPA was disbanded, HSC began to support substantive research studies. In 1964 HSC was merged with INPC and began to provide grants to research projects based in the Irish universities.

John Vaizey's advocacy and OSTP's support were factors that operated in favour of Ford Foundation grant aid for the establishment of the Economic Research Institute (ERI) in 1960. Two figures active in the international economics of education network, Patrick Lynch and Henning Friis, were subsequently involved in the developments that widened the remit of ERI and transformed it into the Economic and Social Research Institute (ESRI). Civil service discussion of planning for social development that would complement ongoing economic expansion plans provided another context for this move.

Integration between the HSC of INPC and ESRI had been envisaged when the latter was created but the two remained separate and did not collaborate to any significant extent. The HSC declined after INPC was reorganised as the Irish Productivity Centre in the early 1970s. Starved of money, its eventual death helped leave university-based social research without a source of funding support for nearly two decades as ESRI dominated the field. These developments established the sharp division between the 'sociology of the research institutes' and the 'sociology of the universities' that has come to characterise Irish social science research.

The Human Sciences Committee, 1958–63

The composition of National Joint Committee on the Human Sciences and Their Application to Industry, as agreed in July 1958, is set out in table 8.1

Table 8.1 **Constitution of committee to operate Project 405 as agreed at the fourth preliminary meeting to consider the establishment of a joint committee to implement EPA Project 405 (1 July 1958)**

Organisation	*Number of representatives*
Federated Union of Employers	1
Federation of Irish Industries	1
Irish Management Institute	1
State Sponsored Companies	1
Provisional United Trade Union Organisation	4
Universities	2
City of Dublin Vocational Education Committee	1
Catholic Workers' College	1

In the case of the university representatives, it was agreed 'that University College Dublin might be asked to nominate a representative skilled in psychology and Trinity College a representative skilled in medicine'. The first meeting of HSC was held in November when it elected as its Chairman the Rev. E. F. O'Doherty, Professor of Logic and Psychology at UCD. Arrangements for liaison between HSC and INPC were agreed between the bodies at a 16 April 1959 meeting. Both committees would communicate directly with Industry and Commerce in relation to financial support. The department provided both committees with secretarial support but neither had a budget: TA grants provided the potential source of national support for their activities. All requests for EPA funding were to be routed through the INPC and the HSC was to make regular progress reports to the INPC.

During the lifetime of the EPA, HSC concentrated on trying to create an Irish human sciences research infrastructure starting more or less from scratch, on promoting ergonomic awareness and on studies of adaptation to industrial and social change, particularly in relation to the Shannon area.

At its first meeting in November 1958 the HSC decided that it would be 'desirable to narrow the field of action' and 'concentrate on a small number of important problems which are regarded as urgent by both management and labour'. A circular letter issued shortly afterwards to a range of interested bodies elicited replies suggesting a wide variety of subjects for study – 'accidents, resettlement of unfit and partially disabled workers, working conditions, job satisfaction, recruitment and training, promotion, vocational guidance, incentives, human relations etc.' Considering these responses at its second meeting in January 1959 the HSC decided 'provisionally to limit consideration to problems coming under the heading "job satisfaction" which was understood to include matters such as human relations and incentives'.[1]

Whatever limits it chose to work within, HSC had to address the reality that in Ireland 'there are no persons or centres specialising in research in the Human Sciences'. EPA projects that offered opportunities for researchers to study abroad and for research institutes to obtain technical assistance were to provide the HSC with a means of beginning to overcome this obstacle. A Trinity College junior lecturer and four holders of UCD postgraduate diplomas were funded under EPA Project 7/07 Section C to go to centres in Britain, France and the Netherlands between 1959 and 1962 (Murray 2004: 13). Project 7/07 Section D made available 'a pool of highly-qualified consultants who would assist existing research institutes in carrying out their programmes or contribute to the setting up of research centres in countries where they do not exist or are too few' but the HSC decided to approach Industry and Commerce on this issue rather than to seek EPA's help.[2]

On 8 July 1960 Fr O'Doherty informed the Minister for Industry and Commerce (Jack Lynch) that the Committee 'could not fulfil its intended function unless some positive steps were taken towards the provision of research facilities'. The ideal to be aimed at, O'Doherty went on, 'would be the establishment of a research unit, either as a completely independent body or in association with one of the University colleges'. A 'less expensive alternative' was also put forward: state funding of a number of research scholarships or fellowships tenable at the Department of Psychology UCD with a suggested value in the range of £800–£1,000 each 'which would be used to promote the study of specific problems recognised as being of particular importance in Irish industry'. A specific proposal for a Research Institute in Industrial Psychology, with an estimated initial establishment cost of £20,000 and an annual running cost of £7,000, was put forward at a 7 October meeting between O'Doherty, accompanied by Rev. M. J. Moloney SJ (the Catholic Workers' College nominee to the HSC), and Industry and Commerce officials. The establishment costs should, the promoters argued, be entirely borne by the state, as they believed the trade unions would not contribute to its support 'and financing by management in these circumstances might prejudice labour against the scheme'. On 3 June 1961 the most senior civil servant to attend the 7 October meeting (an Assistant Principal) wrote to O'Doherty asking the HSC to 'submit detailed proposals related to a specific fellowship project' and inquiring 'if a project could be selected which could be carried out in participation with EPA'.

The day before this letter was issued, O'Doherty had sent his research institute proposal directly to the EPA. The reply of 14 June from the Head of the Social Factors Section informed him that EPA had no means of providing such an institute with financial assistance. The best way to proceed, it suggested, would be to select a few concrete projects dealing with issues relevant to the Irish context, such as the training of rural manpower for industrial work. EPA's Project 7/07 schemes could be used to provide suitable study placements for the researchers who would carry out these projects on their return to Ireland and also an opportunity for an Irish person to acquire abroad the type of management skills that would need to be available in order to establish a research institute back home. But funding for the selected projects would need to be sought from Irish sources or from 'the great research foundations such as the Ford Foundation or the Rockefeller Foundation'. O'Doherty then turned to UCD for support in establishing the proposed institute but again without success (Murray 2004: 13–15)

Fitting the job to the worker

Although the HSC was not in its own estimation 'a suitable body to undertake or direct research' it was better adapted to the purpose of sending delegations to or organising its own conferences and seminars. Here the EPA's promotion of ergonomic awareness through its Fitting the Job to the Worker project provided a focal point. This project had commenced in Ireland's period of minimal EPA involvement with the two-month visit to the USA of a European mission comprising eight specialists and a European Free Trade Union's representative in late 1956. This was followed up by a technical seminar at Leiden in Holland in March 1957. To this point there was no Irish participation, but by late 1958

EPA preparations for a major conference to be held in Zurich were coinciding with the Irish process of creating the HSC and the INPC. Industry and Commerce's TA budget paid for a delegation comprising the HSC's two university representatives, an employer and a trade union nominee as well as a member of its factory inspectorate added by Department to attend this conference in March 1959.

Back in Ireland, the HSC organised a national follow-up conference to promote public awareness of ergonomic issues. This was held in the Rupert Guinness Hall in November with five speakers from Britain and continental Europe. This attracted an attendance of over two hundred people. At the European level the Fitting the Job to the Worker project continued with an EPA study seminar aimed at those responsible for the programmes of schools of engineering held in Liege in September 1961. The Irish delegation nominated by the HSC consisted of representatives from UCD, Trinity College and the City of Dublin Vocational Education Committee's Bolton Street College of Technology. As with the Zurich conference, the HSC organised an Irish follow up to the Liège seminar to which 'teachers of engineering and architecture together with others to whom these principles [of ergonomics] may be important, e.g. industrial medical officers and engineers in national concerns' were invited. In September 1962 seven speakers from Belgium, Britain, France and Sweden addressed a Dublin seminar held over four days. A further Dublin 'Joint Engineering-Psychological Meeting' was organised in February 1963 but HSC involvement with ergonomic issues faded thereafter until, as discussed below, it was revived at the end of the 1960s.

Planning and studying industrial and social change

In addition to events promoting ergonomic awareness, the HSC also organised a May 1962 seminar entitled 'The Impact on the Individual of Change in Industry'. The creation of the 'first Air-Age Industrial Development Zone in the world' at Shannon Airport in 1958 (Callanan 2000: 82–105) also provided a site for extensive HSC collaboration with INPC, EPA and EPA-backed Dutch researchers. This aspired to develop plans for a radically new kind of industrial community in Ireland. The Shannon area's special industrial development status had arisen out of fears that the advent of larger airplanes requiring fewer stops would render the airport redundant and make its workers unemployed. The new zone was envisaged as 'a regional growth point within the total framework of national development with the accent on effective manpower utilisation, community development, good social conditions and sound industrial relations'.

With encouragement from Lemass and Erskine Childers, whose new Department of Transport and Power had taken over responsibility for Shannon, this initiative started in November 1959 with a visit from EPA's Adrianus Vermeulen to Shannon and Dublin. Vermeulen highlighted as central issues the supply, recruitment and training of the labour force together with the provision for employees, preferably through employer/worker co-operative bodies, of housing and welfare facilities. An official request that EPA arrange visits to Shannon by vocational training, housing and social welfare consultants was submitted in December while the Shannon Free Airport Development Company (SFADCO) at the same time set about reviewing the adequacy of its management structure in these areas. A memorandum by SFADCO's Chairman identified the need for an Adminstration Manager who would work with a range of support organisations including EPA, INPC and HSC as well as supervising and co-ordinating the activities of a Housing and Estates Officer, an Employment Officer, a Welfare Consultant and a Labour Liaison Officer. This team's main human science input was to be provided by the Employment Officer:

> Mr McNabb (BA Hons in Philosophy, Post Graduate Studies in Social Psychology and in Sociological Survey Work in Wageningen University, Holland) who will be the Company's *Employment Officer* responsible for conducting introductory training courses for potential new workers. This officer will be assisted by Dr O'Doherty, the Chairman of the National Joint Committee on the Human Sciences and Their Application to Industry. Mr McNabb will also consult with factory Managers, draw up definitions of the characteristics and aptitudes required for various positions, and conduct aptitude tests in manipulative skills. It will be this officer's special task to ensure that potential new workers understand the overall aims and responsibilities of work at Shannon, and that they can secure by lecture and discussion group methods, the outlook that will enable them to commence to work enthusiastically in the special environment of Shannon. Mr Nabb [sic] because of his special qualifications will also assist in the Social planning required in connection with Housing for workers.[3]

Prior to his employment by SFADCO Patrick McNabb had worked on the Limerick Rural Survey which Muintir na Tire carried out with funding from

Agriculture's portion of the £350,000 Grant Counterpart Fund TA allocation. In the course of this work he had gone for a period of initial research training to the University of Wageningen whose Professor Hofstee (the 'doyen of European rural sociologists') was one of the overseas experts to whom Muintír na Tire had turned for advice (Newman 1964: vii–ix). In September 1960 McNabb was one of two HSC nominees to attend an EPA seminar held in Groningen on the adaptation and training of rural workers moving to industrial centres.

Shortly afterwards, a proposal emerged for a study of Shannon and its hinterland to be carried out with EPA support by the Sociological Institute of Leiden University. After a preliminary visit to Ireland by Professor Emile Vercruissje in December 1960, McNabb and UCD's Francis D'Arcy, whom O'Doherty described as 'attached to my department of psychology and trained in sociology at Columbia, New York', spent two weeks in Leiden in February 1961 discussing Irish society and observing the functioning of the Dutch sociological institute. In April four members of the Institute staff came to Ireland for a month, divided between the Shannon area, where three parishes were selected for the survey, and Dublin where meetings were held with two government ministers (Industry and Commerce, Transport and Power), the Director of the Central Statistics Office, the sociological staff at UCD and the National Farmers Association among others.

Subsequent refinement and revision focused the survey on five issues: the nature and prospects for expansion of the Shannon Airport complex's local labour market, the information local people had about this labour market, the educational preferences of different strata of the local community, the kinds of jobs preferred in different social strata and tendency to emigrate existing among the different strata. In May a party of six staff members and 30 students arrived to carry out the fieldwork. This lasted for three weeks, during which 769 people were interviewed. The students, who stayed in family homes, 'were also required to keep a diary of their experiences, and to make written observations on the families with whom they lived'. In October D'Arcy and McNabb revisited Leiden to take part in the analysis of the data (Murray 2004: 18–19).

By this time, however, the idea of Shannon as the site of a model industrial community was fading fast. SFADCO had presented Transport and Power with a plan entitled 'Review of Residential and Community Requirements of New Industries at Shannon' in April 1960. This drew on EPA advice and the British New Town experience, particularly that of Crawley, and was later supplemented by proposals based on further work carried out for SFADCO by

Irish architects. A Memorandum which Transport and Power brought to the government in April 1961 noted that 'in assessing the future position the Company is convinced that considerable further expansion of the Free Airport Industrial Estate is possible; that the Estate presents an opportunity of a model for an Irish Industrial Community; that the result should be more than a justification of the State capital invested in Shannon and that it should set standards for industrial development elsewhere throughout the country.'[4] But the memorandum also revealed the strength of the opposition to this view.

SFADCO's plans envisaged Shannon having a resident population of 25,000–30,000 people and an industrial estate employing up to 10,000 workers within a 10–15 year period. Finance argued that the scale of investment involved could only be considered within the context of the development of the economy as a whole and opposed any increase at Shannon in the extent to which housing costs were currently subsidised by the state. Reflecting the views of the affected County Councils and averse to disruption of the administrative *status quo*, Local Government favoured expansion of Limerick, Ennis and smaller existing centres rather than the building of a new town at Shannon. Locating industry in existing centres was the preference of Industry and Commerce which found the size of Shannon's projected population and the concentration of industrial workers it would contain disquieting. A concentration of export industries sustaining a population of up to 30,000 could, it observed, be particularly vulnerable to trade recessions or to unsettled international conditions: 'if, for any reason, the impact of such conditions were to cause a collapse of the industries at Shannon the Company and Government would be faced with a colossal task in dealing with a five figure resettlement problem.'[5]

The Cabinet agreed to provide SFADCO with some additional finance to build factory units and a small stock of housing in the short term but referred consideration of the longer-term development to an interdepartmental committee dominated by unsympathetic departments. This committee recommended that planning for Shannon be based on a population of between 1,500 and 2,000 while 'provision for community services should be on a minimum, but expandable, basis'. EPA enthusiasm had contributed to SFADCO's formulation of expansive plans but now Finance based its arguments in favour of a conservative approach on the uncertainty regarding Shannon's position in EEC conditions while Transport and Power concurred that 'it would be well at this stage to hasten slowly'. By the end of 1962 the bulk of the Committee's recommendations had been adopted as government policy.[6]

The cost of HSC during the last year in which it enjoyed EPA support was, as table 8.2 shows, a little over £1,000.

Table 8.2 **Expenditure of the Human Sciences Committee in the year ended 30 June 1962**

Project	*Irish TA* £	*EPA* £
September 1961 Study Seminar in Liège for those responsible for teaching programmes in Schools of Engineering	–	227
September 1961–June 1962 Training of junior research workers in the human sciences	300	300
October 1961 Participation for training purposes in survey of Shannon hinterland conducted by Sociological Institute, Leiden University	46	46
January 1962 Study Seminar in Paris for research workers on the adaptation and training of rural workers	16	35
May 1962 – Dublin Seminar on The Impact on the Individual of Change in Industry	94	20
Total	456	630

HSC after EPA's demise

The minutes of HSC's February 1962 meeting conclude that 'the date of the next meeting will be fixed by the Rev. Chairman when OECD announce their future programme'. But EPA's encouragement of human science research suffered the fate of death by protracted, indeterminate committee discussion. At the beginning of 1963 HSC began to plan its own programme of work and to discuss its future relations with INPC in the light of a suggestion from Vermeulen (who had been appointed INPC's Technical Consultant) that it become a sub-committee of the productivity centre.

The programme envisaged three funded scholarships 'at a recognised institution in Ireland' worth £1,200 each; a grant of £1,000 to the Sociological Institute of Leiden University – where Patrick McNabb was now a Research Fellow – to carry out a study of Limerick that would explore 'what has hindered Irish urban-industrial agglomerations developing at a quicker pace' and an initial grant of £400 for a migration case study proposed by J. A. Jackson, an English-based sociologist who had already published a major study of the Irish in Britain. In March Industry and Commerce forwarded the application for a grant of £5,000 from its TA funds to Finance. Finance indicated to Industry and Commerce that the future relationship between HSC and INPC should 'be clearly defined before the grant question is decided' as 'once the Human Sciences Committee were given the status of a grant receiving body it would be difficult to cut off the grant subsequently'. By the time sanction for a grant of £2,400 issued in October, the revamped INPC into which HSC was being absorbed had been publicly unveiled. By then the Leiden project, whose fieldwork like that of its Shannon predecessor was to have been carried out in the early Summer months, had fallen by the wayside. In the interim HSC agreed to sponsor without funding 'research into some problems of human relations in C.I.E. which the Tavistock Institute of Human Relations would be undertaking'.[7]

The integration arrangements, agreed in July 1963, and coming into effect in February 1964, provided for INPC to appoint five Labour and five Management members to its HSC and for these members to co-opt 'not more than eight people qualified in the Human Sciences field'. In practice the numbers co-opted were much larger than eight: by the second meeting of the new HSC they had reached 11 and by 1968 stood at 18. Of the first 11 co-opted members, four had engineering or technology backgrounds and in most cases connections with earlier ergonomics activity, three were from psychology, two from medicine and two from social science (broadly defined). Two of those initially co-opted had been recipients of EPA-funded training abroad. O'Doherty stepped down as Chairman at the time of the HSC's reconstitution and was succeeded by a trade union nominee, Charles McCarthy, who was to hold the position for more than a decade.

Operating within the INPC from January 1964 the HSC provided grants to support research projects, with the amount devoted to this purpose running at approximately 10 per cent of the INPC's grant-in-aid in the late 1960s (see table 8.3).

Table 8.3 **INPC grant-in-aid and HSC research project expenditure 1963–79**

Year	*Grant-in-aid* £	*HSC grants* £	*% of Grant-in-aid*
1963–4	40,000	2,000	5
1964–5	58,000	4,182	7
1965–6	72,000	7,250	10
1966–7	80,000	6,875	9
1967–8	80,000	6,077	8
1968–9	84,500	9,000	11
1969–70	110,000	9,000	8
1970–1	108,400	9,491	9
1971–2	163,000	15,890	10
1972–3	183,000	13,775	8
1973–4	205,000	8,439	4
1974 (nine months)	220,000	11,997	5
1975	300,000	13,000	4
1976	300,000	16,330	5
1977	350,000	7,300	2
1978	385,000	750	0.2
1979	439,400	-	-

Source: INPC and Irish Productivity Centre Annual Report and Accounts, Various Years.

After four years in operation it had, as table 8.4 shows, provided almost twenty such grants with an average value of almost £1,500. Apart from the Tavistock Institute, the grant recipients were all based in Irish institutions with HSC explicitly assuming a capacity-building responsibility for stimulating research activity in the Irish universities. Publication of the Dublin busmen study (Van Beinum 1967) and the Skibbereen survey (Jackson 1967) was followed by the launching of a Human Sciences in Industry Monograph Series in which ten titles appeared up to 1975. By 1970 'a reasonable record so far in producing research of an acceptable quality at a reasonable price' was being claimed on HSC's behalf.[8]

Table 8.4 **Projects Sponsored by Human Sciences Committee 1964–7**

Project	*Director(s)*	*Cost*	*Location*	*Progress*
The Morale of the Dublin Busmen	H. Van Beinum [Tavistock Institute]	£2,000	Dublin	Report published 1967
Skibbereen Social Survey	J. Jackson [Sheffield]	£900	Skibbereen	Report published 1967
Management/Worker Communications	G. Scaife [TCD]	£1,100	Ireland	Report completed
Management Control Systems	J. Murray [TCD]	£2,000	Ireland	Report completed
Attitudes of Workers to their new Industrial Environment in Shannon	H.Van Beinum, E. McCarthy [Tavistock]	£2,000	Shannon	Report completed
Extended study of data from the Shannon Survey	Ditto	£1,200	Shannon	Completion in 1968
Industrial Medical Services	T. Murphy (UCD)	£500	Ireland	Report published 1967
Leaders and Innovators Irish Management	D. Egan ([MI]	£2,000	Ireland	Journal/book in publication forthcoming
Mobility and Resettlement	J. Kavanagh (UCD)	£2,650	Ireland	Completion in 1968
Juvenile Employment	T. Roseingrave [UCD]	£1,000	Ireland	Completion in 1968
Managerial Emigration	D. Forrest [TCD]	£1,500	Ireland	Report completed
Psychological Investigation of Incentive Schemes	D. Forrest [TCD]	£1,250	Ireland	Report completed
Motivation of Female Textile Factory Workers	E. O'Doherty [UCD]	£1,200	Dublin	Completion in 1968
Industrial Supervisors	P. Dempsey [UCC]	£1,500	Ireland	Report completed
Extension of Supervisors Project	Ditto	£750	Ireland	Completion in 1968
Productivity in Galway port	E. O'hEideain [UCG]	£1,615	Galway	Completion in 1968
Organisational change and resistance to change	F. Dreschsler [TCD]	£1,925	Ireland	Completion in 1969
Development of a test disposition	P. Dempsey [UCC]	£1,500	Cork	Completion in of 1968
Job Satisfaction and Occupational Stratification	E. O'Doherty [UCD], D. Egan [IMI]	£1,000	Ireland	Completion in 1968
Total		£27,590		

The Ford Foundation and the Economic Research Institute

In the form of a request from the Director of EPA, the initiative that led to the foundation of the HSC came from outside Ireland. HSC's funding department, Industry and Commerce, played a relatively passive role in the process, handing over the task of acting on the request to IMI. By contrast, active moves initiated by Irish governmental actors were much more in evidence when the Ford Foundation was approached for a grant to support the foundation of an Economic Research Institute (ERI) in 1959.

In April of that year, reports reached the Department of the Taoiseach from New York that the Ford Foundation 'seemed prepared to consider economic aid' to Ireland. When other departments were circulated with this information, Finance put forward the idea of seeking grant aid to establish an economic research centre. As meetings of department secretaries and diplomats advanced the idea, it was judged best to submit the application through a non-governmental body, and the Statistical and Social Inquiry Society of Ireland (SSISI) took on the role of the centre's sponsor. The application was received by the Ford Foundation in late August and was discussed at a luncheon meeting in its offices on 9 October. Present on the Irish side were Frank Aiken, the Minister for External Affairs, T. K. Whitaker, Secretary of Finance and an Honorary Secretary of SSISI, J. J. McElligott, Whitaker's Finance predecessor and now Governor of the Central Bank as well as two diplomats based in New York – Frederick Boland and Jack Conway.[9]

But while the Irish side came away from the meeting in an optimistic mood, the supporting documentation subsequently sent from Dublin seems to have raised as many questions as it answered and the International Affairs Division was reluctant to become involved with yet another country. Reviewing the material, Stanley Gordon recommended either 'a very neutral note to Whitaker indicating that early action is not practicable and that . . . [a] member of the Foundation staff will try and pay a visit during the coming year' or, 'if, on the other hand, it is decided that the Foundation should stretch to give more active consideration', taking the immediate step of communicating with John Vaizey, 'who wrote such a good letter to me about Ireland a month or so ago'.

Vaizey's letter, written on 1 November, dealt in turn with 'the economic and political situation, 2) the state of the Universities in relation to education, 3) hopeful and helpful people, 4) the proposed Institute, and 5) how we might break into education'.

For Vaizey, Ireland's economy was indissolubly linked with that of the UK while inefficiency in agriculture and industry underlay its recurrent economic crises. A new realism was emerging among politicians and civil servants but had to struggle against the power of a church 'responsible for a terrible education system' and of a backward-looking nationalism exemplified by Irish language revival policy. Turning to the universities, Vaizey stressed their poverty. Of his fellow economists, he wrote: 'they all teach inordinately, their salaries are so low that they have to hold innumerable jobs and hardly any of them do any research'. However, 'the *innate quality* of the academic staff is high (no other employment opportunities probably explains a lot)' and their existing deficiencies were curable by adequate time and money.

Appearing on Vaizey's list of 'hopeful and helpful people' were T. K. Whitaker, M. D. McCarthy, Patrick Lynch and George O'Brien of UCD. These were linked through SSISI, but they lacked 'coherent research', 'a forum for debate and dissemination of their ideas' and – with the exceptions of Charles Carter and Vaizey himself – 'outside informed experts'. The proposed economics institute could supply these wants as well as being 'above all . . . a means of educating the informed public (members of the Dáil included) in the realities of the Irish situation'. Education should be a priority area of study – 'in its present state it is an immense handicap to the country and above all to the individual emigrant who can only go to England in an unskilled capacity'.

With its 'ray of light', Vaizey's letter provided a narrative – an inward looking country reintegrating with the Atlantic Community under guidance from an enlightened group that was struggling to overcome entrenched resistance to necessary change – around which subsequent recommendations that the Foundation support the Irish application were framed by its staff. Another key point of reference was OSTP, with whom Vaizey was working and from whom the Foundation obtained all the reports written in the course of the 1959 annual review of Ireland. To OEEC was attributed the conclusions that 'the time is now propitious to get at Ireland's problem through education' and 'the improvement of economic and social research and training programs would establish the best base on which further educational steps could be taken'.[10]

After the ERI became operational, Vaizey continued to be a source of information and comment for the Ford Foundation on how the new institute was taking shape. In September 1960, when he complained of a lack of attention to the economics of education and an over-emphasis on econometrics, Shephard Stone, head of the International Affairs Division, raised the issue with T. K. Whitaker when the two met while Whitaker was in the USA attending World Bank meetings. Educational research continued to be urged on ERI by the Ford Foundation until early 1962 when a firm government commitment to the OECD's pilot study proposal emerged.[11]

Apart from the type of economic research it was carrying out, the other issue to spark debate about the ERI's work was whether it should become involved in social as well as economic studies. There had been ambiguity from the outset about the scope of the work to be carried out by the proposed institute. Muintir na Tire, which had become active in the social research field through its Limerick Rural Survey, complained to Lemass about the absence of sociology from the new institute in January 1961. This prompted discussion of whether social research should be referred to in the Taoiseach's speech at the ERI's official opening ceremony later that year. It was agreed that it should be and the speech stated that 'the Institute's net will be cast wide . . . it does not intend to confine itself to purely economic affairs, important as these are . . . it is planning also to undertake research into wider social and community affairs'. Hosting visiting scholars from a variety of disciplinary backgrounds provided a foothold for non-economic research within ERI prior its mid-1960s restructuring.[12]

HSC and the emergence of the Economic and Social Research Institute

Overlap between HSC and ERI was not initially a serious issue as HSC delimited its field of operation to specifically exclude economics:

> The Human Sciences Committee is concerned with the development of research bearing on the human problems of work in all sectors of the economy. This includes problems which are external to the enterprise and which have a direct influence on attitudes and behaviour at work and on the organisation and conduct of the work. Consequently, the Committee is concerned with the applied human sciences and more particularly industrial sociology, psychology and physiology. Purely economic and medical research are excluded in principle.

However, in 1963, as HSC was formulating a post-EPA programme of work and discussing its future relations with INPC, a Social Research Committee (SRC) was formed under the auspices of the Institute of Public Administration (IPA) with UCD economist Patrick Lynch as its chairman. A friend of Vaizey – and one of 'the hopeful and helpful people' he identified to the Ford Foundation – Lynch was at this time Chairman of Aer Lingus, an influential

NIEC member and the central figure in the two seminal OECD-supported team studies of early 1960s Ireland discussed in chapter 7 above. As was the case with Lynch's career, SRC straddled the civil service (it included seven department secretaries) and academia (UCD, Trinity College and St Patrick's College Maynooth) as well as including a number of state-sponsored research institute directors (ERI, IIRS, IPA and the Agricultural Institute). A document it drew up envisaged a scheme of university-based postgraduate research fellowships whose holders 'would investigate specific problems of Irish sociology, preferably of an applied nature'. The cost of such a scheme would, it was estimated, average a minimum of £10,000 a year over an initial three-year period (Friis 1965: Appendix 1).

An 'indication of how our thoughts are forming' on this proposal was provided by T. K. Whitaker in September 1963. Social research was unquestionably desirable, but so was avoidance of 'the proliferation of agencies and duplication of functions' by organisations looking to the state for funds and competing for scarce expertise. Quoting the passage that had been inserted into the speech delivered by the Taoiseach at ERI's June 1961 opening ceremony in response to Muintir na Tire's criticism that sociology was being neglected, Whitaker observed that 'the ambit of the Economic Research Institute covers social as well as economic research and there is much to be said for having both carried out by one organisation'.[13]

At a meeting in October, Lynch and other SRC representatives accepted that in the longer term an economic and social research institute was to be desired but argued that its establishment at the outset 'would be a mistake'. Lack of trained social research workers was an immediate task to be tackled and here 'the Economic Research Institute had no special advantage, organization or skill'. Social studies 'would at this time be wholly overwhelmed by the superior sophistication of economic studies and the standing of the Economic Research Institute would not, in any event, be enhanced by operating at two contrasting levels of sophistication'. The civil service secretary members of SRC had, it was pointed out, been invited 'from specifically non-economic departments' – 'they were ready to co-operate in social studies; their co-operation was essential in much of the possible research, but a number of them would be likely to be highly suspicious of a preponderantly economists' approach to their problems'. The need for research-based improvement of policy making in social spending departments was 'so urgent that those who wanted to get it started should be permitted to do this'.[14] But, hopeful that foundation funding could be obtained for social research, Whitaker resisted the commitment of domestic funds sought by SRC.

Thus, like the HSC before it, SRC did not succeed in sourcing funds for a scheme of fellowships. Unlike the HSC, it did pursue to a successful conclusion the acquisition of expert analysis from abroad:

> The United Nations Organization had expressed a desire to help with the assignment of experienced directors of research, should the committee be able to get funds to conduct this research. When this failed that project fell through. The occasion of a recent visit to New York by the Chairman of [IPA] . . . and the Director . . . was taken to discuss with the United Nations what might possibly be done to help clarify the whole situation concerning social research in Ireland, and to see what allocation of roles might be made so that the advance of knowledge, the training of research workers and the formulation of social policy might all be best developed. It was suggested that the United Nations might be able, say as from September 1964, to send over to the Committee, if the Committee so wished, a very senior and experienced administrator in the social field who might draw up a report for the guidance of all the interested parties on the best allocation of roles.[15]

In July 1964 SRC met to consider this proposal and 'to discuss, from amongst a list of very eminent social administrators supplied by the UN, the one whose experience would best commend itself to the Committee for that purpose'. The chosen expert nominated in the application for assistance to the UN was Henning Friis, Director of the Danish National Institute of Social Research. Earlier in 1964 ERI had, at the suggestion of Patrick Lynch, invited Friis to speak on the topic 'The Organisation of Social Research on a National Basis'. Friis had accepted but indicated that his schedule would not enable him to come to Dublin until the spring of 1965. Difficulties that for a time prompted the UN to seek another expert having been overcome, it was as a consultant rather than as a lecturer that Friis visited Ireland between February and May 1965.[16]

At a meeting with HSC on 30 March, Friis outlined his thinking, which converged with the view expressed earlier by T. K. Whitaker rather than with that of the SRC:

> His investigations so far led him to believe that a permanent central organisation was desirable to carry out social research in this country – especially in view of its small size. In the absence of such a body there was likely to be a mushrooming of minor institutes all operating in this field. Small scale studies were currently being undertaken which were not bringing up the evidence for

> national policy formation. In regard to research on policy formation, many questions could not be answered by one discipline and the co-operation of many disciplines was, in fact, necessary. Moreover it was extremely difficult to build up social research on an ad hoc financing basis – people tend to move to other countries or areas. Therefore he was of the view that it was necessary to establish a permanent body for policy related research in the social sciences.[17]

Completed in May, the Friis report set the stage for the conversion of the existing ERI into the Economic and Social Research Institute (ESRI). In August the matter was brought before the government by a memorandum from Finance entitled 'Social Development Programme'. This obtained approval for two proposals. One was that the Friis recommendation of an integrated economic and social research institute with a survey unit attached be accepted in principle. The other was that M. D. McCarthy, the CSO Director, be asked 'to formulate a preliminary programme for the organisation and integration of the studies and inquiries on which the official aspects of a social development programme should be based'. The two were linked by the expectation that, when the ERI's Director Roy Geary retired in the following year, McCarthy would succeed him. In June 1962 a visiting Ford Foundation officer had noted:

> The close relationship between the Institute and the Ministry of Finance is especially interesting and could make this investment very meaningful over the long run. The influential members of the Executive Board have in the past been associated with the Ministry of Finance and the present Minister [*sic*], T. K. Whitaker, is in daily touch with Geary on virtually every question he faces. It would probably be too much to say that Whitaker 'runs' the Institute, but such an assessment would not be too far from the truth. Under the circumstances at present this appears to be a good thing because it guarantees that the work of the Institute will be closely focused on policy questions of interest to the government and may have a significant impact on the future development of the Irish economy. More difficult to assess is the question of what this relationship does to the independence of the Institute as a center of free scholarly research.[18]

Departmental discussion of social research within the context of some sort of social development programme that would be linked to the ongoing programmes for economic expansion had begun in 1964. An ERI paper by a visiting scholar from outside economics, P. R. Kaim-Caudle, was the main stimulus for a Department of the Taoiseach document entitled 'Some Notes on Department of Social Welfare'. This also made reference to a variety of other manifestations of 'the growing interest in social, as opposed to economic, research' and concluded that 'as the Minister for Social Welfare may have to contend with the results of much of this sociological study work, there may be a case for giving him the responsibility for [social research]'. Apparently in response to this, Lemass indicated that he wanted the idea of a programme for social development – covering social welfare, housing and other social amenities but not education – discussed informally.

This initiative became entangled with another by Finance suggesting an interdepartmental committee to consider how Social Welfare might be improved as Second Programme for Economic Expansion targets were met. Lemass, when he learned of the Finance proposal, fell in with its envisaged production of 'an internal confidential study focused on rational evolution of policy rather than a published programme'. Unwilling to proceed were the 'social' departments. Local Government wanted its services (principally housing) left out of any review while Social Welfare insisted on proceeding departmentally rather than interdepartmentally with ferocious obduracy. The programme idea was dead before the end of the year, bearing out the SRC representatives' view in the previous one that 'a number of them [Secretaries of "specifically non-economic departments"] would be likely to be highly suspicious of a preponderantly economists' approach to their problems'.[19]

The social programme concept was nonetheless revived by Finance in the different form of McCarthy's 'programme of studies and inquiries' when the Friis report was published. As the formalities required to turn ERI into the ESRI were completed in October 1966, McCarthy succeeded Geary as Director and the government was required to fulfil its undertaking to provide the institute with funding once Ford Foundation aid had ceased. However, McCarthy directed the ESRI for barely a year before returning to his native Cork to become President of UCC. The link between the Directorship of the CSO and that of the ESRI was broken by the appointment of Michael Fogarty, an academic with an Irish family background but an English (specifically Oxford) educational formation, to succeed him. Also lost was the catalyst role in preparing a social development programme it had been hoped McCarthy would play while ESRI Director. As a Finance minute put it in August 1967, 'pressure of other duties has prevented [McCarthy] doing much in this area and, while he is still hopeful, I think that we will have to go it alone'.[20]

The transformation of ERI into ESRI had raised the issue of what the HSC's relationship to the new institute should be. Friis had been positive in his assessment of the job HSC had done and had wanted to see its structure preserved within the new institute. 'To develop programmes for particular areas of research', his report suggested that 'the Council [of the restructured institute] might set up committees with experts in the particular field', supplying the example that 'the existing Human Sciences Committee of the Irish National Productivity Committee might be re-organized so as to function as the committee on labour market research and human relations in industry' (Friis 1965: 24). After the government's decision in October 1965 to accept the recommendations made by Friis, a meeting between HSC and ERI took place in January 1966 which concluded that 'the position might be left flexible for about a year and then examined again'. In October 1966 approval for a government grant-in-aid to ESRI was accompanied by the expression of Finance's view that a formal approach to HSC to discuss the relationship between the two bodies was desirable, but no move appears to have been made during McCarthy's brief period as ESRI Director.[21]

Fogarty's academic career included a long stint as Professor of Industrial Relations at University College Cardiff, but his expertise in this field found its main Irish outlet in conducting enquiries set up by the Department of Labour whose subject matter included major industrial disputes affecting electricity supply and banking. He appears to have had virtually no contact with HSC during his period as ESRI Director. In February 1970 he put forward the idea of joint sponsorship by INPC and ESRI of a study of pay claim formulation, but in two internal memoranda he wrote shortly afterwards, reflecting on the ESRI's first decade and seeking to stimulate discussion of its next five years, the issues of overlap and liaison with other organisations involved in research are discussed without any mention being made of either INPC or its HSC.[22]

In 1969 the chronic conflicts within INPC alluded to in chapter 4 were analysed in a comprehensive review of the organisation by Svein Dalen and Tony Hubert of the European Association of National Productivity Centres. They concluded that 'there is little, if any, valid future for the Irish National Productivity Committee as it now stands'. The worthwhile applied social science work of HSC they wished to see continued by a new Irish Productivity Centre (IPC). The transfer to some other organisation of the advisory service, on the other hand, they regarded as an essential break with the past. However, IPC took shape rather differently. The name change took place but the proposed transfer of the advisory service did not. ICTU and FUE assumed control of

IPC in 1972 with all the other constituents bodies either withdrawing or being shown the door (Murray 2005b: 77–9).

Although praising the work HSC had got through at a time when INPC was in a state of civil war, Dalen and Hubert had commented that 'the direction of the research policy process' was 'somewhat peculiar'. Research policy should, they considered, be defined and implemented by 'the top-most body of the [productivity centre]: the dog must wag the tail, and not vice-versa'. In October 1972 IPC's Director sent a memorandum on research expenditure to its Chairman. This argued that IPC needed to invest in research to attain its objectives and that, insofar as it studied human problems at work, HSC research was in line with IPC research needs. But HSC had also sought to 'to develop a body of knowledge in the behavioural sciences on the Irish situation' and 'to develop a social science research capability in Ireland'. IPC could not assume responsibility for funding projects serving these ends in the future. Clarification of objectives and roles was now called for – 'there is no possibility that the [IPC] Council would continue to [*sic*] practice (if not the policy) of the [INPC] Committee of Management to transfer an annual sum to HSC and forget it'.[23]

In July 1973 four HSC representatives attended the IPC Council meeting. Here discussion was initiated by the Director who presented a view of research as a support to the IPC field services working to enhance the productivity and profitability of the enterprise as well as to improve its labour–management relations. In this context 'the emphasis would be on application of knowledge to practical situations rather than on the generation of new knowledge'. Responding, Charles McCarthy argued for a mix of the 'once off' projects that HSC had supported for nearly a decade with the evolution of a more strategic approach. The other HSC representatives emphasised either the importance of HSC for the development of a pool of skilled researchers or unique features of the Irish environment that justified ongoing IPC involvement in knowledge-generating research.[24]

Attempts to develop the more strategic approach that might secure HSC's survival within IPC focused on a turn towards action research and on a revived ergonomics involvement. The idea of developing an emphasis on action research – 'projects in which the researcher would analyse specific situations, suggest solutions to problems identified and monitor the attempt to implement solutions' – had emerged out of discussion between McCarthy and Hans van Beinum, who had headed the Tavistock Institute team that carried out the Dublin busmen study in the mid-1960s and was now a university professor in

Rotterdam. However, this proposal was perceived as a threat, and successfully lobbied against, by another division within IPC. After EPA's demise, HSC ergonomics activity had fallen away for a number of years but had been revived with the funding of a research fellowship in Trinity's engineering school in 1970. A proposal for the setting up of a permanent HSC-supported ergonomics unit was subsequently developed. In the July 1973 discussion McCarthy had pointed to this as the potential starting point of a 'strategic approach' convergence between HSC activities and IPC concerns. This hope was dashed after 'both FUE and ICTU had been lukewarm in their reaction to the proposed Unit because it seemed "research" rather than "plant" oriented'.[25]

In relation to its project funding, HSC had set up a Future Work Sub-Committee to identify 'priority themes' in November 1972. Here two focal points emerged – unemployment and married women workers. At HSC's meeting in May 1973 'the proposal for a project in the Unemployment Area was discussed and even though the area of the project was socio-psychological, it was felt by some members of the Committee that it might duplicate work being done by the ESRI and in any event the area was not an appropriate one for the Human Sciences Committee'.[26] Support was given to further exploration of the married women workers area by UCD's Eunice McCarthy up to 1976.

By this time HSC was being starved to death financially while inconclusive meetings on its role within IPC continued to be held. At the IPC Council meeting in November 1975 it was pointed out that the amount available to HSC was diminishing as a percentage of the Centre's grant-in-aid and that no money was available for new projects. The Chairman's response was that 'it was unlikely that more money could be made available under present conditions.'[27] In 1976 IPC's annual report acquired a new format and shrank to half its previous length. Within these shrunken confines no announcement marked the ending of twenty years' involvement in human sciences research activity when it came. In 1979 the heading 'Human Sciences Committee research project grants' simply disappeared from IPC's accounts.

Conclusion

Writing in 2002, Goldthorpe suggested that, while a distinction between 'the sociology of the research centres' and the 'sociology of the university departments' had relevance in many states, it applied with particular force in the case of the Republic of Ireland (Goldthorpe et al. 2002). A subsequent overview of

Irish social science research policy and practice echoed this view (Jackson 2004). The division became deeply embedded between the early 1980s and the mid-1990s when no significant source of public funding for social science research other than the grant-in-aid to the ESRI existed. Within this wider context, the demise of the HSC is of some significance as it removed the earliest and longest sustained source of government support for university-based social science research.

The origins of the Irish divide between the two sociologies can be traced back to the mid-1960s. Then Friis argued that while a dedicated research institute with a policy focus was essential, social research within the universities also needed support. He noted that university research was restricted by the combination of heavy teaching loads with 'very limited funds' and pointed out that 'most other countries have a publicly sponsored science foundation or council to which researchers from various disciplines can apply for research funds, and part of the problem of financing university research is thereby solved'. He concluded by hoping that this problem would be 'studied in the context of the Irish science and technology survey' (Friis 1965: 29–31). But, while critically noting that Friis 'gave little space to observations on the need for more basic research in the fundamental social sciences', the Lynch team took the government decision to approve the Friis report's organisational recommendations as a *fait accompli* and did not specifically advance proposals to give additional structural support to social science research (Department of Industry and Commerce 1966: 141–3). In January 1966 an OECD meeting of Ministers of Science was devoted to the social sciences. OECD was keen to see social science research councils established in member countries but, shaped by M. D. McCarthy who was at one with Friis on the desirability of prioritising policy-oriented research in Ireland, the speech delivered to the meeting by the Irish minister kicked for touch on this point.[28] Three decades would pass before this ball was to be retrieved and thrown back into the field of play (Jackson 2004).

CHAPTER NINE

The Impact of Innovations and the Context of Institutions

Introduction

At the outset of this study, three objects of technical assistance and productivity activities were identified: public opinion, education and industry. In relation to public opinion it has to be said that these were only two of a very wide range of influences feeding into a remoulding of attitudes towards acceptance of the desirability of becoming outward-looking and embracing far-reaching economic, political and social changes.[1] Political parties (Bew and Patterson 1982), pressure group lobbies (Murphy 2003) and the media, whether directed to mass (Horgan 2001) or more selective (Fanning 2008) audiences, were undoubtedly much stronger agents of attitudinal change in society at large. It should, however, be noted that the key political champion of change, Seán Lemass, attached great importance to the adherence of the trade unions to the productivity movement (Murray 2005b) and could on occasion hold productivity out as the means of overcoming most of the Republic's most pressing difficulties:

> Productivity is the key to the solution of most of our economic and social problems. Increased productivity is the only solid and permanent basis for higher living standards. On it depend the improvement of social conditions, the relief of need, the ending of emigration, the strengthening of the country's international position, the solving of unemployment and, in general, the advancement of the economic life of the nation.[2]

Of Denis Hegarty, Ruaidhrí Roberts 'and other hard-working [INPC] members who laboured with them' Lemass declared that 'when the story of Ireland's progress in the 1960s comes to be written, their individual contributions will occupy a very important chapter'.[3] Readers of the preceding chapters may decide for themselves whether this should be regarded as a formulaic pleasantry flattering participants in 'joint economic discussions in the drafty acres of a deserted holiday camp'[4] (McCarthy 1977: 573) or a substantive judgement that deserves serious consideration.

Costs and benefits

For the most part technical assistance and productivity were not the stuff of Dáil debates, political party manifestos or – more than occasionally – newspaper editorials. Instead they were an institutional interface between external and internal possessors or brokers of industrial expertise and Irish governmental, business and trade union actors. Irish official belief in the efficacy of industrial consultants can be traced back to the earliest days of TA with the minutes of a December 1949 meeting of the Interdepartmental ERP Committee making reference to a 'British firm of industrial consultants with whose help several Irish firms have significantly increased their production and profits'.[5] With American TA abruptly suspended, Industry and Commerce stated its intention to turn Irish manufacturers from tariff reliance to technique improvement (see chapter 3 above). During the 1950s a steady stream of consultants made themselves known to the department which, by the time it was in a position to actually subsidise individual company projects at the end of the decade, had a list of almost 50 such firms.[6]

Concern about 'abnormally high' fees was being expressed within Industry and Commerce by early 1961, although 'where this question has already been raised with applicant firms they have stated that they considered the benefit to be obtained from the scheme would more than justify the high fees involved'. A schedule of the fees of 15 consultants that had carried out state subsidised TA projects in firms by this date showed a range from £52 per week to £426 per week, with most firms charging in or around £150 per week.[7] By late 1963 the 'four leading consultant firms' whose weekly fees in early 1961 ranged from £150 to £173 were stated to be charging from 185 to 210 guineas. A department conference to which this was reported considered that 'no useful action could be taken with regard to the regulation of fees of technical consultants':

> The possibility of fraud through collusion between industrialists and consultants was also considered but it was felt that such possibility was very remote in view of the standing of industrialists and consultants alike.[8]

Supplying information to the Dáil Public Accounts Committee in March 1967, Industry and Commerce stated that 'no overall information is available as to the extent to which they [more than 60 consultancy companies that had carried out grant-aided assignments] may have increased their fees in the last few years' but noted that 'the four better known companies have increased their fees on two occasions in the last two years and that the cumulative effect has been an increase of 15% to 20% above the fees operative in early 1965'.

As regards the benefits associated with such escalating costs, Industry and Commerce put forward to the Public Accounts Committee a variety of reasons why 'it has not been found possible to evaluate in any precise way the overall benefits derived by industry in general from consultancy schemes'. But, in the unspecified proportion of cases 'where actual figures have been quoted' in departmental follow-up with grant recipient firms, productivity had increased by between a third and a half while production had risen by between a third and 40 per cent. Moreover 'it is only in very rare cases that firms express any dissatisfaction with results from consultancy schemes'.[9] In December 1967 the same issue was addressed by a consultant working in one of the four leading firms who was interviewed by Finance civil servants researching the NIEC report on industrial adaptation incentives:

> The assessment of results varied in difficulty according to the nature of the recommendations made. It was difficult to assess them where the changes made were in management structure, less difficult in relation to marketing and relatively easy in relation to production improvements. Under the latter heading increases of 40%–50% in output per head were typical but there were a fair number of cases where really massive increases ranging up to 200% had been achieved. Some firms absolute output rates compared favourably with the best firms in the United Kingdom, following implementation of consultant's recommendations by the Irish firms. They had also brought about improvements of 4 to 5% in materials use. There had also been in many cases quite large increases in profitability due to improvements brought about by consultants in management accounting and profit planning.[10]

The 60 or so industrial consultancy providers implementing state-subsidised schemes in the late 1960s were practitioners of what in ECA terms had been Type B TA, whereby expertise came to an industry. Irish Type A TA, involving team visits abroad to inspect superior technique in action, also flourished in this period. Between 1963 and 1967 almost 30 study team visits abroad were funded by INPC and others were supported by Industry and Commerce or IIRS. Greater doubt about benefits is evident in relation to this activity, however, with the NIEC secretariat being told that no INPC team visits took place in 1967–8 as 'we felt that some fairly substantial changes would be necessary in the method of handling visits of this type . . . the arrangements both for preparing for visits and more particularly for reporting and analysing these visits could be substantially improved'.[11] The abortion of the US industrial TA programme, described in chapter 2 above, had meant that mechanisms for the wider diffusion of either Type A or Type B Irish experiences were not created during the formative early 1950s period while the development of such mechanisms in the 1960s was hamstrung by the absence of industry level joint action (or even concerted business action) bodies, discussed in chapter 4 above, and the presence of the interest group antagonisms that all but paralysed INPC. Had functioning diffusion mechanisms existed, TA and productivity programmes might have been of greater significance in relation to general attitude and opinion change. Britain's Anglo-American Council of Productivity experience indicates that exposure to a productivity message by no means ensures its adoption by the target audience. But in Ireland, absence of effective diffusion mechanisms meant that a wider industrial audience than those participating in the projects was seldom if ever reached by the message.

Education

By channelling resources to educational and training provision for managers and trade unionists, the productivity drive certainly ensured that an inquiry about 'facilities for the study of Mass Production, Industrial Management, Time and Motion and Trade Unionism in Ireland' could be answered in the affirmative by 1970. The movement also provided a forum within which defects of the Irish education system – notably its low post-primary participation rate and the neglect of science and technology within its schools and universities – could be raised. For instance, when the newly established HSC, seeking to identify topics it should prioritise, met a group of industrial managers for a general discussion in June 1959 'the most noteworthy feature was the emphasis laid on problems relating to education'. Here 'there was general agreement that many entrants to industry, who have had only national school education up to 14 years of age, are hampered by deficient basic education, by lack of self-confidence and by an absence of ambition towards self-improvement'.[12]

The transnational networks of the productivity drive, through which resources to develop specialised management and trade union provision flowed, also played a significant part in preparing the ground for the transformation of the mainstream of the Irish education system that occurred during the 1960s. The catalytic effect of the OECD-linked study that produced *Investment in Education* is a much-celebrated episode of Ireland's modernisation (O'Sullivan 1992). A remarkably broad consensus supported the initiative. Bureaucratic caution and ministerial self-preservation were set aside to allow a warts and all portrait of Irish education to be painted by the study team (O'Connor 1986: 63, Walsh 2005: 150). Special efforts were made to focus public attention on the findings of a damning report that legitimated a quickening pace of government action to increase access to an expanded, rationalised and reoriented education system (Walsh 2005: 158). This consolidated a fundamental change in social structure with the acquisition of educational credentials replacing the familial inheritance of property as the key determinant of life chances in Ireland. An expanding supply of educated labour, with business and technical skills featuring strongly, was an attraction to mobile capital investment that was marketed heavily by the IDA after its late 1960s revamp.

The political rhetoric surrounding the agency's overhaul had heralded an end to the wooing of foreign industrialists to the neglect of native ones. Henceforth, IDA was to place native and foreigner on a similar footing.[13] But through the 1970s the new IDA embarked on a push for US investment that had previously gravitated mainly towards the United Kingdom, proffering grants that its critics claimed were extravagantly large. At the beginning of the 1980s the Telesis report highlighted the extent to which Irish industrial policy had become IDA policy and the neglect suffered by indigenous industry in the process (NESC 1982). In the S&T field, extreme dependence on a flow of foreign high technology investment underlined the perpetuation of a weak national system of innovation (Mjoset 1992, Yearley 1995). By this point Irish-owned industry was contracting sharply with 27 per cent of jobs in this sector being lost between 1980 and 1987 (O'Malley 1989: 101–2). With foreign investment also stalling over this period, unemployment rose until it neared 20 per cent and mass emigration returned. The consequences of failures in the adaptation process set in motion by the CIO were now fully apparent. The route out of the 1950s slump had led into something remarkably similar in the 1980s. Some institutional factors that contributed to the manner in which the industrial adaptation agenda floundered will now be discussed.

Business community attitudes

The lack of business commitment to either intra-industry co-operation between firms in adaptation councils or the operation of joint approach bodies such as development councils, in spite of an FII subscription to the CIO and NIEC reports that advocated the creation of these different kinds of council, is particularly striking. It is also very difficult to interpret in the absence of access to FII records. A consultant to FII who also attended NIEC General Purposes Committee meeting as an alternate for its Director General, Garret FitzGerald (1968: 66) attributed the blocking of Development Councils to 'a reluctance to embark on a further experiment and . . . doubts about the wisdom of participating in joint bodies which would concern themselves with the future of each industry, and in which industrialists would face both trade unionists and officials'. Another NIEC insider on the trade union side, Charles McCarthy (1968: 97) considered the main factor in grassroots FII attitudes on the question to be 'the remarkably low level of sophistication of Irish management'.

Industry generally appears to have responded with considerable indifference to movements for management development that aimed to increase this sophistication. A Review Committee questionnaire on management development schemes sent out in 1961 to 450 IMI corporate members elicited a 'most disappointing' response rate of around 20 per cent. IMI's Director commented that 'it was obvious that, up to recently anyway, industry in this country was not alive to the importance of management' adding that 'this was in striking contrast to the attitude in European countries which he had visited'.[14] Presenting initial findings from the CIO industry surveys in April 1963, C. H. Murray concluded that 'in many Irish firms the survey reports showed that those at the head had not a proper grasp of the functions of management and how these functions should be discharged' (Murray 1963: 90). One of the general problems in industry's performance highlighted by Murray was insufficient specialisation, but when IMI organised a December 1962 seminar on variety reduction with a speaker from Imperial College in London the response was 'disappointing'.[15] 'Disappointing' was also the term quoted by the IMI managerial resources survey to describe local industry's response to the range of courses, including TWI, offered by the Cork and Limerick VEC colleges (Tomlin 1966: 314–15).

The prevalence of family-owned firms – in many of which, as we have seen, the CWC Jesuits detected an outlook of amoral familialism – was generally held to be chiefly responsible for both the extent of management shortcomings and the absence of positive interest in tacking this problem. Speaking at an IMI conference in May 1961, Lemass earmarked this ownership pattern for change:

> In the structure of Irish industry the main features are the comparatively small size, by international standards, of most of our industrial undertakings and the number of them which are still family concerns in the sense that they are controlled by the members of one family from which their top management personnel is drawn. In the circumstances of the years ahead, as we can now foresee them, changes in this pattern of ownership and control may be desirable and are possibly inevitable. Encouraging the right kind of changes may become an important purpose of national industrial policy.[16]

The management consultant interviewed for the NIEC industrial adaptation incentives report in late 1967 similarly observed that:

> In general he considered Irish management to be as good as management in Britain and Scotland. There were deficiencies in some areas such as marketing and management accounting; these were mainly due to a shortage of qualified people, which was in the process of being remedied. It seemed to him that there was also a larger proportion of managers who were prepared to accept the 'allright' or mediocre. Many of these were in family firms.[17]

The familial pattern was, however, one with deep societal roots. While southern Ireland's Catholic majority progressively acquired political control over the course of the nineteenth and early twentieth centuries, the commanding heights of the economy's private sector remained in Protestant hands. Employment discrimination against Catholics was being highlighted by the beginning of the twentieth century, but the form of remedial action prescribed for the sphere of owner-managed businesses and professions was that of 'favouring our friends', with preferential dealing by consumers being urged as the means of strengthening existing Catholic enterprises or creating new ones. Within an economy whose balance was to be altered in this way, religious discrimination in employment was accepted as a legitimate prerogative of the proprietor of a family firm. By contrast, even if privately owned, larger corporate institutions like railways companies and banks were not, it was argued, entitled to discriminate but had a duty to recruit and promote employees fairly (Murray 1987: 64–70). A tilting of the family firm sectarian imbalance by consumer action remained a pipedream, however, with only extreme sectarian violence in the north prompting periods of effective consumer boycotting against Belfast firms (Johnson 1981).

State introduction of tariff protection was to prove a much more practical agency of sectarian rebalancing through which 'the emergence of a new economic elite dependent on government helped redress the largely unionist sympathies of the dominant Irish business establishment in 1922' (Daly 1992: 180) and 'Fianna Fáil . . . kept its promise to consolidate and expand the national bourgeoisie' (Dunphy 1995: 160). Although Protestant businessmen remained prominent in some parts of the new protected economy, such as motor assembly (Jacobson 1989: 179), the lion's share of the opportunities accrued to Catholics against a backdrop of differential emigration rates that even involved the departure of older Protestant men already established in their careers (Kennedy 1973: 110–38). A rebalanced, but still segregated, business world took shape in the 1930s of which it could still be said in the early 1980s that 'until recently, most businesses in Ireland could be readily identified as either Protestant or Catholic' (Bowen 1983: 94). This reality was tacitly recognised by IMI:

> From the end of Sir Charles Harvey's term [in 1956] to the mid-1960s an informal pattern had developed with the chairmanship alternating between private enterprise and semi-state bodies, An astute member, noticing this, also observed a coincidental alternation between Protestant private sector businessmen and Catholic semi-staters! That, indeed, was the case: T. F. Laurie (private/Protestant). D. A. Hegarty (public/Catholic), A. H. Masser (private/Protestant), J. F. Dempsey (public/Catholic), M. Rigby-Jones (private/Protestant) (Cox 2002: 107)

Here, the absence of Catholic private sector businessmen is striking. If Catholics tended to accept the private sector business code of the long-dominant Protestants, as the CWC Jesuits argued they did, their acceptance encompassed recruitment and promotion practice based on ascriptive family and segregated religious community ties rather than achieved educational credentials. Of the 'remarkable degree of segregation' that disadvantaged them in the 1950s, Bowen (1983: 96) writes that 'no doubt many Catholics were envious, but they too thought along the same lines', citing the finding of a sociological study of the period (Alexander Humphreys' *New Dubliners*) that Catholics in the capital subscribed to the view that 'the greatest economic obligation of kinship in the city' was 'to get a relative a job'. By the 1970s, although by no means dead, 'the segregationist tendencies of the minority had undergone a very striking decline' that Bowen interprets as principally 'a product of the rapidly industrializing economy of the 1960s and 1970s which required an increasingly educated and technically skilled labour force in its pursuit of productivity and profit . . . increasingly employers were looking for technical and other educational qualifications that often could not be provided by the Protestant school system' (Bowen 1983: 98–103).

A wider perspective on the changing relationship between managerial recruitment and qualification is provided by a survey carried out by IMI in 1973 (Gorman et al. 1974). Taking Tomlin's 1964 data as a baseline for comparison, this found that over the period there was a 31 per cent increase in the number of managers employed in Irish transportable goods industries, accompanied by a marked increase in the proportion of managers holding degrees or professional qualifications. The result was that managers in Ireland 'seem to be rather similar to British managers in the extent to which they hold formal qualifications'. The increase in the number of managers employed was brought about by an increase in the number of large (500 or more employee) and medium-sized (100–499 employee) firms operating in these industries with neither the average number of managers per firm nor the employee-to-manager ratio changing significantly over the period. The population of firms had risen from 3,000 to around 3,400, as had the proportion of firms with more than 100 employees, from 10 to 14 per cent. One contributor to this was the merger activity that state adaptation policy had increasingly come to rely on. Also striking in 1973, but not comparable with 1964 owing to underestimation by the earlier date's sample, was the proportion of foreign firms within the large and medium categories – over a third in the case of the large firms and over a quarter in the case of the medium-sized ones (Gorman et al., 1974: 1–29). Concern with the adaptation of existing Irish firms to free trade conditions had been the dominant note when management education began to grow rapidly in the early 1960s. A decade later the competencies created by this expansion were being absorbed to a large extent by the rapid nativisation of management that characterised the burgeoning of the predominantly foreign-owned 'New Industry' sector.

Divisions within a weak state

That 1960s economic planning was a project of Finance that evoked a desultory response from others departments has often been acknowledged. Garret FitzGerald (1968: 68) noted how in its early days EDB's 'attempt to get some new projects off the ground met with resistance from a number of quarters, as other departments reacted against initiatives which they felt to be within their own areas of responsibility'. In 1969 C. H. Murray, referring to the Third Programme, noted the prevalence of 'a rather parochial attitude by departments to aspects of programmes which affect their own areas' that 'leads to the existence of as many pressure groups as departments and to the fragmentation of pressures for change' (quoted in Fanning 1978: 603). The preceding chapters have provided a number of concrete supporting illustrations. These include the blocking of EDB's proposed inquiry into the state of management education in 1960 and the negative response to suggestions for a programme of social development in 1964.

In relation to TA and the productivity drive, the key relationship was that between Finance and Industry and Commerce. This was at best uneasy with Garret FitzGerald (1991: 59) characterising interaction within CIO as 'Finance, the CII and ICTU endeavouring as a troika to nudge [Industry and Commerce] into psychological acceptance of free trade'. By 1967–8, the correspondence between Whitaker and J. C. B McCarthy in the context of prospective EEC entry negotiations shows that the divergence in outlook evident around the time of the OEEC free trade area exchanges continued. At a time when new initiatives were being brought forward to fill the vacuum left by the failure to operationalise the CIO's adaptation blueprint, Industry and Commerce had in George Colley an assertive post-protectionist minister. He was, however, one whose ambitions to lead Fianna Fáil and become Taoiseach may have inclined him towards constant emphasis on his department's territorial prerogatives in dealings with Charles Haughey, his chief party rival and holder of the 'premier' ministerial post.[18]

In this context there emerged not only 'as many pressure groups as departments' but as many as departments plus the organisations funded by grant-in-aid through their Votes. In the case of TA and the productivity drive, non-governmental organisations – principally IMI, RGDATA and the slowly reuniting trade union movement – had pushed for positive engagement with EPA at a time when government departments were satisfied with keeping up a modicum of appearances through the most minimal involvement. But, when

EPA was disbanded while domestic TA funding provision was expanded greatly within a context of freer trade and EEC membership pursuit, some of these organisations – whose scale of activities, staff numbers, and ambitions had also considerably enlarged[19] – became rival fishers in the same pool of resources.

When rivalries between organisations engaged in the promotion of greater efficiency and productivity (principally IMI and INPC) escalated into open turf warfare, government departments failed to initiate any action that went beyond deploring duplication and overlap between such bodies. Responding to questions put to him by a consultant reviewing INPC in May 1970, Ruaidhrí Roberts identified a need for 'a more selective and informed system of grant aid less dependent on particular organisational pressures'. He added that 'from this point of view an overall advisory committee would appear to be desirable to avoid financing duplicate activities and even, in a sense, financing organisation time spent on organisational competition for grant aid'.[20] Following a visit in 1966 during which he was based at IPA, Louis B. McCagg of the University of Pittsburgh's Graduate School of Public and International Affairs wrote a memorandum suggesting that better use needed to be made of Ireland's research and training institutes. Here McCagg was critical of 'uncoordinated, dispersed and isolated institutes', antiquated management practice, small scale of activity leading to low spin-off effect as well as 'an excessive exaggeration of stress between persons for the right to control and make decisions'.[21] Location on a common campus was suggested as a means of promoting cross-fertilisation but the expanding organisations concerned continued to make their accommodation arrangements separately and remained able to rely on the support of a departmental sponsor whilst waging their turf wars.

At a meeting with a deputation from FIM in April 1953 Lemass was asked for his definition of efficient production. He replied that 'he had stated over and over again that he would be satisfied with production of goods here at comparable prices with those produced in Great Britain quality for quality'.[22] This British benchmark would be an increasingly treacherous one, given the extent to which Britain experienced worsening problems of industrial competitiveness in the post-war period. Even if it were achieved, comparability or convergence with Britain on various measures did not ensure an adequate level of industrial adaptation to a European free trade environment. Of relevance here is the contrast drawn by Mjoset (1992: 9) between Ireland's position as 'a free rider on Britain's economic decline' and that of industrially successful small European states that were free riders on Germany's 'economic miracle' (see also Girvin 2004). Moreover, its relations with Britain did not merely yoke Ireland to an economic power in long-term decline. They also bestowed an institutional legacy that blocked the achievement of the kind of historical compromise between collective actors that might have provided a basis for breaking out of the resultant vicious circle. A comparison of Sweden, West Germany and the United Kingdom in the decade after 1945 concludes that, although its initial circumstances were in many ways the most favourable to the achievement of this outcome, the United Kingdom failed, relative to the other two states, to institutionalise a functioning productivity coalition:

> An effective productivity coalition requires a proactive state to persuade, threaten, or even coerce institutions into a cooperative bargain and to develop the machinery of coordination that consolidates such bargains (Booth et al. 1997: 436).

Analysing this British failure, they argue that 'perhaps the key lies in its liberal and reactive state tradition'. 'The British legacy of a weak state without a significant tradition of government economic intervention' has been held to be 'of crucial importance' both in limiting the scope of the transformation of the Irish economy wrought by Fianna Fáil policies in the 1930s and in subsequently inhibiting action to tackle inefficiencies in the protected industrial sector these policies created (Daly 1992: 176–9).

Having had its strong 1946 efficiency proposals watered down, Industry and Commerce added to the Bill it brought forward provisions for the creation of industrial development councils. Of these Lemass later said that:

> his hope had been that through these councils there would develop a sense of common responsibility for industrial efficiency, for the giving of good service by industry to the people, and that by a joint approach to these problems of costs by reason of obsolete equipment, working methods and labour rules, a remedy for them would be found which would on the one hand reduce the price of industrial products to our own people and on the other enable industrial expansion to march ahead to the benefit of the whole nation, and not least to the workers who were looking to industry for the creation of an ever widening pool of employment.

But because 'that provision became the focus of controversy and was strongly assailed by the Federation of Irish Manufacturers which saw it as a danger to the integrity and independence of industrial managements' he did not, having returned to office in 1951, intend to revive it as 'there would be no sense in reawakening the controversy it engendered'.[23]

In earlier chapters we saw how Industry and Commerce's intention to turn manufacturers from tariff reliance to technique improvement was thwarted by a firm's unchallenged refusal to avail itself of subsidised technical assistance. We also saw this department admit that it had no effective means of enforcing the price undertakings it had been given by protected industries. The protectionist Irish state could enmesh the industrial sector of its economy in a thick jungle of minute regulation, but it lacked the capacity to supply consistent developmental direction to that sector.

By the late 1960s, a new proposal for development councils had met with the same fate as the old one. On this occasion, as we saw in chapter 4, the NIEC's observation that 'new institutional arrangements take time' provided its elegy. Yet, if this was the case, the whole rationale of the dash for free trade embarked on when the decision was made in 1961 to seek full EEC membership is called into question. Whether the CIO's framework for tackling the adaptation to free trade was ever a feasible one may be questioned. What is certain is that, deprived of forceful state action to support its implementation, its mix of technical assistance and productivity mobilisation techniques was doomed to failure.

Bad timing?

A problem of timing would admittedly have faced even a forcefully adaptive Irish state. The heyday of technical assistance and productivity drive for most of Europe was in the middle of the 1950s. In Ireland the activity peak came almost a decade later. By this stage the industrial environment across much of Europe was becoming more turbulent. Irish industry-level joint action was being attempted within a context of extensive conflict between unions, employers and government over wage restraint and industrial relations regulation in what has been dubbed 'the decade of upheaval' (McCarthy 1973). Denis Hegarty had informed the members of EPA's Governing Body in February 1960 that in Ireland 'though the Employers' organizations and the Trade Unions are well organised and there is a fairly good relationship between them on the negative side of industrial relations (absence of serious strikes etc.) it was only very recently that a climate of opinion was created which made possible the kind of joint action necessary to support a productivity drive'.[24]

However, serious strikes were far from absent during the decade that followed as strong grassroots pressure for wage increases made its presence felt (Allen 1997). Increasingly drawn into the economic planning machinery, the trade union leadership was constrained by an acute awareness of the need to watch its back and was resistant to government pressure to accept the introduction of a national incomes policy. Accompanied by calls for new punitive legislation, lack of discipline within the union movement was denounced by the employers' organisations and by government ministers overseeing strike-prone semi-state companies like CIE (see Murray 2005a) and the ESB. Thus the climate of opinion changed over time in ways that significantly diminished the degree to which 'the kind of joint action necessary to support a productivity drive' was possible. As Ruaidhrí Roberts put it in 1970, 'it is unrealistic to envisage a situation in which workers and employers end a morning "bargaining" meeting having failed to resolve a dispute about interests, and proceed in the afternoon to a joint meeting about how to expand production'.[25]

Adaptation and Labour incorporation

But if the adaptation process failed to bring unions and employers together in functioning industry level institutions, it did provide a framework in which a relationship between government and unions of great political benefit to the Fianna Fáil party was forged:

> Although from a purely institutional point of view Ireland was deficient in its corporatist structures, a substantial enough set of institutions did exist, which when taken together with expansionist programmes of public expenditure initiated in the early 1960s, elicited a crucial union commitment to Lemass's economic strategy. The political significance of his achievement should be appreciated – especially since its actual technical economic success was not substantial (Bew and Patterson 1982: 189)

The process of successful incorporation emphasised here is one that can also be seen to have framed the development of Irish trade union education and training services. Ostensible enthusiasm for joint approach bodies operating within an overall planning process masked significant misgivings within the trade union movement, according to some of its leading figures. Fear of being saddled with the responsibility for redundancies and unemployment was central to these doubts. Business hostility to encroachment on the prerogatives of management allowed trade union reservations to remain unexpressed. Akin to this fundamental tenet of business was the independence of the trade union movement from the state. But being both a substantial TA payments recipient and a productivity drive supporter was to bring this independence into question.

Historians of the WEA in Northern Ireland note that 'the pioneering period of workers' education took place before partition and in theory at least could have developed in Dublin, Galway or Cork as much as in Belfast' (Nolan and Johnston 2003: 24). That it did not is attributable to a combination of industrial structure and ideology. Structurally British industrial cities and Belfast had a mass of better-paid and/or securely employed workers sufficiently large for movements like consumer co-operation to take root in a way that was absent in the industrially undeveloped south. In 1914 co-operative societies had built up a membership of between 15,000 and 20,000 in Belfast and the industrial towns adjacent to it but outside the north-east Irish consumer co-operation had established itself only in isolated enclaves and around specific untypical occupational communities, such as railway company workers in Inchicore, Greenore or Rosslare (Murray 1987: 228–30). At the time of the 1913–14 lockout James Larkin aspired to create in Dublin the type of self-contained and self-sufficient proletarian culture whose development was a feature of the growth of the socialist movement in Britain and many European countries in this period (Holton 1976: 187–8).

A three-city comparative study notes that 'in Bristol and, to a lesser degree Belfast, the "middle class" began to support "labour" institutions such as the Fabians or the WEA', while 'in Dublin the professional and white collar classes were involved in the National party and its cultural and language activities' (Lynch 1998: 56). Provided recognition is given to the existence of contending 'orthodox' and 'radical' nationalist groups in Dublin, and to the significantly 'non-political and non-sectarian' basis upon which most cultural nationalist activities were organised (Murray 1987: 175–251), this is accurate. In the absence of a vibrant socialist milieu, the type of white collar or skilled manual worker whose British (or even Belfast) equivalent tended to gravitate towards WEA, Labour Colleges, co-operative societies or the Independent Labour Party was often recruited into Gaelic revival organisations which provided a not dissimilar mix of social activities but in a distinctly different ideological context. As a young Alfred O'Rahilly put it in the *WEA Handbook 1918*:

> It may surprise English readers to be told that in no country is adult education so flourishing as in Ireland. The Gaelic League and related activities are really

> the Irish equivalent of the Workers Educational Association. The greatest educational achievement of Ireland is to be found in the Gaelic Movement (quoted in Lynch 1998: 55)

The Dublin lockout of 1913–14 prompted the Catholic hierarchy to issue a pastoral letter containing an exposition of the papal teaching on the relations between social classes in industrial society as set out in the encyclical *Rerum Novarum*. However, Catholic social action movements did not really prioritise or pay sustained attention to educating trade unionists until O'Rahilly began wielding the cudgel of anti-communism in the mid-1940s. The Catholic movement he began dominated adult education and marginalised the labourist alternative sponsored by one of a split union movement's two congresses.

Productivity one of its US exponents in 1951 declared to be 'a mid-twentieth century alternative to Marxism'.[26] Irish circumstances hardly called for such an alternative to be promoted but Ireland's OEEC membership made it accessible to Irish trade union leaders. The prospect of workers receiving a share of the benefits of higher productivity and of unions coming together with employers and government in pursuit of productivity gain was rather more attractive than the frugal comfort regarded by Catholic social thinking as sufficient to satisfy workers' legitimate entitlements. In the field of trade union education, the productivity drive offered the leadership of a movement reunited only after the most protracted efforts a seductive combination of reasonably substantial resources and a legitimacy largely unassailable from the powerful forces to its right. The courses provided might be characterised as narrow training rather than broad education but a process of de-radicalisation was hardly involved as earlier educational provision for workers had been forced to eschew even moderate labourism in order to survive.[27]

A decade after ICTU embarked on the provision of an education service with EPA assistance, it declared that:

> The trade union movement . . . is formed of organisations controlled by trade union members. It cannot perform its functions properly if it is subsumed in governmental or other such organisations. Its autonomy must be jealously preserved if it is to fulfil its function, and to retain the trust and confidence of its members . . . education which is concerned with the field of trade union policies and practices must be the responsibility of the trade union movement . . . [there is a] need for a strong and well organised trade union education organisation, apart from and independent of all other organisations. It is for

this reason that, over the past ten years, the ICTU has consistently followed a policy of building up, under its own control a trade union education service. This educational service requires further development (ICTU Annual Report 1969–70: 85)

This rhetoric of trade-union movement control over the aspects of education specifically relevant to its discharge of a vital social role jarred with the reality of its financial dependence, first on international organisations and then on the Irish government. At the beginning of the 1970s developments north of the border briefly attracted attention to such dependence. In the immediate post-war period the ITUC found itself discriminated against on account of its British-based unions by a Dublin government that favoured the rival CIU. It was at the same time refused recognition by the Stormont government on the grounds that, although it had a more-or-less autonomous Northern Ireland Committee, its headquarters were in Dublin and it was therefore controlled from a foreign state. Attempts to form a Productivity Council for Northern Ireland in the late 1950s and early 1960s foundered on this obstacle despite business and Protestant church support. Finally, in 1964, Lord Brookeborough, having been succeeded as Prime Minister by Captain Terence O'Neill, a formula for ICTU recognition was worked out and tripartite economic planning bodies got off the ground (Boyd 1972, Mulholland 1997).

Within five years, relations between the Stormont government and ICTU had moved from standoff to subvention with the offer of a £10,000 annual grant to support in the north the kind of educational and work study advisory service ICTU had established in the south with INPC funding. This proposal aroused opposition that reflected both the northern trade union tradition of independent working-class education and the political context in which Stormont's system of sectarian domination was breaking down in the face of the challenge mounted by Northern Ireland's insurgent Catholic minority. ICTU accepted the grant nonetheless, a course of action defended by leaders like John Swift and the Belfast Communist Andy Barr (Boyd 1972, 1984, 1999).

The attention focused in the north on state subvention of trade union education spilled over into the south with the publication in the *Irish Independent* between 22 and 26 February 1971 of a series of articles by its industrial correspondent, John Devine, entitled 'State Money and the Unions'. The flavour of the series is conveyed by the article headlines – 'From the Irish taxpayer – £23,000 a year', 'No political strings – but is the position healthy?', 'Cold look at the annual report', 'Is movement behind the involvement?', 'Contrast in attitude of British TUC'. The series failed, however, to spark off any significant debate about the issues which it highlighted. State subvention continued to increase both north and south while the British TUC soon ceased to provide an example of financial independence and embarked down the same path (Smith 1984). An explanation of why debate was absent is provided by a 1970 survey that placed trade union education in the wider context of adult education of all kinds in the south. This observed that:

> While some trade unions are developing educational services for their members, it is obvious both from the response and lack of response to this Survey that trade unions generally give little attention to this question. This is not for want of the appreciation of the value of such services by trade union executives. We believe that the explanation is to be found in the general attitude of trade unionists . . . and their understanding of the role and purpose of trade unions in society. Education is not regarded by any means as an important service to be provided by the trade unions for their membership. Resources (both financial and otherwise) are, therefore, scant, and many trade unionists would be reluctant to provide them by means of increased subscriptions which they would have to pay in order to sustain an education programme (Department of Education 1970: 121)

Contentious as its content and control became at times, trade union education thus appears to have been a peripheral concern for the mass of the members. What they were seen as being reluctant to fund was proffered support by EPA for a short but crucial period. With adaptation to free trade conditions for EEC entry prioritised, technical assistance grant aid became so ubiquitous in 1960s Ireland that significant subvention rather than financial independence was the norm for a wide range of bodies that appeared to belong to civil society rather than to the state. Within such a generalised state of dependency, relativity claims with the 'wage leader' of Irish technical assistance recipients, the Irish Management Institute, became the effective frame of reference within which the organisation of trade union education came to be discussed.

Notes

Chapter One: Protected Irish Industry and Post-War European Free Trade

1 NAI DIC R303/11/3 OEEC: proposals for technical assistance projects, D. Neligan to Secretary, Department of Industry and Commerce 1/1/1950: draft reply undated.

2 NAI DT S 13814 A Control of Prices and Promotion of Industrial Efficiency Legislation 1947–.

3 NAI DIC 315/13 Proposed European Free Trade Area Div. 'A' File: European Free Trade Area First Meetings of OEEC Working Parties nos 21, 22 and 23; Report by Department of Industry and Commerce Delegate.

4 NAI DFA 305/57/343 F Part 2 FTA – WP23 Financial Experts attached to Working Party 23 (including visit to Dublin, May, 1958) Report of Meeting, Visit of Financial Experts of OEEC Working Party no. 23, 5 May 1958.

5 NAI DFA 305/57/343 F Report of Meeting, European Free Trade Area: Visit of Financial Experts of Working Party no. 23, 8 May 1958.

6 NAI DFA 305/57/343 F Report of Meeting, Visit of Financial Experts of OEEC Working Party no. 23, 2 May 1958.

7 NAI DFA 305/57/343 F J. C. B. McCarthy, Secretary, Industry and Commerce to W. P. Fay, Head of Irish Delegation to OEEC 11/6/1958.

8 NAI DIC 315/13 Draft Memorandum for British, June 1959.

Chapter Two: Marshall Plan Innovations

1 NAI DFA 305/57/112 Dollar Fund for Special Technical Assistance Part III H. McCann, Washington Embassy to Secretary, External Affairs 5/9/1951.

2 NARA RG 469 Europe Ireland Division 1948–1953 Box 2 folder Industrial Development: the quotation is from the December 1949 issue of *Irish Industry*; NAI DFA 305/57/112 Part 1 Note of Meeting held on 28/11/1949.

3 NAI DFA 305/57/112/6 Technical Assistance Project Phases I and II (44–80): industrial survey of Ireland Part 1 H. McCann, Washington Legation to Secretary, External Affairs 13/1/1950.

4 NARA RG 469 Mission to Ireland Director Subject Box 1 folder ECA/W – General, 1948–9 E. T. Dickinson Jr, ECA Washington. to J. Carrigan, ECA Mission to Ireland 28/12/1949.

5 NARA RG 469 Europe Ireland Division 1948–1953 Box 2 folder Industrial Development: W.H. Taft III, ECA Mission to Ireland to J. R. Nelson, ECA Washington 26/11/1949.

6 NARA RG 469 Mission to Ireland Director Subject Box 1 folder ECA/W – General, 1948–49 E.T. Dickinson Jr, ECA Washington to J. Carrigan, ECA Mission to Ireland 28/12/1949.
7 NARA RG 469 entry 1245 Director Subject Box 1 folder ECA/W – General 1950 J. Carrigan, ECA Mission to E. T. Dickinson, Jr, ECA Washington 15/2/1950.
8 NAI DFA 305/57/112 Dollar Fund for Special Technical Assistance F. H. Boland, External Affairs to T. Murray, Industry and Commerce, 16/2/1950: J. Leydon, Industry and Commerce to F. H. Boland, External Affairs 10/3/1950.
9 NARA RG 469 Mission to Ireland Director Subject Box 1 folder Department of External Affairs 1948–49 (Mr MacBride) J. Carrigan, ECA Mission to Ireland to S. MacBride, Minister for External Affairs 5/1/ 1950.
10 NAI DT S 14504 A/1 European Recovery Programme: Funds for Provision of Technical Assistance: Department of External Affairs Memorandum to the Government 'Technical Assistance Projects', 10/2/1950.
11 NARA RG 469 Taft General Box 1 folder 1033 Industrial Development Authority W. H. Taft III, ECA Mission to J. P. Beddy, IDA 6/1/1950.
12 NAI DT S 14504 A/1 European Recovery Programme: Funds for Provision of Technical Assistance: Department of External Affairs Memorandum to the Government 'Utilization of Technical Assistance Facilities provided by the Economic Cooperation Administration', 17/4/1950.
13 See NAI DFA 305/57/112/6 Technical Assistance Project Phases I and II (44–80): industrial survey of Ireland Part 1: see also Murray (2008: 14–16).
14 NARA RG 469 entry 1251 Taft Technical Assistance folder 304 TA Budget copy of J. A. Cassidy, IDA to Secretary, External Affairs, 21/10/1950.
15 NAI DFA 305/57/245 Department of External Affairs Memorandum to the Government, 'Expectations of Continued Marshall Aid and Technical Assistance', 28/12/1950.
16 NARA RG 469 Entry 1245 Director Subject Box 1 folder Depart. Of External Affairs 1948–49 (MacBride) P. Miller, ECA Mission to S. MacBride, Minister for External Affairs, 15/1/1951: NAI DFA 305/57/112 Part III 'Progress Report on Implementation of Expanded Programme of T.A. Submitted to Mr Miller on 27th December 1950' 8/3/1951.
17 NAI DFA 305/57/112 Dollar Fund for Special Technical Assistance part III B. Gallagher, External Affairs note to Minister on meeting with Harry Clement, 7 February 1951.
18 This envisaged 'a panel of five highly qualified technicians and economists to be available to the Irish Government for advice on the over-all utilization of the results of technical assistance projects, and on such other technical aspects of the national economy as may be referred to them from time to time. The panel might include one commodity specialist, one general, one agricultural and one industrial economist, one labour-training and evaluation expert'. The proposal does not seem to have developed further and appears to have been overtaken by the inter-party government's disintegration in the spring and early summer of 1951. Clement records MacBride as telling him in March that 'he still wanted to go ahead with it and that I should phone him as soon as he returns to Ireland. He feels that he would be personally involved in the development of this project and that the advisors concerned should be assigned to the Taoiseach who would then reassign them to the various Ministers', NARA RG 469 Entry 1246 Director Misc. Subject folder Memos Clement to Miller memorandum

from H. Clement, ECA Mission to P. Miller, ECA Mission 'Conversation with MacBride, March 8', 8/3/1951.

19 NAI DFA 305/57/112/57 P. Miller Application for Technical Assistance 'Special Industrial Problems', 4 June 1951.

20 NAI DFA 305/57/112/53 J. Cassidy, IDA to Secretary, External Affairs, 9 June 1951.

21 NAI DFA 305/57/112/58 Paul E. Miller 'Ireland TA 44–77 Direct Productivity Assistance', undated.

22 On the military side, the US Ambassador reported that 'they felt that by so doing they would be undertaking to render military assistance to other nations which they had as yet in no instance agreed to do, and to which they are not at this time prepared to commit themselves' (quoted in Davis (1998: 216)). The External Affairs Memorandum to the Government 'Enactment of Mutual Security Act by US Congress – Demarche by American Ambassador', 17 December 1951 (NAI DFA 305/57/275 The Mutual Security Act, 1951 (The Foreign Aid Bill)) also noted that 'apart from the emphasis on military-security, it will be noticed that the preamble to Section 101 (a) mentions as an object of the appropriations authorised by that section 'to further encourage the economic unification and political federation of Europe'. This goes much further than any previous statement of the desire of the American legislature to see the creation of a unified Europe'.

23 NAI DFA 305/57/275 The Mutual Security Act, 1951 (The Foreign Aid Bill) J. Hearne, Washington Ambassador to Secretary, External Affairs, 14 January 1952.

24 NAI DIC R303/8/18 European Recovery Programme: Formation of new Mutual Security Agency to replace ECA: report from H. McCann, Washington Embassy, 9/7/1952.

25 NAI DIC R303/8/18 Secretary, External Affairs to Secretary, Industry and Commerce 1/8/1952, Secretary, Industry and Commerce to Secretary, External Affairs 27/8/1952, Industry and Commerce minute O'Riordan to St John Connolly 18/8/1952.

26 NAI DFA 305/57/112/53 Note 'Technical Assistance Projects Sponsored by the Industrial Development Authority' attached to J. Haughey, IDA to T. Commins, External Affairs, 7 March 1951.

27 NARA RG 469 Entry 1250 Records of US Foreign Assistance Agencies, 1948–61 Mission to Ireland Industry, Tourism and Special Projects Officer, Willam. H. Taft, III Subject Files 1949–51 Box 1 Folder Industrial Produc. meeting, Paris 27–29 March 1950,W. H. Taft III, ECA Mission to John Quinn, Technical Assistance Division, Office of the Special Representative, Paris 16/3/1950.

28 NAI DFA 305/57/226 Establishment of a Productivity Centre in Ireland.

29 NAI DFA 305/57/226 J. P. Beddy, IDA to S. McBride, Minister for External Affairs 9/4/1951.

30 NAI DFA 305/57/226 memorandum 22/6/1951: handwritten note conveying Minister's suggestion dated 3/7/1951.

31 NAI DFA 305/57/226. copy of Report of Meeting, Agency for Securing Increased Productivity, 8/8/1951.

32 NAI DFA 305/57/226 H. McCann, Washington Embassy to Secretary, External Affairs 29/8/1951.

33 NAI DFA 305/57/226 Report of Meeting, Technical Assistance, 8 September 1951.

34 NAI DFA 305/57/112 Dollar Fund for Special Technical Assistance: H. Clement, ECA Mission to Ireland to T. Commins, External Affairs 18/10/1951: Secretary, External Affairs to Secretary, Finance 7/12/1951.

Chapter Three: US innovations after US Aid

1 NAI DIC R303/8/18 European Recovery Programme: Formation of new Mutual Security Agency to replace ECA: Government Secretary to Secretary, External Affairs 15/2/1952.

2 NAI DFA 99/3/70 OEEC Grant Counterpart Fund Establishment of a Fund for defraying in whole or part the cost of Technical Assistance Projects: F. Aiken, Minister for External Affairs to J. Matthews, US Ambassador 4/6/1952.

3 NAI DETE 2000/13/6 Minutes of Departmental Conference no. 244, Item 15 Technical Assistance Schemes Relating to Manufacturing Development, 10/3/1952.

4 NAI DETE 2000/13/6 Minutes of Departmental Conference no. 240, Item 19 Coras Trachtala, Teo: Technical Assistance Schemes 4/2/1952.

5 CTT was a marketing rather than a production-focused organization with limited capacity to follow up on the myriad problems identified. It did, however, subsequently sponsor a technical assistance project that got under way in the mid-1950s in which a Belgian consultant worked with a number of woolen and worsted manufacturers to improve the design of their products. In September 1954 CTT ceased to be a purely dollar export agency when an extension of its promotional activities to include non-dollar areas was approved by the Government: see NAI DT S14818 C Industry and Commerce Memorandum for the Government Extension of the Activities of Coras Trachtala, 9 September 1954.

6 See NAI DFA 305/57/112/58/3 for correspondence.

7 NAI DETE 2000/13/6 Minutes of Departmental Conference no. 244, Item 16 Technical Assistance for Industries, 10/3/1952.

8 Ibid. Minutes of Departmental Conference no. 256 Item 14 Tariff Applications: General, 9/6/1952.

9 NAI DETE 2000/13/9 Minutes of Departmental Conference no. 322, Item 32 Industrial surveys and Item 33 Tariff reviews, 30/11/1953.

10 NAI DETE 2000/13/8 Minutes of Departmental Conference no. 296, Item 6 Industrial Surveys, 28/4/1953.

11 NAI DETE 2000/13/8 Minutes of Departmental Conference no. 288, Item 10 Protection: Compliance with undertakings etc. 23/2/1953.

12 NAI DETE 2000/13/9 Minutes of Departmental Conference no. 322, Item 33 Tariff reviews 30/11/1953.

13 NAI DETE 2000/13/10 Minutes of Departmental Conference no. 346 Item 5 Tariff Reviews, 26/4/1954.

14 NAI DETE 2000/12/1138 Technical Assistance Scheme Division B Solus Teo. Cork Abbey Bray, D. O'Donohue, Solus Teo to Secretary, IDA 9/10/1950: Industry and Commerce minute JM to Mr Cassidy 14/11/1951.

15 NAI DETE 2000/12/1138 Minute B. Devlin to Mr Murray 19/5/1952.

16 NAI DETE 2000/12/1138 D. O'Donohue, Solus Teo To Industry and Commerce 27/5/1952: various minutes May–June 1952.

17 NAI DETE 2000/12/1138 copy O. J. Redmond, Finance to Secretary, Industry and Commerce, 14/4/1953.
18 NAI DETE 2000/13/8 Minutes of Departmental Conference no. 301, 1/6/1953, Item 19 Manufacture of electric lamps: French proposal.
19 NAI DETE 2000/12/1281 Electric Filament Lamps – Survey, 'Report of Interview manufacture of electric lamps by Solus Teoranta' 30/4/1954: various minutes May 1953–May 1954.
20 NAI DETE 2000/12/1281 Submission for Departmental Conference 'Proposed manufacture of electric filament lamps by the Philips Radio Manufacturing Co. Ltd.' 7/1/1955: Report of Interview Proposed manufacture of electric filament lamps by the Philips Radio Manufacturing Co. Ltd 1/2/1955: Minute 6/2/1958.
21 NAI DETE 2000/13/13 Minutes of Departmental Conference no. 383, 18/1/1955 Item 14 Proposed manufacture of electric filament lamps by the Philips.
22 See NAI DIC R303/13/11/1 Negotiating of Technical Assistance Sub-Agreement between Ireland and U.S., governing the disposition of balance in Counterpart Special Account; also NAI DFA 99/3/70 OEEC Grant Counterpart Fund Establishment of a Fund for defraying in whole or part the cost of Technical Assistance Projects.
23 According to the project description, 'practically all our imports come from Britain. On a number of occasions in the past imports from Britain have been curtailed, due to production difficulties in that country, while the cost of imported coal has been rising steadily for the past few years. It is not unreasonable to assume that, in future, there will be recurring difficulties in securing from Britain our full import requirements of coal, and it is probable that imports will become still more expensive': for the Director of the Geological Survey's optimism see NAI DETE 2000/13/13 Minutes of Departmental Conference no. 424 Item 24 Technical Assistance Project: Coal Exploration 31/11/1955.
24 See project description in NAI DIC R303/13/11/1 Negotiating of Technical Assistance Sub-Agreement between Ireland and US governing the disposition of balance in Counterpart Special Account.
25 NAI DIC R303/13/11/1 for 1955–6 interdepartmental correspondence and Interdepartmental ERP Committee discussions.
26 NAI DT S 15453 A European Productivity Agency.
27 NAI DIC R303/7/59 Establishment of National Productivity Centre in Ireland, Extract from Report of Industry and Commerce Departmental Conference 2/3/1954.
28 NAI DIC R303/7/59 Industries Division A 'European Productivity Agency', January 1958.
29 See NAI DL W93 Organisation for European Economic Co-operation: European Productivity Agency Human Relations in Industry EPA Project no. 312 Stage B Rome Conference minute Miss Brewster to Mr McCarthy 27/8/1955.
30 NAI DL W93 for memoranda and correspondence.
31 For full details see NAI DIC R303/8/12 State Aid to Participants in EPA Projects.
32 See NAI DFA 305/57/204/69 OEEC Technical Assistance Programme: Irish participation in OEEC missions following suspension of US aid.
33 NAI DFA 305/57/168/34 OEEC Productivity and Applied Research Committee: European Productivity Agency: proposal for setting up a centre Part 6 Secretary, Agriculture to Secretary, External Affairs 17/6/1956; Industry and Commerce to Secretary, External Affairs 27/6/1956.

34 NAI DFA 99/3/70 OEEC Grant Counterpart Fund Establishment of a Fund for defraying in whole or part the cost of Technical Assistance Projects: B. Durnin, Washington Embassy to Secretary, External Affairs 29/8/1955.
35 NAI DETE 2000/12/1586 Irish Management Institute Request for Technical Assistance Grant towards Management Development Unit: minute 28/5/1957.
36 See NAI DT S 14,504 B European Recovery Programme: funds for provision of technical assistance Industry and Commerce Memorandum for the Government, Technical assistance for Industry, 6 January 1958 and Secretary to the Government to Private Secretaries, Minister for Finance and Industry and Commerce 13/1/1958 conveying decision of Government meeting on 9/1/1958. The maximum state contribution was cut from half to one third of the cost of a project at this point.
37 See NAI DFA FA 305/57/168/421 Areas in the process of economic development 1957–61.
38 NAI DFA 444/23 Proposals for continuation of certain EPA activities in OECD: OEEC EPA/D/7513 21/1/1960 1960–61 Programme of the 'New Agency' Sector I Industry and Commerce Statement by the Delegate for Ireland.
39 NAI DFA 444/23 EPA/GB/M (60) 1 Dated 18 March 1960 Extract from the Minutes of 12 Session of the Governing Body of the European Productivity Agency Held on 4 and 5 February 1960.
40 NAI DFA 444/23 memorandum PC-9 'Preparatory Committee on Reorganisation of OEEC' 19/10/1960.
41 NAI DFA 444/23 Secretary, Taoiseach to Secretary, External Affairs 27/10/1960.
42 NAI DFA 444/23 memorandum 'Question of Irish Participation in the Technical Assistance Programmes of the OECD for countries in the process of economic development'.
43 NAI DFA 444/23 Note of Meeting of secretaries held in Department of Finance 8 February 1961: Brief for Irish Member of the Preparatory Committee on the reorganisation of the European Productivity Agency in the new organisation, February 1961; Observations of the Department of Industry and Commerce on the proposals contained in Document OECD /P (61) 30, 24/6/1961.
44 NAI DFA 444/23 Note 'European Productivity Agency' 8/5/1962: S. Murphy minute 21/5/1962; S. Murphy note of telephone conversation with J. Gannon, INPC Secretary 26/5/1962.
45 See conference material in NAI ICTU Box 352.
46 NAI DFA 444/23 Proposals for continuation of certain EPA activities in OECD: S. Murphy, Irish Delegate to OECD Preparatory Committee to Secretary, External Affairs 21/1/1961.
47 NAI DFA 305/57/15 Draft Minutes of Meeting of the Interdepartmental ERP Committee 5/10/1962.
48 See 'Government Notice Technical Assistance Grants to Promote Productive Efficiency in Industry' dated 6/9/1962, *Management* 9 (10), October 1962.
49 See also NAI DF 2001/3/643 Productivity of industrial consultants.

Chapter Four: Partners in Adaptation?

1 NAI DIC TIC 33339 Industrial Research Council: proposed establishment of a separate research institute. Proposed establishment of Institute for Industrial Research and Standards: preparation necessary legislation: Industrial Research and Standards Act 1946. Industrial Research and Standards Bill 1946.

2 NAI DIC 2000/13/7 Minutes of Departmental Conference no. 267, 22 September 1952, Item 9 Industrial Research and Standards: Amending Legislation.

3 NAI DIC R303/7/59 Establishment of National Productivity Centre in Ireland: D. Flood, Director IIRS to Secretary, Industry and Commerce 26/7/1955.

4 NAI DFA 305/57/226 Establishment of a Productivity Centre in Ireland: J. P. Beddy, IDA to S. MacBride, Minister for External Affairs 9/4/1951.

5 NAI DIC R303/7/67 Papers regarding Productivity Committee: Report of Third Informal Meeting Held on the 5 July, 1955, in the Institute for Industrial Research and Standards to Discuss the Setting up of a Productivity Centre.

6 See NAI DFA 305 /57/112/28 Technical Assistance project no. 44/93, 44/94 Central Council of Congress of Irish Unions application to send a team of trade unionists to the USA to study American industrial productivity and production methods etc.: NAI DFA 305/57/204/31 Technical Assistance Mission no. 88 to study productivity methods in US and participate in international productivity congress in November: NAI DL W113 ECA. Mission to USA to study labour relations and productivity – employers; NAI DL W117 ECA Mission to the United States to study labour relations and productivity.

7 See NAI DT S13,700 Congress of Irish Unions: Uniformity of State action following recognition of.

8 NAI DIC R303/7/59 Establishment of National Productivity Centre in Ireland Chairman and Director, IIRS to Minister for Industry and Commerce 30/11/1956.

9 NAI DIC R303/7/59 Extract from report of Departmental conference 28/1/1957: extract from report of Departmental conference 6/5/1957.

10 See NAI DIC R303/8/12 State Aid to Participants in EPA Projects.

11 See NAI DIC TIW/1280/1 for draft, related notes and memoranda: see NAI DETE 2000/13/18 Minutes of Departmental Conference no. 496 Item 19 European Productivity Agency suggestion for establishment of a Joint Committee to study human problems in industry 1/7/1957 for the decision.

12 NAI DIC TIW/1280/1; NAI DIC R303/7/59 Establishment of National Productivity Centre in Ireland and ICTU 4/268/Box 30 Establishment of Human Sciences Committee and of Productivity Committee.

13 NAI DIC R303/7/75 Statement of Productivity Principles.

14 Ibid., also NAI DIC R303/7/74 Statement of Productivity Principles and NAI DT S 15,453 D/1 European Productivity Agency: Industrial Productivity: Irish National Productivity Committee: National Employer/Worker Conference, 1962, S 15,453 D/2/61 Industrial Productivity: Irish National Productivity Committee and S 15, 453 E/61 Industrial Productivity: Irish National Productivity Committee.

15 NAI DT S 15,453 F/61 Industrial Productivity: Irish National Productivity Committee.

16 During the 1960s, the FIM changed its name first to Federation of Irish Industries (FII) and then to the Confederation of Irish Industry (CII). The changes of name coincided with a shift in stance from being a protectionist lobby group to participating in the structures designed to promote the adaptation of industries to free trade.
17 NAI DIC 2000/12/114 Organisations Which Have as an Objective the Improvement of Efficiency in Industry.
18 NAI DT S 15,453 F/61 Industrial Productivity: Irish National Productivity Committee and S 15,453 G/62 Industrial Productivity: Irish National Productivity Agency.
19 NAI DT S 15,453 G/62 Industrial Productivity: Irish National Productivity Agency, Jack Lynch, Minister for Industry and Commerce to Sean Lemass, Taoiseach 30/3/1962.
20 NAI ICTU Box 216: 3505 INPC Advisory Services 1965–6 'Proposed Discussions on Future of Advisory Service Background Document INPC 6 May 1968': for the wider context see also NAI ICTU Box 215: 3502 IPC Committee of Management From February 1970 to October 1971: Memo from Chief Executive Officer to Committee of Management 'Development and representation of the recommendations made by Messrs. Dalen & Hubert about the future of the Irish National Productivity Committee' 14/11/1970.
21 NAI DF 2001/3/1034 NIEC Planning at Level of Industry: FII to NIEC 28/4/1965 enclosing Statement on the Irish National Productivity Committee by the Independent Chairmen of Adaptation Councils.
22 NAI DT 96/6/325 Establishment of Industries: Underdeveloped Areas Acts 1952 to 1957: Undeveloped Areas Amendment Act 1962: Lemass speech to National Convention of Junior Chambers of Commerce, Galway, 30/4/1966.
23 See NAI DF 2001/3/57 IDA activities.
24 NAI DF 2001/3/1303 1 Survey of Grant-aided Industries 2 Re-appraisal of the approach to attracting foreign industry to Ireland 3. Engagement of A. D. Little Inc. as consultants: Patrick Hillery, Minister for Industry and Commerce to Jack Lynch, Minister for Finance 31/1/ 1966.
25 Ibid.; NAI DF 2001/3/651 Arthur D. Little and Cabot, Cabot and Forbes: research-based industries: NAI DF 2001/3/1615, 1616 and 1617 IDA review: NAI DF 2001/3/1300 Little Review of IIRS.
26 NAI DF 2001/3/1500 Industrial preparations for free trade – Discussion with Department of Industry and Commerce: especially Report of Meeting between Finance and Industry and Commerce 28/9/1967.
27 NAI DF 2001/3/1500 T. K. Whitaker, Finance to J. C. B. McCarthy, Industry and Commerce 20/10/1967 and McCarthy to Whitaker 18/1/1968. On 31/1/1968 Whitaker suggested reviewing the Finance/Industry and Commerce joint action proposals he had made in the light of progress made in Third Programme working groups; on 2/2/1968 McCarthy assented to this suggestion.
28 NAI DT 99/1/563 Free Trade: Preparation of Industry: G. Colley, Minister for Industry and Commerce to C. Haughey, Minister for Finance, 1/5/1968 (Taoiseach Jack Lynch, to whom this letter was copied, responded 'I entirely agree with your proposal' on 3/5/1968): Haughey to Colley 8/5/1968 (Haughey wrote to Lynch on 8/5/1968 'I agree with his objective but am not happy about the machinery imposed'); Colley wrote again to Haughey on 22/5/1968 receiving a reply on 13/6/1968; Colley wrote again on 27/6/1968 and Haughey acquiesced in his proposal on 8/7/1968.

29 NAI DF 2001/3/1530 Mergers and amalgamations: J. P. Beddy, ICC to C. Haughey, Minister for Finance 25/6/1968.

30 NAI DF 2001/3/1530 G. Colley, Minister for Industry and Commerce to C. Haughey 26/6/1968 and 18/7/1968.

31 NAI DF 2001/3/1530 Secretary, Industry and Commerce to Secretary, Finance 26/9/1968 and 4/10/1968; Report of Meeting Proposed Establishment of Mergers Ltd 19/12/1968.

32 See also NAI DF 2001/3/1530 'Take-Overs and Mergers – The Shape of the Seventies?' a Talk to Secretaries and Accountants given by a Mergers Ltd Director F. A Casey on 2/2/1971 which points to significant merger-led 1960s restructuring in banking, paper and printing, textiles and construction.

33 G. FitzGerald 'Redundancy in Perspective', *Irish Times*, 29 July 1964.

34 See NAI DT 97/6/173, 97/6/174 and S 17626 A/95 manpower policy and redundancy.

Chapter Five: Educating Trade Unionists

1 NLI [William] O'Brien Gift L.O. P93 National Labour Party 'Communist Victory over Irish Labour: Story of the Red Coup in the Party Reprinted from the Standard 17th March 1944'; National Labour Party '"Inquest" on Labour Inquiry Reprinted from the *Standard*, 5 May 1944'.

2 NLI William O'Brien Papers MS 13, 960 A. O'Rahilly, UCC to P. J. O'Brien, ITGWU, Cork 14/2/1944.

3 IJA CIR/21 A. O'Rahillly, UCC to Fr Devane, Rathfarnham Castle 13/7/1948.

4 NAI DFA 324/339 Ford and Rockefeller Foundations: copy of H. Atkins, UCC to Secretary, Ford Foundation 13/8/1958.

5 NAI DIC R303/13/6 Application from the Congress of Irish Unions for Assistance from the Grant Counterpart Fund towards the development of trade union education: L. Crawford, Secretary CIU to S. Lemass, Minister for Industry and Commerce 31/5/1957; 'Note On Application of Congress of Irish Unions for a Grant to develop trade union education on similar lines to Management Education' undated.

6 NAI ICTU/2/378 (a) Economic Policy, Industrial Development, Industrial Productivity: A. Vermuelen, EPA to Secretary ITUC 14/11/1957; V. Agostinone, EPA to R. Roberts, ITUC 13/12/1957; NAI DIC R303/7/59 Establishment of National Productivity Centre in Ireland: Industries Division 'A' 'European Productivity Agency' Eanair [January] 1958.

7 NAI DIC R303/7/41 Activities undertaken by Irish Congress of Trade Unions with assistance of EPA, Joint General Secretaries, ICTU to R. Cottave, Trade Union Section, EPA, 9/9/1959.

8 NAI DIC R303/7/41 R. Cottave, Trade Union Section, EPA to R. Roberts, Joint General Secretary, ICTU 11/5/1960.

9 NAI DIC R303/7/41 R. Roberts, Joint General Secretary, ICTU to Mr O'Grady, INPC 26/2/1962.

10 IJA CIR/20 1–55. Memorandum on the Catholic Workers' College 1947–1962 Section B: Growth of Other College Activities.

11 IJA CIR/113 Fr. E. Kent, CWC to Fr O'Grady, Provincial 14/4/1960.

12 IJA CIR/20 1–55 Memorandum on the Catholics Workers' College 1947–1962. Part Two Guiding Principles and Policy Section A The College Courses and their Need, Aims and Importance.

13 Ibid.
14 Ibid.
15 IJA CIR/20 1–55 Memorandum on the Catholics Workers' College 1947–1962.
16 Ibid. Appendix B.
17 Ibid. Appendix C.
18 Ibid. Appendix D.
19 IJA CIR/56 Proposal to change the name of the Catholic Workers College: proposal one and proposal two.
20 NAI DETE 2001/50/57 The Catholic Workers College, College of Industrial Relations 'Education for Industrial Relations' statement released at a press reception 28/3/1966.

Chapter Six: Developing Managers

1 NAI DIC R303/13/5 Irish Management Institute request for financial aid for technical assistance: copies of C.O. Harvey to John Leydon 11/9/1952 and 15/9/1952.
2 NAI DIC R303/13/5 Extract from Report of Departmental Conference 332, 28/1/1954 Irish Management Institute: Use of Grant Counterpart Fund.
3 NAI DIC R303/13/5 Report of Interviews, Visit of US expert to advise the Irish Management Institute 23/4/1956 and 25/4/1956.
4 NAI DIC R303/13/5 Report of Meeting, Technical Assistance for Irish Management Institute 10/2/1956.
5 NAI DIC R303/15/26 Suggested training of nominee of Irish Government under the British Ministry of Labour and National Service Scheme for Training Within Industry for Supervisors.
6 NAI DETE 2000/12/1586 Irish Management Institute Request for Technical Assistance Grant towards Management Development Unit: Application of the Irish Management Institute for a Grant of £27,000 – For Departmental Conference – TID 3073/2 Industries Division 'A' 23/3/1956.
7 NAI DETE 2000/12/1586 Education to Industry and Commerce 6/4/1956; Extract from Report of Departmental Conference no. 441, 10/4/1956 – 'Minister directed that the Minister for Finance should be made aware of the fact that the Institute's application was for £27,000'; handwritten addition 'Minister subsequently altered this to £6,000 – see relevant file', JM 23/4/1956.
8 NAI DIC R303/15/26 Suggested training of nominee of Irish Government under the British Ministry of Labour and National Service Scheme for Training Within Industry for Supervisors, minute by J. Gannon, January 1956.
9 DIC R303/7/74 Statement of Productivity Principles: covering letter with IMI memorandum 21/6/1960.
10 NAI ICTU 2 378a Economic policy, industrial development, industrial productivity: handwritten note on document Draft Proposals for an Irish National Productivity Centre circulated by J. J. Stacey of FIM for discussion at fourth informal committee meeting 6/9/1955.
11 NAI DETE 2000/12/1586 Irish Management Institute Request for Technical Assistance Grant towards Management Development Unit, Department of Education to Department of Industry and Commerce 3/4/1956.

12 NAI DF Finance 2001/3/118 Education for Management: Secretary, Industry and Commerce to Secretary, Finance 2/1/1968.

13 NAI DIC R303/15/10 'Education for Management', Memorandum by the Economic Development Branch of the Dept of Finance.

14 NAI DIC R303/15/10 J. Murphy, Industry and Commerce to C. H. Murray, Finance, 26/5/1960.

15 NAI DIC R303/15/10 Bhreathnach, Education to C. H. Murray, Finance, 10/1/1961.

16 NAI DETE 2000/13/27 Minutes of Departmental Conference no. 852, 16/5/1966 Item 11 State Financial Assistance For the Irish Management Institute and the Federation of Irish Industries also Conference no. 887, 12/6/1967 Item 6 Irish Management Institute – Proposed Reorganisation of Structure.

17 NAI DIC 2000/12/78 Committee on Industrial Organisation Joint Committee on Education and Training for Management: NAI DIC 2000/12/62 Selection and Training of Supervisors in Industry.

18 NAI DT 98/6/937 Report of Committee on Supervisors.

19 'The New Materialism in Scientific Management', *Irish Catholic* 21 Jan. 1960.

20 IJA CIR/20 1–55 Memorandum on the Catholics Workers' College 1947–62.

21 NAI DETE 2001/50/57 The Catholic Workers College, College of Industrial Relations: 'Proposal to Establish an Industrial Relations Advisory and Research Centre, memorandum, 15/5/1965, Edmund Kent SJ, Superior and Director of Studies'; Extract from Report of Departmental Conference no. 817, 21/6/1965; Report of Meeting, Proposal by the Catholic Workers College that a 'National Centre of Industrial Relations' be established, 27/7/1965; P. Hillery, Minister for Industry and Commerce to Fr E. Kent 2/9/1965.

22 NAI DETE 2001/50/57 Report of Meeting, Activities of College of Industrial Relations 2/12/1966; Report of Meeting, the Secretary accompanied by Mr B. Maghnuis visited the College of Industrial Relations on invitation, 3/1/1967.

23 NAI DETE 2001/50/57 Report of Meeting. Future of College of Industrial Relations, 17/9/1968.

24 NAI DT 2001/6/385 College of Industrial Relations memorandum enclosed with Fr M. O'Grady SJ to J.Lynch, Taoiseach 4/12/1968.

25 NAI DT 2001/6/385 Report by an Interdepartmental Committee on a proposal, submitted to the Taoiseach by the College of Industrial Relations, Ranelagh, Dublin for the establishment of a National College of Industrial Relations.

Chapter Seven: Remoulding Mainstream Education and Inaugurating Science Policy

1 In the early 1940s 'the future of the vocational education sector was in some doubt. De Valera, who was then acting Minister for Education, openly questioned the value of the sector in the Dáil in 1940. His public preference was for the system to be absorbed by the primary schools, but in private he offered the entire sector to a religious order to remove it from state control' (Girvin 2002: 122).

2 NAI DIC TIC 33345/21 Institute for Industrial Research and Standards Request by Industrial Research Committee for enquiry into shortage of scientific manpower in Ireland: 'Memorandum for the Industrial Research Committee relating to a shortage of Scientific Man-Power in Ireland' undated.

3 NAI DIC TIC 33345/21 memorandum 'Scientific Manpower' April 1951; Extract from Report of Departmental Conference no. 209, 18/6/51 Item Scientific Manpower.

4 NAI DIC TIC 33345/21 IIRS to Industry and Commerce 28/7/1951, Extract from Report of Departmental Conference no. 219, 3/9/1951 Item Scientific Manpower.

5 NAI DIC TIC 33345/21 Education to Industry and Commerce 30/5/1953.

6 NAI DIC TIC 33345/21 IIRS to Industry and Commerce 19/2/1954.

7 NAI DIC TIC 33345/21 Industry and Commerce Memorandum 'Shortage of Scientific Manpower' 12/3/1954.

8 NAI DIC TIC 33345/21 Education to Industry and Commerce 17/11/1955, Industry and Commerce to IIRS 16/3/1956, IIRS to Industry and Commerce 19/4/1956.

9 NAI DT S 16,213 A (I) Establishment of Scientific Policy Committee: Suggestion by Professor E. T. S. Walton (II) Science Teaching in Schools Proposed Committee: E. T. S. Walton to E. de Valera 2/4/1957, T. Nevin to E. de Valera 9/4/1957 with enclosure 'The Need for Scientific Education in the Schools', Note of telephone call from E. de Valera to E. T. S. Walton 15/4/1957.

10 NAI DT S 16,213 A T. S. Wheeler to E. de Valera 25/4/1957 with enclosures 'Science Teaching in Irish Schools' and 'Science Subjects in the Secondary Schools'; T. S. Wheeler to E. de Valera 26/4/57 enclosing memorandum of evidence given by Wheeler to Science Sub-Committee of the Council of Education on 25/4/1956, E. T. S. Walton to E. de Valera 4/6/1957 enclosing memorandum 'The need for more attention to science in Eire with some suggestions for its encouragement'. Joseph Doyle, Professor of Botany at UCD, also wrote to the Taoiseach on 19/6/1957 enclosing 'Notes on Science in Secondary Schools'.

11 NAI DT S 16,213 Leo J. Close, Chief Inspector, 'The Advancement of Science in Secondary Schools' 26/8/1957.

12 NAI DT S 16,213 Secretary, Council of Education note 'Science in the Secondary School Programme' 30/1/1958.

13 NAI DFA 305/57/67/19/1 Part 1 OEEC Scientific and Technical Manpower Programme A. King, EPA to Mr Kennan, Irish OEEC Delegation 10/7/1957.

14 NAI DFA 305/57/67/19/1 Minutes of Interdepartmental ERP Committee meeting 7/1/1958.

15 NAI DFA 305/57/67/19/1 Industry and Commerce to External Affairs 28/1/1958.

16 NAI DFA 305/57/67/19/1 Part 2 W. P. Fay, Paris Ambassador to Secretary, Industry and Commerce 26/2/1958.

17 NAI DFA 305/57/67/19/1 Part 1 Notes on OEEC Science and Technical Manpower Programme 19/8/1957.

18 NAI DFA 305/57/67/19/7 Annual Review – Scientific and Technical Personnel: Industry and Commerce to External Affairs 6/8/1958.

19 NAI DFA 305/57/67/19/10 OEEC Scientific Co-operation Visit to Europe of Mr L. D. Wilgress 1959 'Note on Visit of Mr L. D. Wilgress of Canada to Ireland' 5/6/1959.

20 NAI DFA 305/57/67/19/10 'C (59) 165 Annex Notes on Each of the Countries Visited', pp. 42–4.

21 NAI DFA 305/57/67/19/10 Miss Murphy to Mr Molloy 1/8/1959 see also 'Ireland Co-operation in the field of Scientific and Technical Research Report of Mr Wilgress (C (59) 165 and Annex) General Report'.

22 NAI DFA 305/57/67/19/7 Annual Review – Scientific and Technical Personnel: 'OSTP/AR/59.12 Office for Scientific and Technical Personnel Annual Review – Ireland 1/10/59 Restricted' quotations are on pp. 5, 8, 9 and in Appendix II.

23 NAI DFA 305/57/67/19/7 Office for Scientific and Technical Personnel Annual Review of Progress in the Field of Highly Qualified Scientific and Technical Personnel (1958–9) Ireland, p. 6.

24 Ibid., p. 7.

25 Ibid., p. 10.

26 Ibid.

27 NAI DT S16213 B (I) Establishment of Scientific Policy Committee: Suggestion by Professor E. T. S. Walton (II) Science Teaching in Schools Proposed Committee: Taoiseach to Education 29/4/1959, Education to Taoiseach 21/3/1960.

28 NAI DF 2001/3/775 Proposed pilot study of future educational needs with Organisation for Economic Cooperation and Development assistance: T. O'Raifeartaigh, Education to T. K. Whitaker, Finance 8/11/1961.

29 NAI DIC R/303/8/4 Irish National Productivity Committee, Minutes of Meeting no. 19, 16/11/1960.

30 TCD Library, T. W. Moody Papers MS 7121 Commission on Higher Education, Minutes of Plenary Meetings, vol. 1, Second Meeting, 13/1/1961.

31 NAI DT S 16,213 C/61 (I) Establishment of Scientific Policy Committee: Suggestion by Professor E. T. S. Walton (II) Science Teaching in Schools Proposed Committee: memorandum 'Mr Hegarty's proposal for the approval of the sending by EPA of a group of experts to examine higher education in Ireland in connection with the work of the Commission on Higher Education, with a view to suggesting how higher education might best be organised here to meet the economic situation of, say, ten years hence', T. O'Raifeartaigh 20/5/1961.

32 TCD Library, T. W. Moody Papers MS 7121 Commission on Higher Education, Minutes of Plenary Meetings, vol. 1, Tenth Meeting, 4/9/1961.

33 Ibid.

34 NAI DF 2001/3/775 Proposed pilot study of future educational needs with Organisation for Economic Cooperation and Development assistance: T. O'Raifeartaigh, Education to T. K. Whitaker, Finance 8/11/1961.

35 NAI DT S 16,213 C/61 (I) Establishment of Scientific Policy Committee: Suggestion by Professor E. T. S. Walton (II) Science Teaching in Schools Proposed Committee: memorandum 'Mr Hegarty's proposal for the approval of the sending by EPA of a group of experts to examine higher education in Ireland in connection with the work of the Commission on Higher Education, with a view to suggesting how higher education might best be organised here to meet the economic situation of, say, ten years hence', T. O'Raifeartaigh 20/5/1961.

36 NAI DF 2001/3/546 OECD policy conference at Washington October 1961 on economic growth and investment in education: Irish representation.

37 NAI DF 2001/3/775 Proposed Pilot Study of Future Educational Needs with Organisation for Economic Co-operation and Development Assistance, Report of Meeting 7/3/1962.

38 NAI DF 2001/3/775 Report of Meeting held on 7/3/1962 OECD Project: Pilot Study on Long-term Needs for Educational Resources..

39 NAI DF 2001/3/775 Conference in Department of Education 17/4/1962 OECD Project: Pilot Study on Long-term Needs for Educational Resources in Advanced Countries.

40 NAI DF 2001/3/775 Handwritten note, undated: Barry Desmond, a fellow member of the Steering Committee, recollects Dr Newman as having been completely out of sympathy with the study's focus on the 'more materialistic manpower aspects' of education (interview with Barry Desmond, 2/1/2006).

41 NAI DT S 16,213 A (I) Establishment of Scientific Policy Committee: Suggestion by Professor E. T. S. Walton (II) Science Teaching in Schools Proposed Committee: memorandum of evidence given by Professor T. S. Wheeler to Science Sub-Committee of the Council of Education on 25/4/1956.

42 DDA, Archbishop John Charles McQuaid Papers AB8/B/XXXX/d Committee on the Public Image of the Church.

43 DDA, Archbishop John Charles McQuaid Papers AB8/B/XXXX/d Studies. The episode also revealed significant divisions within the Department of Education. There, 'the Minister had withdrawn his permission for publication (at the intervention of the Secretary Dr O'Raifertaigh)'. Only a substantially amended version of O'Connor's article, which was unacceptable to the author, was now to be permitted to appear in print. After taking legal advice, *Studies* published O'Connor's original text: see Fanning (2008: 247, note 37).

44 NAI DFA 99/3/178 Pilot teams to study the needs for scientific research and technology in relation to economic growth.

45 NAI DF 2001/3/417 OECD conference of Ministers for Science: Inter-departmental science group: NAI DETE 2000/13/26 Minutes of Industry and Commerce departmental conferences, no. 806, 15 March 1965 Item 7 Formulation of National Science Policy.

46 NAI DF 2001/3/415 Organisation for Economic Cooperation and Development Committee for Scientific Research: Pilot study of scientific research and technology needs in relation to economic growth.

47 NAI DF 2001/3/417 OECD conference of Ministers for Science: Inter-departmental science group.

48 Ibid.

49 NAI DT 96/6/80 OECD Scientific Research: National Science Council: Establishment.

50 NAI DFA 99/3/178 Pilot teams to study the needs for scientific research and technology in relation to economic growth.

51 Such institutions do not appear to have come under any actual pressure to accept the Commission's recommendations as a high-level committee within Education that reviewed them did not support either the establishment of a National College of Agricultural and Veterinary Sciences or a Technological Authority. In relation to the latter, it concluded that 'the activities proposed by the Commission for a Technological Authority are too diffuse. It would appear to be expected to roll up into one web the entire tapestry of technological and industrial education, training and research, to set industrial standards and to provide industry with field and information services': NAI DT 99/1/438 Commission on Higher Education:

Report, Department Committee's Observations on the Recommendations of the Commission on Higher Education pp. 12–14: quotation is from p. 13.

52 NAI DFA 99/3/178 Pilot teams to study the needs for scientific research and technology in relation to economic growth, Department of Education Memorandum for the Government 'Science and Irish Economic Development' undated.

53 NAI DT 98/6/682 OECD Scientific Research: National Science Council: Establishment, Department of Finance Memorandum for the Government 'National Science Council' 21/7/1967 Paras. 16 and 18.

54 NAI DF 2001/3/775 Proposed Pilot Study of Future Educational Needs with Organisation for Economic Cooperation and Development Assistance, T. O'Raifeartaigh, Education to T. K. Whitaker, Finance 4/5/1962.

Chapter Eight: Shaping Social Science Research

1 DIC MIS/1/5 National Joint Committee on the Human Sciences and Their Application to Industry Meetings to 31/12/1961, Minutes of Committee Meeting no. 2, 16/1/1959.

2 DIC MIS/1/2 Human Sciences Committee Technical Assistance to Research Institutions (project no. 7/07 – section D).

3 NAI DIC R303/7/84 Productivity Project for Shannon Development Area.

4 NAI DT S 16622 B/61 Shannon Free Airport Development Co. (1) Legislation (2) Housing at Shannon: Department of Transport and Power Memorandum for the Government 'Amending Legislation to Provide for the Financing of the Shannon Free Airport Development Company Limited'

5 NAI DT S 16622 B/61 Department of Transport and Power Memorandum for the Government 'Amending Legislation to Provide for the Financing of the Shannon Free Airport Development Company Limited' Appendix IV Views of Minister for Industry and Commerce.

6 NAI DT S 16622 B/62 Shannon Free Airport Development Co. (1) Legislation (2) Housing at Shannon, record of Cabinet decisions of 28/12/1962 on Interdepartmental Committee on Housing at Shannon Report of February 1962.

7 NAI ICTU Box 356 File Research Department Human Sciences Committee – Minutes: Minutes of Meetings no. 23, 11/1/1963 to no. 27, 24/10/1963.

8 NAI ICTU Box 218 3509 INPC Human Sciences Committee (December 1963 to December 1974) 'Report on Work of Committee' presented to annual meeting, 18/12/1967.

9 NAI DFA 324/339 Ford and Rockefeller Foundations: NAI DT S 16,645 A Ford and Rockefeller Foundation Aid to Ireland NAI DT S 16,705 A Centre for Economic and Social Research in Ireland: Establishment.

10 FFA Reel no. 620 Grant no. PA 60–285 Section 4 memo S. Gordon to J. McDaniel 18/12/1959: Reel no. 620 Grant no. PA 60–285 Section 4 corres. J. Vaizey, Oxford to S. Gordon, Ford Foundation 1/11/1959; J. Pognan, OSTP to S. Stone, Ford Foundation 3/2/1960.

11 FFA Reel no. 620 Grant no. PA 60–285 Section 4 J. Vaizey to S. Stone and S. Stone to J. Vaizey, various dates 1960–1; NAI DF 2001/3/775 Proposed Pilot Study of Future Educational Needs with Organisation for Economic Co-operation and Development Assistance copy M. Cullen, Ford Foundation to R. C. Geary, Director, ERI 13/6/1962.

12 NAI DT S 16,705 A Centre for Economic and Social Research in Ireland: Establishment: N. O'Nuallain, Taoiseach to T. K. Whitaker, Finance 5/5/1961; T. K. Whitaker, Finance to N. O'Nuallain, Taoiseach 8/5/1961: copy of speech is in file.

13 ESRI Box 1 History of ERI/ESRI File 'Institute of Public Administration, 59 Lansdowne Road Dublin 4 Social Research Council', T. K. Whitaker, Finance to C. S. Andrews, Chairman IPA 12/9/1963.

14 ESRI Box 1 History of ERI/ESRI File 'Institute of Public Administration, 59 Lansdowne Road Dublin 4 Social Research Council', 'Social Research' 21/10/1963.

15 ESRI Box 1 History of ERI/ESRI File 'Institute of Public Administration, 59 Lansdowne Road Dublin 4 Social Research Council', 'Social Research Committee' 7/7/1964.

16 ESRI Box 1 History of ERI/ESRI, File 'Dr Henning Friis', P. Lynch, Aer Lingus, to R. C. Geary, ERI 8/4/1964: R. C. Geary, ERI to H. Friis, Danish National Institute of Social Research 27/4/1964: Friis to Geary 1/5/1964. See also NAI DFA 98/3/258 Institute of Public Administration: Request for UN Expert in Social Research 1964–6.

17 NAI ICTU Box 356 File Research Department Human Sciences Committee – Minutes: Minutes of Meeting 30/3/1965.

18 NAI DT 97/6/209 Programme for Social Development: J. Lynch, Minister for Finance to S. Lemass, Taoiseach 26/5/1965; FFA Reel no. 620 Grant no. PA 60–285 Section 4 memo M. Cullen to Records 11/6/1962.

19 NAI DT S17,678/95 Programme for Social Development.

20 NAI DF Finance 2001/3/1468 Third Programme for Economic Expansion: Social Development Aspects: Memo C.H. Murray to M. Breathnach 25/8/1967.

21 See NAI ICTU Box 356 File Research Department Human Sciences Committee – Minutes of relevant meetings.

22 NAI ICTU Box 218 3509 INPC Human Sciences Committee From December 1963 to December 1974: M. Fogarty, ESRI to D. Walsh, INPC 20/2/1970; ESRI Box 1 History of ERI/ESRI 'ESRI 1960–1970' pp. 28–9; 'ESRI And The Next Five Years', p. 17.

23 NAI ICTU Box 216 File 3506 INPC November 1971 to June 1973: memo from Director, IPC to Chairtman IPC 'The IPC and its Expenditure on Research' 16/10/1972.

24 NAI ICTU Box 3506 INPC November 1971 to June 1973: Memo from Director, IPC to Chairman, IPC 'The IPC and its expenditures on research'16/10/1972; NAI ICTU Box 217 3506 Irish Productivity Centre From July 1974 to June 1976 Irish Productivity Centre Council Meeting no. 13 13/7/1973.

25 NAI ICTU Box 216 3506 INPC November 1971 to June 1973: on action research see P. Clancy, Promotions Division, IPC to R. Roberts, ICTU 17/7/1972; on the ergonomics unit see IPC Council Meeting Minutes 26/2/1974.

26 NAI ICTU Box 218 3509 INPC Human Sciences Committee, December 1963 to December 1974: Minutes of Meeting no. 77, 31/5/1973.

27 NAI ICTU Box 217 Minutes of IPC Council Meeting no. 33 4/11/1975: NAI ICTU Box 218 3509 IPC Human Science Committee (from February 1975).

28 NAI DF 2001/3/952 Programme for Social Development, Statement by the Minister for Education at the OECD Ministerial Meeting on Science, Paris, 13 January 1966.

Chapter Nine: The Impact of Innovations and the Context of Institutions

1 Deep disagreement continues to prevail in relation to the specification of these influences and the weighting of their effects – see especially Garvin (2004) and Kirby (2006).

2 'Inspection of New IMI Premises by An Tanaiste' *Irish Management* 4 (5), Sept./Oct. 1957, pp. 151–7: quotation is on p. 155.

3 NAI DT S15,453 H/63 European Productivity Agency: Irish National Productivity Committee, speech of Seán Lemass to INPC Labour–Management Conference, Red Island, Skerries, 19 September 1963.

4 From their initiation in 1959, INPC's annual Labour-Management conferences were held in late September in Red Island holiday camp (on whose history see Hugh Oram 'An Irishman's Diary', *Irish Times*, 6 May 2003) near Skerries. In the mid-1960s they moved to hotel venues in and around Dublin.

5 NAI DFA 305/57/112 Part 1 Special Dollar Fund for Technical Assistance Minutes of Interdepartmental ERP Committee Meeting 3/12/1949.

6 NAI DIC R303TA/68/1and R303TA/68/2 Industrial Consultants Offer of Services – General File.

7 NAI DIC R312/156 Technical Assistance Division B General File, C.A. Barry to Mr Devlin 4/1/1961: Schedule Technical Assistance Consultants.

8 NAI DIC 2000/13/24 Minutes of Departmental Conference no. 757, 25/11/1963 Item Technical Assistance Scheme – Consultants Fees: the four leading firms are identified as Personnel Administration Ltd., Associated Industrial Consultants, Urwick Orr and Partners and Production Engineering Ltd.

9 NAI DF 2001/3/1343 NIEC Review of Industrial Adaptation Incentives, copy of Appendix XXI 'Industrial Consultancy Projects', 23/3/1967; as noted in chapter 4 above, quantification of consultancy scheme benefits later eluded the CIP survey teams as well.

10 Ibid. W. Kirwan note of meeting with Mr Hancock of P.A. Consultants 'who acts as contact man for the Management Consultants Association . . .', 20/12/1967.

11 Ibid. J. B. Ryan, INPC to N. Coghlan, Finance 26/6/1968; Irish National Productivity Committee Study Visits Abroad 1963–7; note 'I&C explained to me [W. Kirwan] that there was no explicit line of demarcation between his Department and INPC in relation to grants for training courses or study visits abroad. The division of functions was founded on the understanding that INPC would assist projects involving participation by labour representatives and also projects involving the smaller firms and that Industry and Commerce would deal with the remainder.'

12 NAI DIC MIS 1/4 Human Sciences Committee: Consideration of Topics for Study, Summary of discussion with representatives of Management concerning human problems in industry (5 June 1959).

13 NAI DF 2001/31617 IDA Review, statement by George Colley, Minister for Industry and Commerce at press conference announcing IDA changes, 5/7/1968: see also FitzGerald (1968) Appendix 6 'Economic Planning and Industrial Promotion'.

14 NAI DIC 2000/12/78 Committee on Industrial Organisation Joint Committee on Education and Training for Management Director, IMI to Secretary, CIO 23/10/1961: Report of Meeting, Industrial Surveys, 7/11/1961.

15 NAI DIC 2000/12/69 Courses on Variety Reductions by the Irish Management Institute, IMI to CIO, 1/12/1962.

16 'The Taoiseach's Address', *Irish Management* 8 (6), June 1961 pp. 200–5: quotation is on p. 201.

17 NAI DF 2001/3/1343 NIEC Review of Industrial Adaptation Incentives, W. Kirwan note of meeting with Mr Hancock of P.A. Consultants 'who acts as contact man for the Management Consultants Association . . .', 20/12/1967.

18 For Industry and Commerce's strong push to have the full set of Little proposals for a restructured IDA implemented despite Finance opposition on some issues see NAI DF 2001/3/1617 IDA Review; for Colley's disparagement of NIEC and his withholding from it of the results of the survey of grant-aided industries between November 1967 and June 1968 see Taoiseach 99/1/563 Free Trade: Preparation of Industry, George Colley to Charles Haughey, 22/5/1968 and Finance 2001/3/1303 1. Survey of Grant-aided Industries 2. Re-appraisal of the approach to attracting foreign industry to Ireland 3. Engagement of A. D. Little Inc. as consultants; in February 1968 Colley informed a Departmental Conference that he would 'not be prepared to take the initiative' in relation to NIEC's Development Council proposal NAI DIC 2000/13/28 Minutes of Departmental Conference no. 911, 19/2/1968, Item 2 Proposed Development Councils for Industry.

19 According to Appendix V of the CIP's Final Report (CIP 1973) IDA, SFADCO, CTT, IIRS, AnCO, IMI and the IPC Advisory Service between them had 1,323 employees in 1971. Expenditure by these bodies had risen from less than £2m in 1960–1 to over £40m in 1972–3. As late as 1967–8 this total was around £10m. and its sharp subsequent rise was largely accounted for by the IDA which by itself was spending almost £30m in 1972–3.

20 NAI ICTU Box 215 3501 INPC General Sept. 1966–Dec. 1970 Personal observations on the questions which you forwarded to me on April 9 enclosed with R. Roberts to T. Hubert 1/5/1970.

21 NAI DF 2001/3/118 Education for Management, copy of Louis B. McCagg 'The Research and Training institutes of Ireland (Why Not Make Better Use of Them?)'. The institutes referred to were the Agricultural Institute, ERI, IIRS, INPC, IMI, IPA, the Dublin Institute for Advanced Studies, the Department of Finance's Civil Service Training Centre and an Foras Forbartha.

22 NAI DIC 315/2 Amendment of Industrial Development Act 1950 (a) Industrial Efficiency (b) Control of Manufacturers' Prices, Report of Meeting between Minister for Industry and Commerce and a Deputation from the Federation of Irish Manufacturers, 7/4/1953.

23 NAI DIC 315/2 Speech by Seán Lemass, Minister for Industry and Commerce, to annual dinner of the Federation of Irish Manufacturers, 10/2/1953.

24 NAI DFA 444/23 Proposals for continuation of certain EPA activities in OECD: OEEC EPA/D/7513 21/1/1960 1960–1 Programme of the 'New Agency' Sector I Industry and Commerce Statement by the Delegate for Ireland.

25 NAI ICTU Box 215 3501 INPC General Sept. 1966–Dec. 1970. Personal observations on the questions which you forwarded to me on April 9 enclosed with R. Roberts to T. Hubert 1/5/1970. But see also Roberts's views in the same document: 'The INPC is not without its achievements. Its National Conferences over the years have had a substantial and beneficial

effect on opinion. Its advisory services, although acting on their own through direct contact [rather than through vertical productivity committees], have continued to create an active demand. The subsidies to ICTU education and advisory services have resulted in the creation and development of these services in a manner which would not otherwise be possible and the ICTU advisory services in particular makes a direct contribution to the introduction, without conflict, of work study and incentive payments schemes. The Distribution Industrial Committee, which refused to be blocked when other committees were brought to an end, has a very good record in the field of developing educational and other services for the distributive sector. The early seminars on labour market policy had a direct bearing on the establishment of the Department of Labour and its manpower services. Nor is this a comprehensive survey of the Committee's achievements. In sum, if INPC is inadequate, it is only in the sense that it could do much more not in the sense that it is barren of achievement. Finally it should be noted that the efforts to establish the INPC were protracted largely because of the reservations of the employer organisations. There existed, and still exists, on the employers' side a reluctance to endorse the principle of joint action, due to fears of workers "interfering in the business of management". These fears can probably be compared with fears on the trade union side that 'productivity means unemployment.'

26 NAI DFA 305/57/226 Establishment of a Productivity Centre in Ireland, William H. Joyce, Jr quoted in *Marshall Plan News* 1 (9) Special Productivity Issue, 'European workers accept the challenge'.

27 Management tools could also be open to subversion. On Merseyside shopfloor trade unionists acquiring a knowledge of work study in the late 1960s which they then turn to their own advantage, and management's disadvantage, see Beynon (1973: 135–8 and 146–7).

References

Allen, K. (1997) *Fianna Fáil and Irish Labour: 1926 to the Present.* London: Pluto Press.

Andrews, C.S. (2001) *Man of No Property.* Dublin: Lilliput Press.

Archer, C. (1990) *Organizing Western Europe.* London: Edward Arnold.

Bew, P. and H. Patterson (1982) *Seán Lemass and the Making of Modern Ireland, 1945–66.* Dublin: Gill & Macmillan.

Beynon, H. (1973) *Working For Ford.* Harmondsworth: Penguin.

Bjarner, O. and M. Kipping (eds) (1998) *The Americanisation of European Business: The Marshall Plan and the Transfer of Us Management Models.* London: Routledge.

Boel, B. (1997) 'The European Productivity Agency, 1953–1961', pp. 113–22 in R. T. Griffiths (ed.) *Explorations in OEEC History.* Paris: OECD.

Boel, B. (2003) *The European Productivity Agency and Transatlantic Relations, 1953–1961* Copenhagen: Museum Tusculanum Press.

Booth, A., J. Melling and C. Dartmann (1997) 'Institutions and economic growth: the politics of productivity in West Germany, Sweden and the United Kingdom, 1945–1955', *Journal of Economic History* 57 (2), pp. 416–44.

Bowen, K. (1983) *Protestants in A Catholic State: Ireland's Privileged Minority.* Dublin: Gill & Macmillan.

Bowman, J. (1993) '"The wolf in sheep's clothing": Richard Hayes's proposal for a new National Library of Ireland, 1959–60', pp. 44–61 in R. Hill and M. Marsh (eds), *Modern Irish Democracy: Essays in Honour of Basil Chubb.* Dublin: Irish Academic Press.

Boyd, A. (1972) *The Rise of the Irish Trade Unions 1729–1970.* Tralee: Anvil Press.

Boyd, A (1984) *Have the Trade Unions Failed the North?* Cork: Mercier Press.

Boyd, A. (1999) *Fermenting Elements: The Labour Colleges in Ireland 1924–6.* Belfast: Donaldson Archives.

Burke. A. (1990) 'Trinity College and the religious problem in Irish education', pp. 95–126 in J. Kelly and U. Mac Gearailt (eds), *Dublin and Dubliners.* Dublin: Helicon.

Byrne, T. P. (1954) 'Training of supervisors' *Irish Management* 1 (4), pp. 139–43.

Callanan, B. (2000) *Ireland's Shannon Story: Leaders, Visions and Networks – A Case Study of Local and Regional Development.* Dublin: Irish Academic Press.

CIO (Committee on Industrial Organisation) (1962) *Interim Report on State Aid to be Granted to Industry to Adapt Itself to meet Common Market Conditions.* Dublin: Stationery Office.

CIP (Committee on Industrial Progress) (1970) *Report On the Women's Outerwear Industry.* Dublin: Stationery Office.

CIP (Committee on Industrial Progress) (1973) *Final Report*. Dublin: Stationery Office.

Communist Party of Ireland (1943) *Ireland Looks To Labour: Second National Congress Communist Party of Ireland Report by W. H. McCullough and Texts of Resolutions* Belfast: Communist Party of Ireland.

Córas Tráchtála (1953) *Dollar Exports: Report of U.S. Consultants. Dublin*: Córas Tráchtála.

Cox, T. (2002) *The Making of Managers: A History of the Irish Management Institute 1952–2002* Cork: Oak Tree Press.

Daly, M. (1992) *Industrial Development and Irish National Identity, 1922–1939*. New York: Syracuse University Press.

Department of Education (1965) *Investment in Education*. Dublin: Stationery Office.

Department of Education (1970) *Adult Education Survey: Interim Report. Dublin*: Stationery Office.

Department of Education (1973) *Adult Education in Ireland: A Report of a Committee Appointed By the Minister For Education. Dublin*: Stationery Office.

Department of Finance (1958) *Economic Development*. Dublin: Stationery Office.

Department of Finance (1968) *Review of 1967 and Outlook for 1968*. Dublin: Stationery Office.

Department of Finance (1970) *Membership of the European Communities: Implications for Ireland*. Dublin: Stationery Office.

Department of Industry and Commerce (1966) *Science and Irish Economic Development*. Dublin: Stationery Office.

Devine, F. (1990) '"A Dangerous Agitator": John Swift, 1896–1990, socialist, trade unionist, secularist, internationalist, Labour historian', *Saothar* 15, pp. 7–19.

Devine, F. (2002) *Understanding Social Justice: Paddy Cardiff and the Discipline of Trade Unionism*. Dublin: Irish Labour History Society.

Duff, T., J. Hegarty and M. Hussey (2000) *The Story of the Dublin Institute of Technology*. Dublin: Blackhall.

Dunphy, R. (1995) *The Making of Fianna Fáil Power in Ireland, 1923–1948*. Oxford: Clarendon Press.

Engwall, L. and V. Zamagni (1998) 'Introduction' pp. 1–18 in L. Engwall and V. Zamagni (eds), *Management Education in Historical Perspective* Manchester: Manchester University Press.

Fanning, B. (2008) *The Quest For Modern Ireland: The Battle of Ideas, 1912–1986*. Dublin: Irish Academic Press.

Fanning, R. (1978) *The Irish Department of Finance, 1922–58*. Dublin: Institute of Public Administration.

Finnegan, R. and Wiles (1995) 'The invisible hand or hands across the water? American consultants and Irish economic policy', *Eire-Ireland* 30, pp. 42–55.

FitzGerald, G. (1968) *Planning in Ireland: A P.E.P. Study*. Dublin: Institute of Public Administration.

FitzGerald, G. (1991) *All in a Life: An Autobiography. Dublin*: Gill & Macmillan.

Fitzgerald, M. (2000) *Protectionism to Liberalisation: Ireland and the EEC, 1957 to 1966*. Aldershot: Ashgate.

Friis, H. (1965) *Development of Social Research in Ireland*. Dublin: Institute of Public Administration.

Garvin, T. (2004) *Preventing the Future: Why Was Ireland So Poor For So Long?* Dublin: Gill & Macmillan.

Gaughan, J. A. (1992) *Alfred O'Rahilly III Controversialist Part 1 Social Reformer.* Dublin: Kingdom Books.

Gaughan, J. A. (2000) *At the Coalface: Recollections of a City and Country Priest 1950–2000.* Dublin: Columba Press.

Geiger, R. L. (1997) 'What happened after sputnik? Shaping university research in the United States' *Minerva* 35, pp. 349–67.

Girvin, B. (1989) *Between Two Worlds: Politics and Economy in Independent Ireland.* Dublin: Gill & Macmillan.

Girvin, B. (2002) *From Union to Union: Nationalism, Democracy and Religion in Ireland – Act of Union to EU.* Dublin: Gill & Macmillan.

Girvin, B. (2004) 'Did Ireland benefit from the Marshall Plan? Choice, strategy and the national interest in a comparative context', pp. 182–220 in M. Browne, T. Geiger and M. Kennedy (eds), *Ireland, Europe and the Marshall Plan.* Dublin: Four Courts Press.

Godin, B. (2002) 'The numbers makers: fifty years of science and technology official statistics' *Minerva* 40, pp. 375–97.

Goldthorpe, J., L. O'Dowd and P. O'Connor (2002) 'Symposium: a sociology of Ireland by Hilary Tovey and Perry Share' *Irish Journal of Sociology* 11 (1), pp. 97–109.

Gorman, L. et al. (1974) *Managers in Ireland.* Dublin: Irish Management Institute.

Gourvish, T. R. and N. Tiratsoo (1998) 'Missionaries and managers: an introduction', pp. 1–13 in T. R. Gourvish and N. Tiratsoo (eds), *Missionaries and Managers: American Influences On European Management Education, 1945–60.* Manchester: Manchester University Press.

Hannigan, K. (1981) 'British based unions in Ireland: building workers and the split in congress', *Saothar* 7, pp. 40–9.

Holton, B. (1976) *British Syndicalism 1900–1914: Myths and Realities.* London: Pluto Press.

Horgan, J. (2001) *Irish Media: A Critical History Since 1922.* London: Routledge.

Ibec Technical Services Corporation (1952) *Industrial Potentials of Ireland: An Appraisal* New York: Ibec Technical Services Corporation.

ICTU (Irish Congress of Trade Unions) (Various Years) *Annual Report.* Dublin: ICTU.

IMI (Irish Management Institute) (1956) *Education and Training For Management: Report of the Joint Committee.* Dublin: Irish Management Institute.

ITUC (Irish Trade Union Congress) (Various Years) *Annual Report.* Dublin: ITUC.

Jackson, J. A. (1967) *Report On the Skibbereen Survey.* Dublin: Irish National Productivity Committee.

Jackson, J. A. (2004) 'Research policy and practice in Ireland: a historical perspective', pp. 23–40 in M. Maclachlan and M. Caball (eds), *Social Science in the Knowledge Society: Research Policy in Ireland.* Dublin: Liffey Press.

Jacobson, D. (1989) 'Theorising Irish industrialization: the case of the motor industry' *Science and Society* 53 (2), pp. 165–91.

Johnson, D. S. (1981) 'The Belfast Boycott' pp. 287–307 in J. M. Goldstrom and L. A. Clarkson (eds), *Irish Population, Economy and Society: Essays in Honour of the Late K. H. Connell. Oxford*: Clarendon Press.

Kavanagh, J. (1954) *Manual of Social Ethics*. Dublin: M.H. Gill.

Kennedy, K. A. and B. Dowling (1975) *Economic Growth in Ireland: The Experience Since 1947*. Dublin: Gill & Macmillan.

Kennedy, R. E. (1973) *The Irish: Emigration, Marriage and Fertility*. London: University of California Press.

Kirby, P. (2006) 'Preventing the future or distorting the past? Tom Garvin on Mancur Olson and the causes of Ireland's underdevelopment', *Administration* 54 (3), pp. 55–68.

Krige, J. (2000) 'Nato and the strengthening of western science in the post-sputnik era', *Minerva* 38, pp. 81–108.

Lee, J. J. (1989) *Ireland 1912–1985*. Cambridge: Cambridge University Press.

Lydon, J. (1992) 'The silent sister: Trinity College and Catholic Ireland', pp. 29–53 in C. H. Holland (ed.) *Trinity College. Dublin and the Idea of A University*. Dublin: Trinity College. Dublin Press.

Lynch, J. (1998) *A Tale of Three Cities: Comparative Studies in Working Class Life*. Basingstoke: Macmillan.

Lynch, P., and J. Vaizey (1960) *Guinness's Brewery in the Irish Economy 1759–1876*. Cambridge: Cambridge University Press.

McCarthy, C. (1968) *The Distasteful Challenge*. Dublin: Institute of Public Administration.

McCarthy, C. (1973) *The Decade of Upheaval: Irish Trade Unions in the Nineteen Sixties*. Dublin: Institute of Public Administration.

McCarthy, C. (1977) *Trade Unions in Ireland 1894–1960*. Dublin: Institute of Public Administration.

McCartney, D. (1999) *UCD: A National Idea: The History of University College Dublin*. Dublin: Gill & Macmillan.

MacCormac, M. (1955) 'Management education in the US', *Irish Management* 2 (5), pp. 208–9.

McCullagh, D. (1998) *A Makeshift Majority: The First Inter-Party Government, 1948–51*. Dublin: Institute of Public Administration.

McDowell, R. B. and D. A. Webb (1982) *Trinity College, Dublin, 1992–1952: An Academic History*. Cambridge: Cambridge University Press.

McGarry, F. (1999) *Irish Politics and the Spanish Civil War*. Cork: Cork University Press.

McGarry, F. (2005) 'Radical politics in inter-war Ireland, 1923–39', pp. 207–28 in F. Lane and D. O'Drisceoil (eds), *Politics and the Irish Working Class, 1830–1945* Basingstoke: Palgrave Macmillan.

Machado, B. (2007) *In Search of a Usable Past: the Marshall Plan and Postwar Reconstruction Today*. Lexington, Virginia: George C. Marshall Foundation.

Maher, D. J. (1986) *The Tortuous Path: The Course of Ireland's Entry into the EEC 1948–73*. Dublin: Institute of Public Administration.

Meenan, J. (1970) *The Irish Economy Since 1922*. Liverpool: Liverpool University Press.

Milotte, M. (1984) *Communism in Modern Ireland: The Pursuit of the Workers' Republic Since 1916*. Dublin: Gill & Macmillan.

Mjoset, L. (1992) *The Irish Economy in a Comparative Institutional Perspective*. Dublin: National Economic and Social Council.

Morrissey, T. (2007) *William O'Brien 1881–1968: Socialist, Republican, Dáil Deputy, Editor and Trade Union Leader*. Dublin: Four Courts Press.

Mulholland, M. (1997) '"One of the most difficult hurdles": the struggle for recognition of the Northern Ireland committee of the Irish Congress of Trade Unions, 1958–1964' *Saothar* 22, pp. 81–94.

Murphy, G. (2003) *Economic Realignment and the Politics of EEC Entry: Ireland, 1948–1972*. Bethesda, Maryland: Academica Press.

Murphy, J. A. (1995) *The College: A History of Queen's/University College Cork, 1845–1995*. Cork: Cork University Press.

Murray, C. H. (1963) 'The CIO Surveys and managements' needs', *Management* 10 (3), pp. 85–90.

Murray, P. (1987) 'Citizenship, Colonialism and Self-Determination: Dublin in the United Kingdom 1885–1918'. Unpublished PhD thesis, University of Dublin.

Murray, P. (2004) *The Transatlantic Politics of Productivity and the Origins of Public Funding For Social Science Research in Ireland, 1950–1979* Nirsa Working Paper no. 22, http://www.nuim.ie/nira/research/pdf/wps22.pdf.

Murray, P. (2005a) *The Pitfalls of Pioneering Sociological Research: the Case of the Tavistock Institute on the Dublin Buses in the Early 1960s*. Nirsa Working Paper no. 25, http://www.may.ie/nirsa/publications/wps25.pdf.

Murray, P. (2005b) 'Ireland and the productivity drive of post-war Europe' pp. 66–81 in B. Girvin and G. Murphy (eds), *The Lemass Era: Politics and Society in the Era of Seán Lemass*. Dublin: UCD Press.

Murray, P. (2008) *Marshall Plan Technical Assistance, the Industrial Development Authority and Irish Private Sector Manufacturing Industry, 1949–52*. Nirsa Working Paper, 34 http://www.nuim.ie/nirsa/research/documents/wp34murrayfeb20081.pdf.

NESC (National Economic and Social Council) (1982) *A Review of Industrial Policy: A Report Prepared By the Telesis Consultancy Group*. Dublin: National Economic and Social Council.

Nevin, D. (1959) 'The worker's share', *Irish Management* 6 (6), pp. 208–10.

Newman, J. (1964) 'Preface' pp. vii–ix in J. Newman (ed.), *The Limerick Rural Survey*. Tipperary: Muintir na Tíre.

NIEC (National Industrial and Economic Council) (1964) *Report on Procedures for Continuous Review of Progress Under the Second Programme for Economic Expansion*. Dublin: Stationery Office.

NIEC (National Industrial and Economic Council) (1965) *Comments On Report of Inter-Departmental Committee on Administrative Arrangements for Implementing Manpower Policy*. Dublin: Stationery Office.

NIEC (National Industrial and Economic Council) (1966a) *Comments on Free Trade Agreement*. Dublin: Stationery Office.

NIEC (National Industrial and Economic Council) (1966b) *Report on Review of Industrial Progress, 1965*. Dublin: Stationery Office.

NIEC (National Industrial and Economic Council) (1966c) *Report on Arrangements For Planning At Industry Level. Dublin*: Stationery Office.

NIEC (National Industrial and Economic Council) (1967) *Report on Review of Industrial Progress, 1966*. Dublin: Stationery Office.

NIEC (National Industrial and Economic Council) (1968) *Comments on Second Programme Review of Progress*. Dublin: Stationery Office.

Nolan, P. and L. Johnston (2003) *An Adventure in Learning: The Workers Educational Association in Northern Ireland Over the Last Century* http://wwww.wea-ni.com/z_pdf/weahistory2.pdf.

O'Ceallaigh, S. (1954) 'The first training course for foremen and supervisors', *Irish Management* 1 (4), pp. 144–5.

O'Connor, E. (1988) *Syndicalism in Ireland 1917–1923* Cork: Cork University Press.

O'Connor, E. (1992) *A Labour History of Ireland 1824–1960*. Dublin: Gill & Macmillan.

O'Connor, E. (2002) *James Larkin*. Cork: Cork University Press.

O'Connor, S. (1968) 'Post-primary education: now and in the future', *Studies* Autumn, pp. 233–49.

O'Connor, S. (1986) *A Troubled Sky: Reflections on the Irish Educational Scene 1957–1968*. Dublin: St Patrick's College Education Research Centre.

O'Drisceoil, D. (1996) *Censorship in Ireland, 1939–1945: Neutrality, Politics and Society*. Cork: Cork University Press.

O'Drisceoil, D. (2005) '"Whose emergency is it?" Wartime politics and the Irish working class, 1939–45', pp. 262–80 in F. Lane and D. O'Drisceoil (eds), *Politics and the Irish Working Class, 1830–1945*. Basingstoke: Palgrave Macmillan.

Ó Gráda, C. (1995) *Ireland: A New Economic History 1780–1939*. Oxford: Clarendon Press.

O'Hearn, D. (1990) 'The road from import-substituting to export-led industrialization in Ireland: who mixed the asphalt, who drove the machinery and who kept making them change direction?' *Politics and Society* 18, pp. 1–34.

O'Maitiu, S. (2003). *Dublin's Suburban Towns, 1834–1930*. Dublin: Four Courts Press.

O'Malley, E. (1989) *Industry and Economic Development: The Challenge for the Latecomer*. Dublin: Gill & Macmillan.

O'Murchu, M. W. (1989) 'Alfred O'Rahilly and the provision of adult education at University College, Cork', pp. 25– 39 in D. O'Sullivan (ed.), *Social Commitment and Adult Education*. Cork: Cork University Press.

O'Riordan, M. (2001) *The Voice of a Thinking Intelligent Movement: James Larkin Junior and the Ideological Modernisation of Irish Trade Unionism*. Dublin: Irish Labour History Society.

O'Rourke, K. (1991) 'Burn everything British but their coal: the Anglo-Irish economic war of the 1930s', *Journal of Economic History* 51 (2), pp. 357–66.

O'Sullivan, D. (1992) 'Cultural strangers and educational change: the OECD report *Investment in Education* and Irish educational policy', *Journal of Educational Policy* 7 (5), pp. 445–69.

Papadopoulos, G. (1994) *Education 1960–1990: The OECD Perspective*. Paris: OECD.

Press, J. (1989) *The Footwear Industry in Ireland, 1922–1973*. Dublin: Irish Academic Press.

Puirséil, N. (2007) *The Irish Labour Party, 1922–73*. Dublin: UCD Press.

Roberts, R. (1986) *The Story of The People's College*. Dublin: O'Brien Press.

Smith, T. (1984) Trade union education: its past and future', *Industrial Relations Journal* 15 (2), pp. 72–90.

Swift, J. P. (1991) *John Swift: An Irish Dissident*. Dublin: Gill & Macmillan.

Tiratsoo, N. (1998) '"What you need is a Harvard": American influence on British Management Education 1945–60', pp. 140–54 in T. R. Gourvish and N. Tiratsoo (eds) *Missionaries and Managers: American Influences On European Management Education, 1945–60*. Manchester: Manchester University Press.

Tiratsoo, N. and J. Tomlinson (1998) *Industrial Efficiency and Conservatism, 1951–1964: Thirteen Wasted Years?* London: Routledge.

Tomlin, B. (1966) *The Management of Irish Industry: A Research Report*. Dublin: Irish Management Institute.

Vaizey, J. (1986) *Scenes From Institutional Life and Other Writings*. London: Weidenfeld & Nicolson.

Van Beinum, H. (1967) *The Morale of the. Dublin Busmen: A Socio-Diagnostic Study of the. Dublin City Services of Coras Iompair Eireann*. Dublin: Irish National Productivity Committee.

Walsh, J. (2005) 'The politics of educational expansion', pp. 146–65 in B. Girvin and G. Murphy (eds), *The Lemass Era: Politics and Society in the Ireland of Seán Lemass*. Dublin: UCD Press.

Whelan, B. (1992) 'Ireland and the Marshall Plan', *Irish Economic and Social History* XIX, pp. 49–70.

Whelan, B. (2000) *Ireland and the Marshall Plan, 1947–57*. Dublin: Four Courts Press.

Whelan, B. (2006) 'Ireland, the Marshall Plan and US Cold War concerns', *Journal of Cold War Studies* 8 (1), pp. 68–94.

Whitaker, T. K. (2006) *Protection Or Free Trade: The Final Battle*. Dublin: Institute of Public Administration.

White, T. (2001) *Investing in People: Higher Education in Ireland From 1960 to 2000*. Dublin: Institute of Public Administration.

Whyte, J. H. (1980) *Church and State in Modern Ireland 1923–1979*. Dublin: Gill & Macmillan.

Yearley, S. (1995) 'From one dependency to another: the political economy of science policy in the Irish Republic in the second half of the twentieth century', *Science, Technology and Human Values* 20 (2), pp. 171–96.

Zeitlin, J. and G. Herrigel (eds) (2000) *Americanization and Its Limits*. Oxford: Oxford University Press.

Index